# Pioneering New Products

## A Market Survival Guide

# PIONEERING NEW PRODUCTS
# A MARKET SURVIVAL GUIDE

Edwin E. Bobrow

Dennis W. Shafer

**Dow Jones-Irwin**
Homewood, Illinois 60430

© DOW JONES-IRWIN, 1987

This publication is designed to provide accurate and
authoritative information in regard to the subject matter
covered. It is sold with the understanding that the
publisher is not engaged in rendering legal, accounting, or
other professional service. If legal advice or other expert
assistance is required, the services of a competent
professional person should be sought.

*From a Declaration of Principles jointly adopted by a Committee
of the American Bar Association and a Committee of Publishers.*

ISBN 0-87094-621-8

Library of Congress Catalog Card No. 86–50777

*Printed in the United States of America*

1 2 3 4 5 6 7 8 9 0 K 4 3 2 1 0 9 8 7

# NEW PRODUCT PIONEERING. . .
# A MARKET SURVIVAL GUIDE

## INTRODUCTION

New product development and marketing has become a vital function of the modern company, a function that happens less by accident and more by direction than ever before in the history of business. In a Department of Commerce study it was found that three fourths of the respondents felt that new products are the key factor in their company's growth. Resurgence of the entrepreneurial spirit is also feeding the recognized business needs of new products for growth. George Gilder, in an article entitled "Capitalists Are Good For You" in the July 6, 1984 edition of the *New York Times*, speaks of the capitalist or entrepreneur:

> He is not chiefly a tool of markets but a maker of markets; not a scout of opportunities but a developer of opportunity; not chiefly a user of technology but a producer of it. . . . He seeks monopoly: the unique product, the startling new fashion, the marketing breakthrough, the novel. These ventures disrupt existing equilibrium rather than restore a natural balance that outside forces have thrown away.

Whether it is the entrepreneur or the newly labeled intrapreneur (the individual within a corporate structure that exercises the entrepreneurial spirit) who is constantly on the search for new opportunity, the search is much more organized. It is taking place more frequently and with a greater conscious effort. Not only have new products been recognized as the lifeblood of business, but the entrepreneur and intrapreneur are being accepted as the people who carry the torch of change. They are the modern-day equivalent of the American pioneer, and every bit as critical to the survival and future growth of American business as they were to the original development of the country.

Much is now being written about new product development and management. Excellent newsletters, articles, textbooks—and even a quarterly journal—are now devoted to the subject. It is being taught at colleges and universities, and executives from many disciplines want to know more about the process of developing and marketing new products.

Entrepreneurs and now intrapreneurs, by their very nature, are pushing us all into the most exciting era of change humankind has ever faced. To stay on top, let alone ahead of change, we have to invent and innovate new products and services that are marketable. And we have to innovate those products with a conscious discipline and a market perspective to ensure their survival. It is toward this end that this book has been written. By creating a practical survival guide for business people, entrepreneurs, intrapreneurs, and marketing people, our new product (this book) deals in a particular way with the subject of "applied" new product development and marketing. It is not an academician's approach, although it does take into account sound principles as well as the latest concepts and theories. It is rather, a "how to" book that will serve as a practical guide for the systematic approach to developing and marketing new products that pioneer new business ground and survive in the marketplace.

*Edwin E. Bobrow*
*Dennis W. Shafer*

# CONTENTS

# 1

# Why Pioneer?

In 1985, an estimated 10,000 new products were introduced to the American market (see Figure 1–1). After five years, some 8,000 of those products will have been discontinued and withdrawn after millions of dollars and thousands of hours were invested in their development and marketing. In many cases, the owners and innovators of new products could have generated a greater return on their investment by purchasing bonds and clipping coupons. Yet they continue to hire people, schedule more projects, and invest in more new product development (see Figure 1–2).

An astute gambler would never play those odds in Las Vegas, so why should any business manager invest in a new product development effort? Why not just wait for competitors to take those foolish risks and then quickly copy and improve on their mistakes? Some companies consciously adopt that strategy, and many companies unconsciously follow it. A few are lucky enough to endure, but most who choose a follower strategy are slowly dying and don't realize it.

All businesses, institutions, countries, and entire civilizations either grow through innovation and change or they die without them. They die because bureaucracy and inertia set in. When institutions and countries lose the desire to change, they become *unable* to react and adapt to a changing world.

World history is evidence of this simple principle. Greek civilization thrived for more than 300 years through the quest for learning. It died when Athens became immersed in internal bu-

**FIGURE 1-1**
New Product Introductions

| | Foods | Drugs | Cosmetics | Durables | Tools | Industrial | Toys/Games | Gadgets | Total |
|---|---|---|---|---|---|---|---|---|---|
| 1985 | 2,314 | 1,340 | 734 | 358 | 431 | 592 | 754 | 3,642 | 10,165 |
| 1984 | 2,209 | 1,314 | 722 | 361 | 462 | 576 | 732 | 3,519 | 9,895 |
| 1983 | 2,307 | 1,401 | 743 | 347 | 484 | 598 | 740 | 3,782 | 10,402 |
| 1982 | 2,213 | 1,229 | 713 | 469 | 586 | 587 | 685 | 3,461 | 9,668 |
| 1981 | 2,142 | 1,142 | 693 | 452 | 493 | 613 | 653 | 3,212 | 9,400 |
| 1980 | 2,107 | 1,087 | 610 | 460 | 502 | 704 | 641 | 3,010 | 9,121 |
| 1979 | 1,860 | 810 | 420 | 310 | 430 | 503 | 645 | 2,970 | 7,948 |
| 1978 | 1,640 | 964 | 501 | 407 | 447 | 584 | 611 | 2,840 | 7,994 |
| 1977 | 2,003 | 985 | 322 | 364 | 411 | 545 | 631 | 2,769 | 8,030 |
| 1976 | 1,475 | 769 | 290 | 385 | 497 | 440 | 567 | 2,850 | 7,273 |
| 1984–1985 CHANGE | +4.7% | +.02% | +.016% | −.008% | −.067% | +.027% | +3% | +3.4% | +2.7% |
| 10-YEAR CHANGE | +57% | +74% | +153% | +.07% | −13% | +34% | +33% | +28% | +40% |

NOTE: Figures are for number of new products introduced, not dollar value. Data based on monitors in ads and editorials in 50 key publications. Survey conducted by New Product Development Newsletter, Point Publishing Co., Inc., Point Pleasant, N.J.

**FIGURE 1–2** _____
Further Findings on New Products in 1985

|  | Yes | No |
|---|---|---|
| Did your company introduce more new products in 1985 than 1984? | 42% | 58% |
| Were the new products designed to sell for a higher price? | 72% | 28% |
| Were the new products more sophisticated than before? | 92% | 8% |
| Did you spend more on new product development than in 1984? | 86% | 14% |
| Did your company employ more people in new product development? | 62% | 38% |
| Was the average person in the new product development area paid more in 1985 than in 1984? | 96% | 4% |
| Did your company have trouble finding enough qualified people for the new product development area? | 82% | --- |
| What is your company's new product success rate? Average: | 34% | |
| Do you consider this rate satisfactory? | 73% | 27% |
| Is this rate satisfactory in terms of dollar profits? | 84% | 16% |
| Is your company now working on more than 10 new products? | 38% | 62% |
| Is your company now working on a "major breakthrough" new product? | 9% | 90% |
| A new product of "significant" merit? | 41% | 59% |
| A new product that will be a "plus" in your product area? | 94% | |
| Are you doing better than your competition in new products? | 56% | 44% |
| Are you now working on new products that will reach the market | | |
| in two years | 45% | |
| in five years | 31% | |
| in ten years | 6% | |
| in twenty years | 2% | |
| Does your company—in general—go for volume over price? | 31% | 69% |
| Does your company see overseas competition as a major threat? | 42% | 58% |
| Will your budget for new product development increase in 1986? | 96% | 4% |

SOURCE: _New Product Development_ 5, no. 12, Point Pleasant N.J.: Point Publishing Co., December 1985.

reaucracy and was unable to react to the events triggered by the Peloponnesian War in 430 B.C. The Romans created a civilization spreading over one third of today's developed world and were responsible for many of the practical innovations of history, their commercialization, and their expansion to widespread use.

Many of the Romans' innovations were actually the refinement of technology invented in the Greek, Mesopotamian, or Egyptian civilizations, but the Romans were powerful innovators and marketers in that they introduced these ideas to a large market. They spread glass making throughout their empire, developed the smelting of brass on a large scale, created central heating and plumbing systems in their homes, and used the concept of credit to promote agriculture and industry, to develop foreign trade, and to finance military operations (a concept practiced to an extreme by many governments today). The Romans are even credited with developing the first mousetraps—many Roman homeowners kept weasels to hunt mice for them.

The Romans became complacent with their successes, however, and focused internally on politics, power, and organization. They were unable to react to the gradual development of new civilizations and cultures around them. The dissatisfaction and desire for change among their own governed people eventually led to the decline and fall of the empire.

Institutions and companies can also turn inward, forgo innovations, focus on organization, and die as a result of the changes around them. The great European monarchies of the 17th and 18th centuries grew because they provided an environment for inspiration and exploration, and they died when they turned inward and refused to acknowledge change or accept creativity. The Industrial Revolution of the late 18th and 19th centuries spawned many large industrial empires in Europe and America and created most of the basic technology of the 20th century.

The first generation of American capitalists put an indelible stamp on the character of modern business, especially in their spirit of pioneering the great American West. The end of the Civil War unleashed thousands of soldiers turned pioneers who raced to stake a claim in the fields of the prairies, the mines of Nevada and California, and the forests of the Pacific Northwest. The resources needed by the pioneers fueled the creation of empires— the Carnegies and Vanderbilts' steel, the Rockefellers' oil, and the Mellons' banking. This surge of industry in turn generated an explosion of technology. The 20 years from 1880 to 1900 generated such major inventions as the motorcar, the radio, the steam turbine, and the combine harvester.

The captains or barons of these industries were agents of change and progress, and they innovated the concept of mass production on an agrarian-mercantile economy. By 1929, however, many of these empires had also planted the seeds of their own destruction by failing to maintain an innovative spirit. Their inability to accept further change, compounded by a fragile economy, ushered in the Great Depression.

Since the Depression the United States has witnessed an unprecedented era of pioneering and technological change. Alvin Toffler, in his book *Future Shock*, dramatizes the rate of change in his description of the progress in transportation:

> In 6000 B.C. the fastest transportation available to man over long distance was the camel caravan, averaging eight miles per hour. It was not until about 1600 B.C. when the chariot was invented that the maximum speed was raised to roughly 20 MPH.
>
> So impressive was this invention, so difficult was it to exceed this speed limit, that nearly 3,500 years later, when the first mail coach began operating in England in 1784, it averaged a mere 10 MPH. . . . It was probably not until the 1880s that man, with the help of a more advanced steam locomotive, managed to reach a speed of 100 MPH.
>
> It took only 58 years, however, to quadruple the limit, so that by 1939 airborne man was cracking the 400 MPH line. It took a mere 20-year flick of time to double the limit again. And by the 1960s men in space capsules were circling the earth at 18,000 MPH.[1]

Product life cycles also demonstrate the rate of change in business. In the first half of the 20th century, technology was advancing rapidly, but the disruptive impact of two world wars and a depression slowed the rate of adoption and assimilation in the marketplace. A good idea could linger in one research lab, one geographic area, or one market niche for years before expanding to other segments. As a result, many companies were able to ride the crest of a product life cycle for 10 to 20 years beyond technical obsolescence. This is not so in the 1980s and 1990s. The quickened pace of consumer psychology has telescoped time. A generation used to be viewed as a 20-year period, but today the data on consumer attitudes, trends, and behavior patterns indicate that a generation has shrunk to 7 years.

The rapid development of communication technology, the opening of international trade, and the concentration and expansion of distribution systems have produced a business world that can react with lightning speed. Kodak introduces a new camera and three Japanese companies and one German company will

---

[1] Alvin Toffler, *Future Shock* (New York: Bantam Books, 1971), p. 26. © 1970 Alvin Toffler.

have film in stores before the cameras get there. IBM announces it will introduce a new personal computer in one year; Apple, Compaq, and two Taiwan companies have enhanced products ready for delivery in six months. Coca-Cola introduces New Coke and obsolesces its own product with Classic Coke in three months.

Even traditionally slow-changing industries are becoming victims of product life cycles. The substitution of plastics and graphite for steel in automobiles to reduce weight has, in effect, made a growing portion of a steelmaker's "product line" obsolete. The rapid advancement of agricultural chemicals and improvement in yields and weed control are obsolescing several farm machinery products and reducing the total market. Deregulation of the banking and finance industries is rapidly making outdated products such as the traditional savings account that have endured for decades.

Product life cycles can be affected from many different directions. A lawn products company introduced new lawn mowers every six to nine months, reacting to a variety of challenges, opportunities, and changing technology: Japanese improvement of two-cycle gasoline engine technology; government-mandated safety regulations requiring blade safety devices; improvement and expansion of dry-powder painting systems providing more cost-effective and durable product finishing; environmental regulation concerns stimulating the design of noise-reduced muffler systems; and advancement of aluminum die-casting technology allowing the use of cost-effective aluminum mower housings with contoured surfaces for vacuum-action cutting. If you think your product or industry is as immune to fast life cycle obsolescence as the old family lawn mower, watch out!

Reacting to life cycles is good but it isn't nearly enough in today's world. Businesses must be "proactive," flexible, and fast product developers to avoid the catastrophic environmental changes that seem to be occurring more often. Peter Drucker describes the situation in his book, *Managing in Turbulent Times:*

> Sometime during the 1920s, the longest period of continuity in economic history came to an end. At some time during the last 10 years we moved into turbulence. The 25 years from the Marshall Plan to the mid-'70s were not only a period of unprecedented economic growth . . . they were also a period of high predictability . . . economically, growth in the major countries proceeded in these years along lines that had been laid out before World War II, and in most

cases well before the Great Depression . . . they were also, a period of high technological continuity . . . rapid change . . . but mostly in areas that were already well mapped before World War II, in areas based on discoveries and innovations that had been made before the Great Depression. . . . This has ended. In technology, too, we are entering a period of turbulence, a period of rapid innovation, a period of fast and radical structural shifts.[2]

Booz-Allen & Hamilton, a large management consulting company, reports from a survey of leading companies throughout the world that the number of new product introductions is expected to double over the next five years. The survey attributes this pace to several external environmental factors.[3] Technological advances were viewed as a major factor by 90 percent of the survey sample, changing consumer needs, 72 percent; shortening product life cycles, 55 percent; increasing foreign market access, 53 percent; increasing foreign competition in the United States, 48 percent; increasing labor costs, 35 percent; government regulations, 35 percent; and increasing capital costs, 18 percent.

Mr. Drucker also offers a solution for dealing with turbulence and discontinuity:

> A time of turbulence is a dangerous time, but its greatest danger is a temptation to deny reality. . . . The greatest and most dangerous turbulence today results from the collision between the delusions of the decision makers . . . and the realities. But a time of turbulence is also one of great opportunity for those who can understand, accept, and exploit the new realities. It is above all a time of opportunity for leadership.[4]

Aggressive business leadership and pioneering are required to survive in an era of turbulence. Some of the giants of industry are demonstrating the type of renewed pioneering spirit needed. General Motors Corporation has acquired a large computer systems company and several technology-based businesses in order to shift from car making to manufacturing technology and services. Sears, Roebuck & Co. has added a variety of financial services to its traditional product retailing business. International Harvester,

---

[2] Peter F. Drucker, *Managing in Turbulent Times* (New York: Harper & Row, 1980), pp. 3–4. Copyright 1980 Peter F. Drucker.

[3] Booz, Allen & Hamilton, Inc., *New Products Management for the 1980s* (New York: 1982), p. 5. © 1982 Booz Allen & Hamilton, Inc.

[4] Drucker, *Turbulent Times*, pp. 4–5.

on the verge of bankruptcy, left the farm machinery business, renamed itself Navistar, and intends to be the largest truck manufacturer in the world.

These examples, some closer to business obsolescence than others, also demonstrate that improvements in internal efficiency are not enough to ensure *market* survival. General Motors was extremely innovative in labor management techniques, cost-effective design, and automobile assembly concepts, but it recognized that ultimate survival would require offering innovative value *outside* the company to the world marketplace. Sears, as the country's largest retailer, developed lending techniques for efficient distribution of merchandise, but realized that shifts in consumer discretionary spending would require innovative service offerings in order to maintain growth and, ultimately, to survive.

Innovation in internal efficiency alone will not guarantee survival for *any* American manufacturing company. Manufacturing competition from Third World and lesser-developed countries will explode in the next 20 years at a rate far greater than the most innovative manufacturing techniques. Low-cost automobiles are already available from Yugoslavia and Korea; Taiwan and Korea are attacking Japan's position in consumer electronics; India and China are replacing New Jersey as America's nuts and bolts source; Indonesia displaced Korea, which displaced the Carolinas a long time ago, as America's clothing manufacturer; and the precision tool industry is being invaded by sources in such unlikely places as Portugal and Sri Lanka. American business must compete with market knowledge, creativity, and new product development skills to survive in this environment.

A few companies can succeed solely by developing intimate market knowledge and product distribution skills and by being a fast follower on technology. These companies are still pioneers, but they are focused on distribution. Danger and management delusion exists, however, when a company adopts a product follower strategy but hasn't pioneered in speed of market introduction and distribution.

With very short life cycles, a market may disappear before a follower can even react. This phenomenon is evident in two vastly different industries, sports clothing and personal computers. The race to become the hot sports shoe of the year has been won and lost annually by such names as Adidas, Nike, and Reebok while the offshore manufacturers struggle to keep up with copy designs. No sooner does Taiwan copy a new Apple personal computer design, than Apple introduces an upgraded version with enhanced memory and peripheral support. Clearly, if a company chooses to be a follower in product design, it better be innovative in product introduction and distribution techniques. And American manufacturers can't count on manufacturing cost efficiency as their pioneering focus for survival.

In addition to offering survival, new product pioneering provides financial rewards despite high failure rates. Most industries have an inherent inertia in their distribution systems which can react to and logistically support only a limited number of alternatives. So once a new product is successfully introduced to a distribution channel, it tends to enjoy a more monopolistic price and profit position for at least 6 to 12 months.

Consumer awareness, attention, and decision time is generally limited to only two or three choices in any product category, which also provides a monopolistic opportunity. The typical supermarket in America has some 18,000 products on its shelves, available to a market where the average new high school graduate has a working vocabulary of about 10,000 words. A successful new product achieving a distribution position in that supermarket and an established awareness and preference with its shoppers will generate attractive financial rewards.

Companies need new product development. Product pioneering is essential for long-term business profitability and survival. New products create the growth that sustains a business just as a civilization thrives on innovation. The rate and degree of change in product life cycles require product pioneering to avoid obsolescence, and the discontinuity and turbulence of today's world require proactive innovation focused on the marketplace. Following rather than leading new product development isn't a practical alternative without unusually innovative introduction and distribution concepts. Good pioneering techniques can generate attractive returns despite the financial risks and low success rate of new products.

Finally, and perhaps most important, new product pioneering *energizes* a company. A product development effort provides a specific, tangible goal that cuts across all company functions. It can create team morale, maintain an environment receptive to change, and stimulate a spirit of creativity, motivation, and enthusiasm extending to all areas of the company.

The choice is not *whether to pioneer, but how.* The rest of this book provides guidelines for success and survival.

# 2

# When Is a New Product New?

The wheel, automobile, jet plane, television, computer, and other pivotal inventions have changed the world. Preexisting knowledge was combined in a new way to bring about something that didn't exist before: an invention. Not all inventions have been world-shaking, however. Many of them will come to market only after someone innovates upon the invention to make it more usable and acceptable in the marketplace. In new product development innovation changes the invention in a way that makes it more acceptable in the marketplace. The wheel may have started as a solid, round stone with a hole through it. Today we have wheels of all configurations, material, and constructions. We have bicycle wheels, wheels for automobiles, for locomotives, for small motors, and so on. All innovations are based on the original invention. In fact, most products are innovations rather than pure inventions and, like the wheel, hardly resemble the first model.

People who create new products are called a variety of terms. Inventors, innovators, entrepreneurs, and lately the term intrapreneurs have all been used to describe those who develop new products or new business concepts. Figure 2–1 puts the various terms in perspective and indicates they do overlap. A manager responsible for new product development as an "intrapreneur" in a business needs to understand the differences in these individuals and when to utilize their varied creative talents. Figure 2–2 shows the general phases of a new product or business development life cycle and indicates the key participants in each

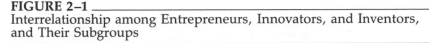

**FIGURE 2–1**
Interrelationship among Entrepreneurs, Innovators, and Inventors, and Their Subgroups

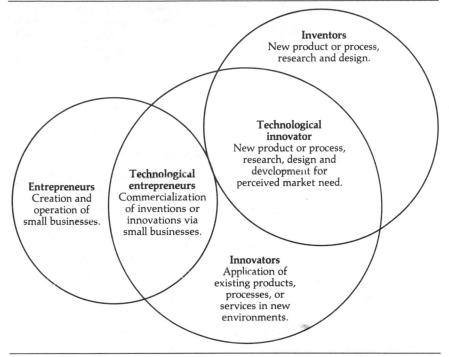

SOURCE: Denver Research Institute, *Final Report, 1: Innovation Center and Technical Assistance to Business Study,* July 1977, p. 7.

phase. Effective managers of innovation develop a network of people, both inside and outside the company, who can provide the perspective required at each stage of development.

Strategic innovation is a term coined by Larry Wizenberg, vice president of YS & W, to describe the approach to developing products or services to achieve specific goals and objectives.[1] By setting clear criteria to meet the goals, it is possible to innovate and, in some instances, invent strategically. Inventing strategically, however, is very difficult, and only companies blessed by inspirational geniuses or unusually aggressive and successful research and development programs are likely to succeed without

---

[1] Larry Wizenberg, "Strategic Innovation Program Guides, New Product Development," *Marketing News* (Chicago, Ill.: American Marketing Association, March 21, 1980), pp. 6–7.

**FIGURE 2–2**

Relationships between the Innovation Process and Its Participants

| Activities | Idea generation | Idea evaluation | Product/process development | New venture initiation / New product introduction | Venture growth reinvestment / Spun-off products | Business maturation |
|---|---|---|---|---|---|---|
| Process phase | Invention | Adaptation | | Entrepreneurial | | |
| Participants | Inventor | Innovators | | Entrepreneurs | | |
| | Technological innovators | | | | | |
| | Technological entrepreneurs | | | | | |

SOURCE: Denver Research Institute, *Final Report, 1: Innovation Center and Technical Assistance to Business Study*, July 1977, p. 7.

an organized approach. On the other hand, successful strategic innovation is possible if the new product or service development system outlined in this book is followed.

The first step in strategic innovation and the process of successfully developing and marketing new products in general is understanding what a new product is in the real world.

A new product or service means something different to the consumer and end user than it does to the manufacturer or marketer. To the consumer or end user, a product or service is new if it has never before been seen, heard of, or used. There are situations, however, where a product may not be perceived as different or innovative until it is already used by the consumer. For example, the consumer might never have heard of a fabric softener for the drier, a product that would eliminate static cling and make the laundry smell fresher and look fluffed up. When Bounce and Cling were advertised, the consumer became aware of the product. It was perceived as new. Some consumers tried the product and others did not. The consumers who did not try the product were resisting a change in the way they laundered their clothes. Those that tried it were willing to change in order to enjoy the benefits promised. For this group the product was new not only in perception but also in utilization.

Many consumers, those we would call "purchase leaders," broke their old laundry habits and tried this new product. They had to change *behavior* and *learn* a new procedure in order to benefit from the new product. Other consumers waited, and after the purchase leaders tried the product and reported liking it, the "purchase followers" started to buy the product. By the time the fabric softener was bought by the purchase followers, it could be said it was no longer a new product. Yet, to the consumers who were purchase followers, the product was new when they used it. In buying and using the product, they learned a new laundry procedure and changed their behavior. If they liked the product and continued to buy it, it then became adopted by that consumer. As many consumers adopted the product, it became diffused in the marketplace. Once the product was sufficiently diffused, it was not considered new, even by a consumer who had never tried it. It was a product they had never tried but not a product new to the market.

Within the change in behavior and level of learning required rests the real measure of newness to the consumer. Many products are marketed as new or improved and may be perceived by the consumer as being new. However, the degree of behavioral change is the objective measure of newness. Marketers need to consider both the measurable behavioral factors as well as the consumer's perception of what is new. To rely on the quantitative factor or qualitative factor alone in defining what is new to the consumer is like relying only on demographics or only on psychographics in targeting a market instead of considering both.

For the end user of industrial products, the measure of newness is much the same as for the consumer, except for the added factors of trade perceptions, which we will discuss later in the chapter. For now, the end user should be viewed in the same way as the consumer. For both, new products must first be used, adopted, and diffused in the marketplace. The degree of newness will relate to the amount of learning required and the behavioral change in using the product. Thomas Robertson attempted to classify new products by how much learning and behavioral changes they required. He divided them into three categories: *continuous innovation*, a low-learning situation, requires the least change in consumption patterns. New car models or packaging changes would fall into this category. *Dynamically continuous innovation* requires a medium amount of learning and involves some disruption of the consumption pattern, for example, the digital clock, which meant reading time in a different manner, or the electric toothbrush. Both of these innovations performed functions that had been done by the consumer before but now involved a new way of performing the same function. *Discontinuous innovation* requires high learning as new consumption patterns are created for previously unknown products. These include products such as videotape recorders, TV games, and Polaroid cameras.[2]

In addition to looking at newness from the consumer's perspective, we must also look at a new product from the trade's perspective. How does the manufacturer, distributor, retailer, or end user perceive newness? It could be a new package, a product new to the company or to the market segment, a new physical form, or a new improved version. An industrial end user might view newness as a consumer would or as the trade would. In consumer goods, you can classify newness as we have already discussed, and separate the consumer measures and trade measures. In industrial goods, the situation will dictate which measures should be taken from the end user categories and which from trade categories.

From a corporate or trade perspective, consumer or industrial products or services can be classified as new if they fall into one of the following categories:

**New Technology.**   This category is the most challenging to market. It requires the greatest change in consumer or end user behavior and often results in replacing existing products. Sometimes the new technology requires developing a new market, as was done for personal computers. A company that embraces a new technology often obsolesces its own products. This calls for a well-planned strategy. Phasing in the new and phasing out the old is not easy.

A company with a new technology often faces breaking new ground, entering unfamiliar marketing areas and markets. It may have to learn one-step direct-to-retailer distribution, when the company was always dedicated to working through a distributor. The new technology might mean a change to independent agents from a company sales force. The company might now need to use national advertising instead of using no advertising.

New technology application and marketing is not easy. It requires knowing the needs of the marketplace, how to apply the

[2] Thomas Robertson, ''The Process of Innovation and the Diffusion of Innovation,'' *Journal of Marketing*, January 1967, pp. 14–19.

technology to the needs in a form acceptable to the ultimate user, and how to achieve adoption and diffusion of the new product. The rewards, however, are limitless.

**New Innovations.**   Most inventions need innovations to make them marketable. The invention, as originally conceived, usually needs design changes, human engineering, or adaptation to market needs. The innovations made to the Polaroid camera made it more acceptable. Faster processing, built-in flash, and other innovations made for new models, which were new and more appealing to consumers.

Old products, too, can take on a new look when a company brings out innovative products. Clocks are an example of a basic technology that has virtually endless innovative possibilities through changes in face, design, shape, color, and size.

**New to the Market.**   When home centers started to sell Pepsi-Cola, this was new. Pepsi wasn't new to the consumer, but it was new to the buyer at such stores, to the merchandise manager, to the field managers, and to the clerks who had to buy and sell it through their stores. New distribution, new displays, and new trade customers and practices came into play.

Selling a product to a new market means it is new to that market. When Nikon began selling to volume retailers, it developed a special camera within a certain price range to service this new market. The special camera opened the new market and paved the way for the sale of standard Nikon cameras in these new outlets.

When entering a new area, there is much to learn about how best to market to this new segment. Sometimes a special sales force, advertising, displays, packaging, and promotions are needed to sell in the new market. It requires looking at the product as that market would and marketing the product accordingly.

**New to a Country.**   Flymo, a lawn mower without wheels that hovers above the ground, was introduced quite successfully in England. But it has met with little success in the United States. Japanese cars, however, have been successfully marketed here. Both products were new to this country and required all the marketing processes that any product new to the marketplace would. Marketing a product in one country does not necessarily give it recognition in another country.

The product must be treated as new. Research, design, and marketing have to be geared to the new market. Transferring the strengths of the new product to the new country without adjusting these strengths to meet the needs of the new market is a mistake too often made. It is essential to look at the product as if it were totally new, factoring in only those elements that are truly transferable from one country to another.

**New Category to the Company.**   Black and Decker's purchase of General Electric's small appliance division is a good example of a company entering a new category of goods. After the purchase Black and Decker had to deal with new buyers, new customers, new distribution systems, new types of packaging, new positioning for a different consumer, and many more factors new to the company. It was a whole new business to be learned and sold in ways dictated by the small appliance industry. If Black and Decker were to take an imperial attitude and try to use the same type of marketing approach used for tools, it would not likely succeed. On the other hand, like any company going into a new category, if it studies the category of goods and develops product and programs for that market, it will succeed.

**New Brand.**   In packaged goods, companies often introduce products that compete with other products from the same company. Procter & Gamble Co.'s multiple brands of detergents are examples of this strategy. On entry in the marketplace, every brand of detergent from Procter & Gamble is new and is treated as new with its own marketing plan.

The multiple brand strategy is used for different reasons. Sometimes a marketer wants to bring out a second brand in order to confine the original brand to a particular market segment. In other cases, an additional brand or brands are brought out to control market share, or they may be marketed to reach different sets of consumers. Whatever the reason a company chooses a multiple brand strategy, when that new brand is brought to market, it should have its own new product marketing plan that positions the brand according to corporate goals.

**Repositioning.**   Old products are often awakened when dressed in new packages, with new features and benefit stories directed at specific target purchasers. Failed products can sometimes find success through repositioning. Whatever the reason for repositioning, the product must be handled as if it were totally new if the repositioning is to work. In repositioning a product, the shape, size, trim, color, or material of the product may be changed. Sometimes, though, just a new marketing approach, with new packaging, new display, new story, new distributor system, new target management, new use or emphasis of uses can be effective.

When Sealtest introduced Light 'N' Lively ice milk as a lower calorie, less-fat substitute for ice cream, the diet image worked for a while. But competition entered the market, watering down the value of Light 'N' Lively's positioning as a diet product. It no longer had the unique selling proposition it had when introduced. Sealtest decided the market for a diet product was limited. Research indicated that although the product was limited in the diet area, if Sealtest could convince consumers Light 'N' Lively tasted good, it could be expanded to compete with ice cream. This required repositioning. A new package, new flavors, and a new advertising campaign featuring good taste were delivered. Even the product's formula was changed by adding milk solids to give it a creamier taste.

Repositioning is a strategy that often works. The key to success is in good research that points to areas of opportunity to which the repositioned product can appeal.

**New Channels of Distribution or Market Segments.**   This category is similar to being new to the market, but there are subtle differences. The new to the market category generally entails a complete market area, such as Nikon selling to the supermarket or drug store market. New channels of distribution can mean selling differently within the same market. For example, if a company is selling tools to hardware stores through distributors and decides to cut out the distributor and sell direct, the tool line might be perceived as new by the retailers that the distributors did not call on. Even those retailers the distributors did call on might perceive the offering as new because it is now presented in a different environment, by a different sales force, under different circumstances.

Selling to new market segments is similar to new markets except the segment is generally a specialized area within the new market. If a company has been selling automotive accessories to automotive chain stores and then begins to sell the same product to the parts houses in the automotive industry, it is now going after a new market segment within the automotive aftermarket.

As indicated, there are subtle differences between "new market," "market segment," and "new channels." When a new market, new market segment, or channel of distribution is opened up by a company, the company and the trade will usually perceive the effort as a new product effort. The astute market-oriented company will treat each category differently, by researching and developing marketing and sales tools that specifically fit that segment, market, or channel.

**New Package.**   Just changing the package can make a product appear to be new. Even without total repositioning, the power of packaging is so important it needs to be singled out as a device that can make a product new. The package repositions the product by its shape, its graphics, and its message. This is particularly true of push-type products: products that need to be pushed through distribution. A toggle switch is an example of this type of product. The consumer generally does not buy this product by a brand name. The consumer will accept the brand that the store carries; seldom will a consumer go to another store because the toggle switch is not a G.E., Eagle, or Leviton brand. The trick for the manufacturer is to get the product on the shelf, and a well-designed, hard-selling package can help convince the trade that shelf space is justified.

With push products, the right package and display is vital. A change in packaging often makes the product or product line look like new and perceived as new by industry and consumer.

On the other hand, pull-type products are usually heavily advertised and asked for. Demand is created and the product is pulled through distribution because the consumer is driven into the store by advertising.

**New to a Product Line.**   Line extensions, additions of sizes, shapes, and colors, create new products. New colors in the Mystic Tape line or new shaped glasses to round out Plastics, Inc.'s line of plastic throw-away glasses are line extensions. A fastener company adding new sizes to its nut and bolt line or American Tack and Hardware Co. adding newly designed electrical switch plates to its line of decorative switch plates are new product offerings. These products have to be sold and added to the merchandise assortment customers are now carrying. Often the line extensions need to be singled out so the customer will know this new size, shape, color, or design is available. Line extensions must be treated as new but don't always require the marketing efforts of the other categories.

A company, not just products, can also be new to a product line. A company may perceive a product as new, but the trade may consider it old. When Stanley Tool Co. started offering plumbing items, those plumbing items were new to Stanley Tool Co. To the trade, Stanley Tool Co. is a new supplier of plumbing items, although not one item in the line is a new invention or even an innovation.

Defining a new product within the context of new product marketing is complex. New product definition is a system that takes into account perception, invention, and innovation and also provides the means of developing categories that help business people create and market what they consider to be new products. It is also the establishing of systems that help look at products from the company's unique perspective as well as from the consumer, end user, and trade point of view. Most important, it should serve a firm's need to organize new product development in a way satisfying to the company's and the market's needs.

Understanding the different types of innovation is critical in getting a company to establish a strategic framework supporting a *balanced* new product development effort. Booz Allen defined six categories of new products in terms of their newness to the company and to the marketplace and identified the following mix of introductions over five years in a worldwide survey of leading businesses:[3]

New-to-the-world products, which created an entirely new market, accounted for 10 percent of total introductions. New product lines, allowing a company to enter an established market, made up 20 percent of new product introductions. Additions to existing product lines were 26 percent of the total, and improvements in or revisions to existing products accounted for another 26 percent. Repositioning, or targeting existing products to new market segments, made up 7 percent of introductions,

---

[3] Booz Allen & Hamilton, Inc., *New Products Management for the 1980s* (New York: 1982), p. 8.

and cost reductions—new products that provide similar performance at a lower cost—accounted for 11 percent.

The survey also found that the 30 percent of New-to-the-World and New Product Line categories accounted for 60 percent of the new products viewed as most successful. A balanced new product strategy accommodates a portfolio of efforts directed at both these "big hits" with greater risks and challenges, as well as the "bread and butter" projects aimed at improving, reducing costs, and adding features to existing products. The degree of emphasis and funding in each category of innovation should be a direct result of the strategic goal-setting process described in Chapter Five.

To help you define new products for your firm, the trade, and potential consumer or end user, here is a check list:

1. How does the consumer or end user perceive your product?
2. Have you measured the degree of learning and behavioral change necessary on the part of the consumer by using the three classifications spelled out early in this chapter?
3. Have you tried to determine the consumer's perception of what is new as it applies to your product?
4. What does the trade or industry consider a new product to be?
5. Do your executives agree as to what is a new product for the company and your trade?
6. Have you measured the new product against corporate and trade classifications offered in this chapter?
7. Has your company developed a system unique to its own needs for measuring and categorizing new products?
8. Have you made the connection between what is defined as a new product and how you will begin to think about marketing the product?
9. Have you begun to think of the different strategies necessary for the different categories of newness?
10. Does your system help organize new products so it helps you see how you can best market them?
11. Is your new product category framework used in developing corporate strategy?
12. Does your new product program have a balanced allocation of resources among categories?

# 3

# Dangers of Pioneering

Just as it is necessary to define what the company, the trade, the consumer, or the end user considers to be a new product, the company must also define its standards for failure or success. Withdrawing a new product from the market doesn't necessarily mean it failed. Perhaps the new product was a test and now innovations can be made to bring the product into a more acceptable form. A product may have been introduced one year and withdrawn the next because its purpose was to meet low-end competition. Other situations occur where a company plans that the new product will become obsolete within a fixed time. When the product is withdrawn from the market, some might see it as a failure when in reality it was planned replacement. An example is the yearly introduction of automobiles that are intentionally changed in order to obsolesce the previous year's model. Automobile manufacturers have a set program for substantial changes to a new model only a few times in a decade, with the basic model cosmetically changed and gadgetry added for newness in the other years. Failure or success of new products, therefore, can be measured only in relation to meeting the company's standards for success or failure.

Statistics on the failure rate of new products should be examined carefully because the data may be based on faulty research, faulty interpretation, or just a lack of understanding. Data may measure the "decay curve rate" or "mortality rate," which tells how many product concepts were dropped before being marketed. Or data may measure the percentage of new products actually marketed. Neither method considers the meeting of company standards. Even if a product is brought to market and remains on the market, only the company knows if the product is meeting standards for success. The basic measurement approaches give rise to statistics that tell us whether more new product introductions are successful this year than last or that new product introduction failures are down.

C. Merle Crawford, author of the excellent textbook *New Product Management*[1] and professor at the University of Michigan Graduate School of Business Administration, studied the percentage of actually marketed new products that succeeded. He found that 25 percent of all new industrial products significantly fail to meet the expectations of their developer, and 30 percent to 35 percent of all consumer products fail to do so. This tabulation refutes the commonly cited claim that the majority of new products fail.

When examining reports on new product failure or success, one should keep in mind whether the report is for a particular group of products, consumer goods, industrial products, packaged goods, consumables, durables, or the sample universal. Are the researchers reporting on products that never got to be marketed or those that were marketed and failed? The way the information is reported may color one's thinking. The perception that only 2.5 percent of new products survive when this figure really applies to all products developed, may lead to pessimism about new product development. On the other hand, the realization that fully 70 percent to 75 percent of products marketed succeed might lead to embracing a policy of new product development.

In the view of many new product developers, the fact that 97.5 percent of products are dropped before going to market is healthy and probably the reason for the success of 70 percent healthy and probably the reason for the success of 70 percent once marketed. The more a company can cull product concepts that do not meet its criteria in the early stages, the less costly new product development will be. It always costs more when a product is dropped late in the development process or after it is marketed.

---

[1] C. Merle Crawford, *New Product Management* (Homewood, Ill.: Richard D. Irwin, Inc., 1983). C. Merle Crawford, "Marketing Research and the New Product Failure Rate," *Journal of Marketing*, April 1977, pp. 51–60.

**FIGURE 3–1** _____
Mortality of New Product Ideas

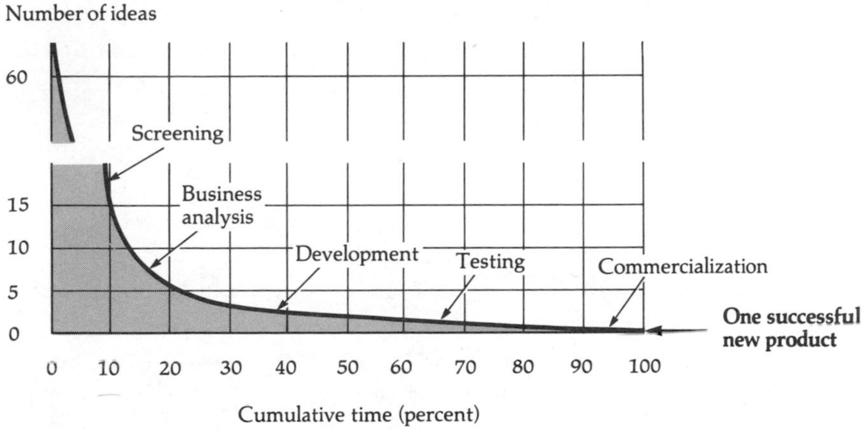

Number of ideas

Cumulative time (percent)

SOURCE: Booz-Allen & Hamilton, Inc.

Figure 3–1 shows how product concepts are dropped over a period of time. It also suggests how a process of new product development that takes new ideas through screening, business analysis, developing, and testing before commercialization can save the developer time and dollars. Later in this book, we will discuss each step in new product development. Figure 3–2 shows the cumulative expenditure over time, reinforcing the importance of early culling of new product ideas. It is essential that clear criteria be established in order to have a means of measuring the qualities and characteristics a new product should have.

Professor Crawford concludes:

> Given that 30 percent of all new market entries fail significantly, it is worthwhile to ask why. There seem to be three key reasons: 1) There was no real need or desire, overt or latent, for the new product on the part of potential buyers, as expected by the developers. 2) The new product did not meet the need that existed, or had overcompensating disadvantages. 3) The marketing effort was mishandled in some major way—especially in the basic communication of product character to the intended buyer.

These reasons for failure are generated by strategic, human, and management execution errors during the new product development process. Strategic errors are associated with whether a real need exists in the marketplace, and how much of a diver-

**FIGURE 3–2**
Cumulative Expenditures and Time

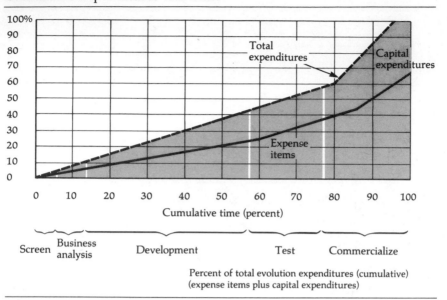

Percent of total evolution expenditures (cumulative)
(expense items plus capital expenditures)

SOURCE: Booz-Allen & Hamilton, Inc.

sification the product represents to the company. A.T. Kearney considers the chance of success to be a direct function of how far from home the new product or venture is aimed.[2] The likelihood of success for an improved product in the present market is assessed as 0.75, declines to 0.50 for a new product with unrelated technology in the present market, and to 0.25 for an existing product into a new market. It is believed the odds of success for external diversification are as low as 0.05, which seems to explain why so many companies use acquisitions to enter new business segments. A study by the *Journal of Marketing* of several hundred new product case histories indicated the success ratio varies significantly depending on the degree of diversification and innovation and the need in the marketplace (see Figure 3–3).

Even if a product is technically innovative, the human element and customer sensitivity can cause failure. A study by Stanford University[3] of 224 product innovations in more than 100 electronic companies concluded that shaping the product for the customer

---

[2] "Analyzing New Product Risk, Marketing for Sales Executives," New York: The Research Institute of America, January 1974.

[3] "Why Products Fail," *Inc.*, May 1984, pp. 98–155.

**FIGURE 3–3** _____

New Product Success Probability

|  | Success Ratio | % Successes | % of Cases |
|---|---|---|---|
| The synergistic "close to home" product | 1.39 | 72% | 12.82 |
| The innovative superior product with no synergy | 1.35 | 70% | 10.26 |
| The old but simple money saver | 1.35 | 70% | 15.38 |
| The synergistic product that was new to the firm | 1.29 | 67% | 10.76 |
| The innovative high-technology product | 1.23 | 64% | 14.35 |
| The close to home, "me too" product | 1.08 | 56% | 8.20 |
| The better mousetrap with no marketing | 0.69 | 36% | 7.17 |
| The "me too" product with no technical/ production synergy | 0.27 | 14% | 10.76 |
| The innovative mousetrap that really wasn't better | 0.00 | 0% | 10.26 |
| Mean | 1.00 | 52% |  |
| Total |  |  | 100.0% |

SOURCE: _Journal of Marketing,_ Spring 1981.

through internal and external communication was the key factor for success or failure. Technological lead and technical capability were named as reasons for success by less than 2 percent of the study sample, an even more startling finding considering the sample focused on high-tech companies.

External communication means establishing a close link with customers and getting feedback throughout the development process, especially a link between top management responsible for moving around the resources necessary to support new products and the lead customers critical to early acceptance of the products. A classic example of a great technological achievement failing because of no customer feedback on real needs was the Lockheed L–1011, one the best jetliners ever produced. It had more backup systems than any other plane, including four or five hydraulic control systems while the DC–10 had only three. But the L–1011 was an overdesigned product, priced out of the range of market acceptance, and it had to be dropped as a commercial airplane.

Internal communication relates to the normal boundaries that exist between the different functions in a company. Lack of communication and different product goals can result in the classic new product comedy of errors shown in Figure 3–4. Internal communication and external communication should be linked to ensure that every time a design trade-off decision is made, it

FIGURE 3–4 _____

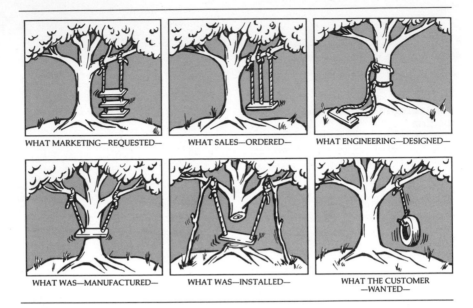

WHAT MARKETING—REQUESTED—   WHAT SALES—ORDERED—   WHAT ENGINEERING—DESIGNED—

WHAT WAS—MANUFACTURED—   WHAT WAS—INSTALLED—   WHAT THE CUSTOMER —WANTED—

represents a common internal decision and relates to the customer need.

Additional human elements to failure include the lack of commitment by top management to new products because of the draining effect on short-term profits, management turnover, and unwillingness to assume risk. The people involved in new product development projects may be inexperienced; market research is fallible, and sometimes misleading; a timely innovative product may require too long a gestation period and management loses patience; or other employees may view new product ventures with animosity because "it's a drain on profits."

Even if a product survives the strategic and human dangers, management or tactical mistakes can still kill it. Additional reasons for product failure listed here can prove a valuable "how not to" guide.

Insufficient analysis of the market is probably the prime tactical reason for failure. There are an endless number of inventors and innovators within the corporate environment and outside of it that get an idea and spend tens, if not hundreds, of thousands of dollars developing it before analyzing the market.

If the design of the product is defective or the manufacturer produces defective products, it can mean a quick death for a new product.

More often than not, planned costs are higher than anticipated. This may mean the product will fail because it is not competitive, or it might meet with minor success for a time until a competitor brings out a similar product at a lower price.

Bringing out the right product at the wrong time can be as devastating as bringing out the wrong product at the right time. Timing relates to analyzing the market. With good knowledge of the market, the right timing is more likely.

Misjudging how competition will react to a new product can bring the product to an early death. This, too, is part of good research and analysis of the marketplace.

Improper or inadequate marketing effort will often cause product failure. Misjudging what is needed to communicate the product to its consumers and to the trade will cause even a good product to fail.

Spending all the money on the development or manufacture of the product, leaving little or no budget to sell it, can doom a product. The developer gets grandiose ideas as to the acceptability of the product. Because it is his child, he believes the product will automatically be adopted.

The market may be too small. Developers who do not check the size of the potential market could find themselves with a new product but not enough potential buyers for economical production.

Improper positioning of the product in the marketplace can cause failure. Usually this can be rectified with repositioning, but unless the needs of the marketplace are understood, proper positioning may never take place.

The product or service may be new, but other products or services may be satisfying consumer or end user needs. Because of this, the product might not be adopted by the market.

The product may take the company out of the field it knows. The product may not fit the company's image, distribution, or even management ability. Sometimes the cost of developing new distribution will be far too great a burden for the new product to carry.

The idea may be new to the company, but distribution may not accept it as new or the consumer may not adopt the product.

Unanticipated change in the marketplace can cause failure, particularly for fashion, color, and design-sensitive products. In the long run, every change in consumer behavior, such as the movement to fast foods or the movement away from junk foods, can affect the success or failure of a new product. Psychographic and demographic shifts are important.

Mistakes in forecasting can cause failures. If test markets are projected incorrectly or if, as is often the case, sales are overestimated, it may stall the marketing of the product.

Failure to study carefully the business aspect of the development and marketing will cause failure. Will it produce the return on investment desired, and pay back within an acceptable period? If it fails in meeting the business goals, it will not be a desirable product for the company to produce.

New government regulations or lack of knowledge of current regulations can cause failure, and development of new technology or new materials can spoil the best plans.

Following are some examples of products that failed because of strategic, human, or tactical problems and some that have been outstanding successes over decades through careful attention.[4] The losers include flavored margarine. Lever Brothers and Kraft knocked themselves out with strawberry and chocolate-flavored margarine. The concept was to simply spread the margarine on a piece of toast and have an instant Danish pastry, but consumers didn't bite.

Artificial bacon is another loser. General Foods keeps experimenting with this product, but has yet to create a winner. Canister-packed potato chips, such as Procter & Gamble's impeccable but costly Pringles, also haven't won the hearts of many consumers. Consumers seem to prefer the regular chips with dark-brown spots that break easily. Pop wines such as Ripple and Annie Greenspring looked like they were going to take over the wine business, but only for a while.

Heinz tried Mexican-flavored and barbecue-flavored catsup, but consumers still prefer ordinary tomato catsup. Peanut butter and jelly in the same jar seemed like a good idea, but it flopped

---

[4] Carter Henderson, *Winners* (New York, N.Y.: Holt, Rinehart, & Winston, 1985), p. 146; "New Products: The Push is on Marketing," *Business Week,* March 4, 1972, pp. 72–77; and Thomas L. Berg, *MisMarketing: Case Histories of Marketing Misfires* (Garden City, N.Y.: Doubleday and Co., 1970).

too. Campbell Soup Co., which should know the soup business better than anyone, has failed a couple of times in introducing frozen soups, but it hasn't given up and is testing a new line. Snack desserts, such as chocolate pudding in little cans, started off strong but faded about a year after introduction.

Some of the other many packaged goods that seemed like good ideas but didn't win enough converts in the marketplace include Bristol-Myers aerosol Ipana toothpaste; Listerine toothpaste; B&W Lyme, lime-flavored cigarette; Frost 8-80's "white" whiskey; three-dimensional movies; and Bell Labs' Picture Phone.

When new products hit it off in the marketplace, it can mean a long-running success story through careful attention from the manufacturer. Some examples are Kleenex facial tissue, introduced in 1924; Oreo cookie, 1921; Coca-Cola soft drink, 1890; Budweiser beer, 1880s; Zippo lighters, 1932; Camel cigarettes, 1913; Ivory soap, 1882; Maxwell House coffee, 1892; and Kodak film, 1900.[5]

Even if all of the most common reasons for failure are consciously evaluated, monitored, and controlled, Murphy's Law can prevail and kill a product for an unexpected reason. In order to succeed despite the crises and disasters that *will occur* in the new product development process, Booz Allen believes companies must adopt identified "best practices" in new product management:[6]

- Make the long-term commitment needed to support innovation and new product development.
- Implement a company-specific approach, driven by corporate objectives and strategies, with a well-defined new product strategy at its core.
- Capitalize on accumulated experience to achieve and maintain competitive advantage.
- Establish an environment—a management style, organizational structure, and degree of top-management support—conducive to achieving company-specific new product and corporate objectives.

How to execute these management practices will be discussed in Chapter Four. Booz Allen further identified several keys to

---

[5] Larry Wizenberg, *The New Products Handbook* (Homewood, Ill.: Dow Jones-Irwin, 1986), pp. 218–219. © 1986 Dow Jones Irwin.

[6] Booz Allen & Hamilton, Inc., *New Products Management for the 1980s* (New York: 1982), p. 3.

successful new product introductions in an international study:[7] Of survey respondents, 88 percent cited product fit with market needs was critical for new product success; 61 percent said product fit with internal functional strengths was necessary; 51 percent cited technological superiority; 44 percent, top management support; 32 percent said use of new product process; 31 percent cited favorable competitive environment; and 15 percent, structure of new product organization.

A slightly more tongue-in-cheek list of new product success factors, but probably not far from reality in many large corporations, was compiled by *New Product Development*, the New Jersey newsletter, after surveying several consultants who specialize in new products. Fifteen or more affirmative answers to the following questions mean the product's success is almost assured:

1. Has the product been in development for a year?
2. Does your company now make a similar product?
3. Does your company now sell to a related customer market?
4. Is research and development at least one third of the product budget?
5. Will the product be test-marketed for at least six months.
6. Does the person in charge have a private secretary?
7. Will the ad budget be at least 5 percent of anticipated sales?
8. Will a recognized brand name be on the product?
9. Would the company take a loss on it for the first year?
10. Does the company "need" the product more than it "wants" it?
11. Have three samples of advertising copy been developed?
12. Is the product really new, as opposed to improved?
13. Can the decision to buy it be made by only one person?
14. Is the product to be made in fewer than five versions?
15. Will the product not need service and repair?
16. Does the development team have a working code name?
17. Will the company president see the project leader without an appointment?
18. Did the project leader make a go of the last two projects?
19. Will the product be on the market for more than 10 years?
20. Would the project leader quit and take the item with him if the company says it won't back it?

---

[7] Ibid, p. 16.

One major way to avoid failure is to set clear standards for the new product development process, because failure in any area is failure for the product. It is important, therefore, to develop a systematic approach around sound principles that will, if adhered to, set off alarms against failure. Consider the following 10 points in establishing a new product development system:

1. Set clear goals for the new product development.
2. Develop specific criteria for each new product.
3. Research thoroughly and analyze the market carefully.
4. Strategically generate new concepts and ideas.
5. Screen the new ideas against the criteria.
6. Do a thorough business analysis, including researching the specific new product concepts.
7. Develop the prototype and refine the business aspects such as tooling cost, production cost, and so on.
8. Test-market and/or further research the product.
9. Commercialize by bringing the new product or service to market.
10. Measure the success or failure against the established standards.

Later in the book, each of the 10 points listed for establishing a successful new product development and marketing system will be amplified. For now, they serve as a guide in preventing failure. By studying why new products fail and at what point in the development system failure can be headed off, it is possible to avoid the pitfalls of failure, or almost avoid them. There is always the human element to account for.

# 4

# Building a Pioneering Spirit

There is no one right organizational structure and process for handling new product development and marketing. Every company, or individual, needs to develop the kind of organization that breeds the pioneering spirit in their company and fits their particular: goals, strategies, economic constraints, personnel capabilities, corporate compatibility, and perception of what will get the job done.

Some companies and entrepreneurs are very research-and-development oriented. Their primary bent is the development of new technology or inventions. Other companies struggle with new product development. They run a good business but virtually stumble upon new product opportunities because they have no organized approach to turning up new products. Between the extremes of the research-and-development oriented company and the company that has no organized approach are companies with many different degrees of organizational development in managing their new product process.

In a small company, new product management will probably be the responsibility of the owner or head of the company. Because new product development is generally a company wide activity, most of the key people will be involved. This involvement may be formalized or it may just be through the entrepreneurial activities of the leader. As companies grow, they need to formalize a management system that will drive toward the corporate goals and overcome the uncertainties that exist in the management of new products. There are seven basic management systems to choose from:

1. An individual leads the way without any formal structure.
2. A new product committee, either formal or informal, is at work.
3. A new product department is established.
4. The product manager system is employed.
5. A matrix team is utilized.
6. Venture teams are used.
7. Outside consultants are hired.

The type of system selected reflects the size of the company and whether the product or service is industrial or consumer oriented. Additional factors that influence the choice include: the industry's custom and practice; budget, and how management views the allocation of time as well as dollars; whether the philosophy is toward developing new products that cut costs or lead technology; the new product strategy of the company; how existing products are marketed; corporate environment; and top management's belief in one structure or another.

All of the above affect the conscious and, too often, subconscious choice of a management system. New product development, although desired by most companies, sits uncomfortably within most corporate environments because new products mean change. Developing and marketing new products upset vested interest and are therefore often short-circuited. No matter what management system is chosen, there is a constant fight: The new product development people have to sell their new products into the corporate system. Despite all of these difficulties, an organized system is needed to increase effectiveness. Few companies can rely only on a stroke of genius or a lucky idea.

For individual entrepreneurs and small business operators, relying on themselves or upon one strong leader is the most basic approach to the management of new products. It is best, however, if all key people in a small company are involved in the process. Not only does the involvement lay the groundwork for building an organizational approach, but it also involves the people so they "own" the new idea. Involvement is probably the best motivator for getting people behind the successful development and introduction of the new product or idea.

For a small business, setting up a formal or informal committee is usually the first organized approach to new product development. It starts with the key individuals of each department—production, finance, marketing, and so on—working together on new product ideas. Formalizing this committee approach can make the effort more productive. Successful use of the committee approach requires clearly spelling out the committee's responsibilities and authority, picking a strong leader to head the committee, and giving the committee specific goals.

One of the strengths of the committee approach is that it involves the people who usually have the responsibility to make a new product development happen. The committee approach also means the company doesn't need to hire additional people to develop new ideas. Ideas, concepts, and expertise are combined in the committee. This approach is flexible. Committees can be ongoing or organized for specific projects. Another strength is that committee members can usually draw upon line personnel without conflict. Also, the committee's decisions are more apt to be accepted because the members are usually top management.

But there are weaknesses in the committee approach to new product development. The committee members' vested interest in their particular departments may color their actions, and the work is an additional demand upon executives' time. Unless clear authority and responsibility is given to the leader of the committee, there may be avoidance of responsibility. Also, if the committee is used just to keep the payroll down, and not because it is the best method under the circumstances, it is not likely to accomplish its goals. Another problem with this approach is that committee members are not expert in new product development and marketing.

The new product committee can be used as the company's complete approach to new product development and marketing, or it may serve only special functions. The committee might only screen ideas, brainstorm, guide consultants, coordinate, or run tests. The degree of involvement depends on the company's objectives, resources, and personnel.

A new product department within the company is another alternative to managing the new product process. This system generally requires strong leadership, someone who can organize a group, who understands the company's focus, and who is able to break into new areas. This approach avoids most of the pitfalls of the committee approach, yet shares the major advantage of drawing upon the company's resources. An independent new product department should have the following qualities:

1. Knowledge of the company's operational abilities and activities.
2. No bias toward particular departments or individuals.
3. Strong analytical abilities.
4. Time to give exclusive attention to new product development.
5. Freedom from functional influences.
6. High visibility within the company.
7. No responsibility for ongoing products.
8. Ability to work with people to marshal internal and external resources.
9. A working knowledge of particular industries and markets, if working toward developing products within a given industry.
10. Ability to integrate a variety of skills.
11. Operating experience, especially helpful for the individual in charge of the department.
12. Drive and ability to push or champion the new concept, idea, or product.
13. Ability to act as devil's advocate as well as coordinator.
14. Repository and processor of ideas that come from employees, the trade, or almost any source.

The new product department should be independent, yet clearly attuned to the goals of the company. It should be able to break new ground but should not become an elitist group. Top management needs to be attentive to this department. Like any other department, it must be managed. Even when, as is often the case, the department consists of one person, it needs the full backing of top management to succeed.

The product manager system is most often used by packaged goods manufacturers like Procter & Gamble, which invented the system more than a half century ago. But other consumer goods as well as industrial companies use this system for new product management. Figure 4–1 shows an organizational chart for a product management system. Each of the product managers may put a portion of his time into new products, but usually one devotes 100 percent to new product development. Product manager 1 under both group directors may devote all of his time to the new product function while product managers 2 and 3 under each

**FIGURE 4–1** _____
Organizational Chart for a Product Management System

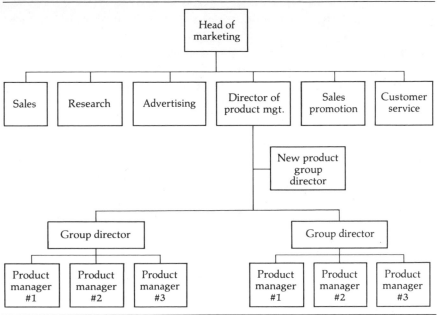

group manager put in part-time efforts. Product manager 1 will work on products applicable to the entire group, but 2 and 3 will be involved only in specific applications to their product area. The new products group director works on products outside the area of the basic group, but within the strategic objectives of the company.

Some companies such as Procter & Gamble refer to their product managers as brand managers. Regardless of the terminology, the managers have a significant influence over existing as well as new products. The influence is strongest over line extensions, repositioning, and innovation.

What the product manager does will vary from company to company. Robert Hisrich and Michael Peters, authors of _Marketing a New Product: Its Planning, Development and Control,_ of Boston College, charted the duties of product managers and contributions from other departments (see Figure 4–2). They say:

> It is evident from this illustration that product managers have numerous duties and responsibilities. In addition to making decisions and recommendations, they generally will have control over signif-

**FIGURE 4–2** _____

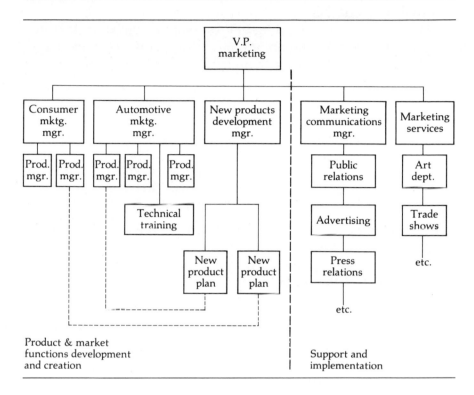

icant funds that must be budgeted for the commercialization strategy of a new product. Product managers receive the expert advice and recommendations of other departments in the decision-making process . . . all decisions must be cleared with top management before product managers are able to continue the development process.[1]

The duties of a consumer goods product manager will vary from that of an industrial goods manager. Industrial product managers will generally be more technically oriented. They might not get involved with the marketing, but act as the bridge, with the R&D people turning the marketing functions over to marketing people. Consumer goods product managers, on the other hand, are usually very marketing oriented. In either case, being attuned to the needs of the market and creating a department that fits

---

[1] Robert D. Hisrich and Michael P. Peters, _Marketing A New Product: Its Planning, Development and Control_ (Menlo Park, Calif.: The Benjamin/Cummings Publishing Co., Inc., 1978), p. 37.

into the company environment helps in the successful introduction of new products.

The matrix team, according to Professor Crawford, is the leading candidate for growth among new product development systems. It is known by many names: task force, project team, or venture team.

> It is a group of people who are actually doing the work, know what is going on, and whose support is critical. These people will expedite the project or stall it; they will achieve the necessary creative breakthroughs, or fail to. They are neither functional heads nor perfunctory representatives. Each of the departments provides one representative to each of the program teams. That representative is responsible both up and across.[2] (See Figure 4–3.)

It is like having a service business within the company. Each functioning department—finance, marketing, manufacturing, and so forth—provides a service that the program team can draw upon. Instead of the team developing its own marketing group or finance group just for the project, it draws upon the functioning departments.

Like every other system, there are advantages and disadvantages to this approach. Dow Corning uses a matrix management system quite successfully. It can be hard on the people involved because they do not have control or authority over the various functions, yet they are responsible for the success or failure of the project. It means they work for many bosses. There is also the struggle for power, with dominant personalities throwing their weight around. This makes it difficult to get a good balance, but when the matrix system works, it is very effective. Generally, it is costly to establish a matrix system, but cost-effective. The smaller business usually will not be able to employ the matrix system in its pure sense. It will tend to operate with a committee, drawing resources from the various functional departments. A demi-matrix system can work for the smaller company if the new product fits the facilities and distribution the company is involved in.

A separate venture group seems to be best employed when the new product does not fit into the company's normal business activities. The venture group is usually autonomous, with most

---

[2] C. Merle Crawford, *New Products Management* (Homewood, Ill.: Richard D. Irwin, Inc., 1983), p. 170.

**FIGURE 4–3**
Matrix Interaction

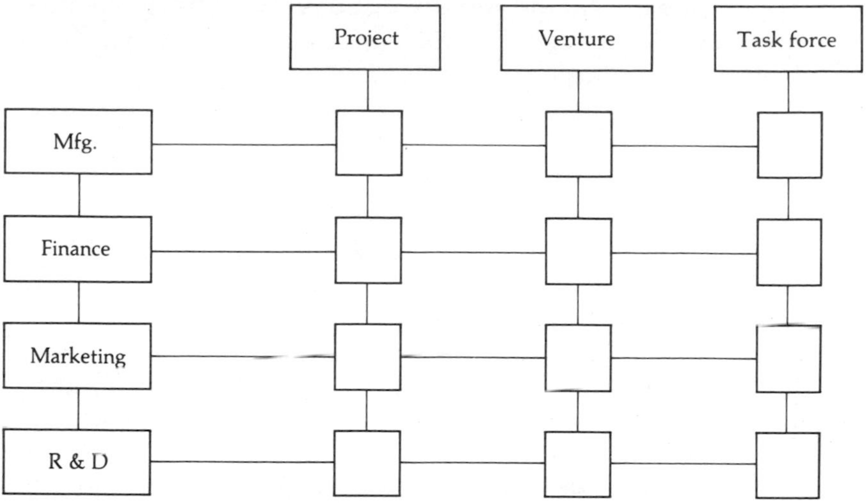

SOURCE: Based on Professor Crawford's Matrix.

of its personnel chosen from the company's various functional departments. Some companies have a permanent venture group, while others set up venture teams for specific projects and may have several venture teams working at once. One individual is generally chosen to head each venture team.

In the venture group or team there is usually no tie to the existing lines of authority. The group or team manager usually will report to the chief executive officer and is given authority and responsibility for major decisions. The group is usually freed from all other company responsibilities and remains together until the job is done.

Venture management groups have the following characteristics:

1. Decisions are in the hands of the group or team leader.
2. The amount of time spent on the project is total.
3. Because a venture team is established, the project takes on great importance.
4. The venture group will generally concentrate on one product or a group of related products, such as bringing the company into a new business.
5. Funding for the project is usually independently developed.

6. The group usually will not have to adhere to company policies.
7. The project should not disrupt usual business activities.
8. The company using venture groups or teams usually has to be fairly large.
9. The project has a high risk coefficient for the company.
10. The group is usually very independent from the rest of the company.

Venture groups and venture teams are different in that teams are usually organized for a specific venture, while groups are permanently established to seek and handle new ventures. The company usually specifies that the venture team or group handle the development and marketing until a certain dollar volume is reached. When that figure is achieved, the functional departments generally take over business operations. At that time, the venture team may be disbanded. The venture group will turn attention to the other projects it may be working on or seek a new project. Figure 4–4 is a summary framework developed by Booz Allen showing the use of different organization structures to meet the varying needs of different product development efforts.

Many companies will turn over all new product development and market planning to outside consultants. Others will use the consultants only for certain phases of the process. There are consulting firms that can do it all and others that specialize in certain phases of new product development and marketing. There are research companies that do only concept testing and others that do quantitative testing. Other consultants specialize in developing new concepts, and still others, in marketing. There are technical consultants, such as Arthur D. Little, Foster D. Snell, and Stanford Research Institute. There are packaging and design firms such as Selame Design, King-Casey, Inc., and Morrison Cousins. There are Booz Allen & Hamilton, The Associate Group, Bobrow Consulting Group, Venture Resource Group, and other broad-based consultants that can deliver virtually every phase of new product consulting. Then there are consultants that specialize in just developing names for new products, such as the Name Lab in California. A good, reliable source of consultants can be obtained from the Institute of Management Consultants at 19 West 44th Street, New York, New York, and the Society of Professional Management Consultants at 163 Engle Street, Englewood, New

**FIGURE 4–4**
New Product Management Environment

| New product opportunity | Organization structure | Management style | Management responsibility | Top management support |
|---|---|---|---|---|
| New to the world products | Venture team | Entrepreneurial | Corporate management | High |
| New lines | | | | |
| Additions to lines | New product department | Collegial | | |
| Improvements/ revisions to products | Marketing or R & D | | | |
| Repositioning | | Managerial | | |
| Cost reductions | Functional | | Functional manager | Moderate |

SOURCE: "New Products Management For the 1980s," Booz Allen & Hamilton, Inc.

Jersey. In general, consultants are probably best used as a member of a larger team that includes internal managers.

In addition to the functional organization of the product development responsibility, the process itself needs a structured, organized approach to ensure success. A broad, strategic process structure includes the following steps: establishing corporate objectives and strategy; identifying growth role for new products; analyzing product life cycles, corporate culture, capabilities, past new product experience, industry, and environment; developing new product strategy; generating ideas; screening and evaluating; analyzing the business; developing; testing; and commercialization.

Figure 4–5 shows one example of a comprehensive process structure for a consumer product and indicates that a new product development effort clearly affects all areas of a company regardless of the specific new products responsibility assignment. Figure 4–6 is an example of the frequent interaction of responsibilities and communication necessary between marketing and engineering during the development of durable goods.

**FIGURE 4–5**
New Product Checklist

| | Research & development | Finance | Production | Distribution | Legal | Communication |
|---|---|---|---|---|---|---|
| **I. Exploration** | | | | | | |
| *Statement of company objective | Policy objective | | | | | |
| Initial exploratory and creative activities | | | | | | X |
| Statement of product idea | Originator | | | | | |
| Judgment evaluation of merit | New product committee | | | | | |
| *Plan to investigate approved | Operations executive | | | | | |
| Profile of products known on the market | X | | | | | |
| Survey of product ingredients, design standards, general technology of the field | X | | | | | |
| Analyze competitive product claims | X | | | | | X |
| Analyze competitive media use | | | | | | X |
| Analyze competitive advertising expenditures | | | | | | X |
| Areas of brand share/volume history | X | | | | | |
| Survey of trade information regarding CGS, wholesale discounts, distribution costs | X | | | X | | X |
| Survey of traditional channels of distribution and other distribution opportunities | X | | | X | | X |
| Survey of general selling practices, promotional allowances, buying standards | | | | X | | X |
| Survey of specific federal and state legal problems in reference to ingredients, sales practices, controls | | | | X | X | |
| Survey to determine marketing opportunity area | X | | | | | |
| Cyclical, seasonal, and long-term marketing considerations | X | | | | | |
| Product class profile study | X | | | | | |
| Survey of potential consumer interest in new product | X | | | | | |
| Definition of the selected market | X | | | | | |
| Preliminary opportunity estimate | New product committee | | | | | |
| **II. Screening** | | | | | | |
| *Appoint project coordinating executive | | | | | | |
| Estimate period of product exclusivity | X | | X | X | | X |
| Research of consumer satisfaction and use habits of current products | X | | | | | |
| Consumer motivation research in area of advertised brand claims, etc. | X | | | | | X |

**FIGURE 4–5**
(*continued*)

| | Research & development | Finance | Production | Distribution | Legal | Communication |
|---|---|---|---|---|---|---|
| Product concept screening | X | | | | | X |
| Analysis of sizes, colors, shapes, textures, types required | X | | | | | |
| Isolation of CGS/price opportunities in distribution mix | X | X | | | | |
| Investigate additional sales outlets—government, export, institutional, premiums | | | | X | | |
| Report of findings and indicated opportunities | X | | | X | | X |

**III. Proposal**

| | Research & development | Finance | Production | Distribution | Legal | Communication |
|---|---|---|---|---|---|---|
| *Request for planned development program, with estimated investment and timetable | New product committee | | | | | |
| Approve research and development budget | Operations executive | | | | | |
| Initial design/formulation of product | X | | X | | | |
| Copyrights or patents | X | | | | X | |
| Prepare product platform | X | | X | | | X |
| Secure required government clearances | | | | | X | |
| Initial costing based on optimum manufacturing levels | X | X | X | | | |
| Local tax, licensing, and other financial considerations | | X | | | X | |
| Life and fatigue tests of materials and finishes | X | | X | | | |
| Performance and efficiency tests | X | | X | | | |
| *Independent laboratory/engineering analysis of prototypes | X | | | | | |
| Prepare a copy platform | | | | | | X |
| Social science evaluation of consumers relative to the new product area | X | | | | | X |
| Panel evaluation of prototype product | X | | | | | |
| Forecast of volume potential | X | | | X | | X |
| Plant capacity and facilities availability | | | X | | | |
| Consumer blind test comparison | X | | | | | |

**IV. Development**

| | Research & development | Finance | Production | Distribution | Legal | Communication |
|---|---|---|---|---|---|---|
| Large-scale research of prototype product | X | | | | | |
| Plant location and transportation considerations | | | X | | | |
| *Basis of appropriation | New product committee | | | | | |

**FIGURE 4–5**
(*continued*)

| | Research & development | Finance | Production | Distribution | Legal | Communication |
|---|---|---|---|---|---|---|
| Develop national media plan | | | | | | X |
| Decide on manufacturer association— identification on/with product | X | | | X | | X |
| Creation of brand name possibilities | | | | | | X |
| Creation of/or agreement on established generic descriptive name | | | | | | X |
| Legal search of brand name possibilities | | | | | X | |
| Register trademark, copyright brand name | | | | | X | |
| Development of basic consumer selling theme | | | | | | X |
| Test of consumer selling theme | | | | | | X |
| Labeling requirements | | | | | X | |
| Initial packaging | X | | | | | X |
| Packaging testing | X | | | | | |
| Approve package design (and inserts) | | | | | | X |
| Prepare instructions/directions to conform | | | | | X | X |
| Adoption of media philosophy, based on selling theme, budgetary consideration, coverage of prospects and availability | | | | | | X |
| Test of advertising execution (in form of basic media) | | | | | | X |
| Creation of total national campaign concept | | | | | | X |
| Labor availability | | | X | | | |
| Labor or union regulations | | | X | | X | |
| Raw material commitments and availability | | | X | | | |
| Special tooling and equipment | | | X | | | |
| Packaging and components commitments | | | X | | | |
| Predict competitive reaction to new product | X | | | X | | X |

**V. Sales Testing**

| | Research & development | Finance | Production | Distribution | Legal | Communication |
|---|---|---|---|---|---|---|
| Assign product manager to work with project executive | Operations executive | | | | | |
| Set test area sales goals—share, penetration, unit, and dollar volume | New product committee | | | | | |
| Determine introductory test area timing | X | | | | | X |
| Service and repair problems and facilities | | | X | | | |
| *Sales representative recruitment | | X | X | | | |
| Sales training | | | X | | | |
| *Manufacturing pilot run | | | X | | | |
| *Approve test area production | Operations executive | | | | | |
| Shipping, storage, and packing tests | | | X | | | |

**FIGURE 4–5** _____
(*continued*)

| | Research & development | Finance | Production | Distribution | Legal | Communication |
|---|---|---|---|---|---|---|
| Define all aspects of available test areas, including demographic, media patterns, trade outlet patterns, and distribution centers | X | | | | | X |
| Plan to meet competitive reaction | | | | X | | X |
| Finalize test areas | X | | | | | X |
| Forecast test area unit and dollar volume (goals) | X | | | X | | |
| *Forecast P/L limits of successful venture and of unsuccessful write-off | X | X | | X | | |
| Test area simulation of national campaign concept | | | | | | X |
| Test area media plan (in line with expansion objectives) | | | | | | X |
| *Determine test area total appropriation | New product committee | | | | | |
| Approve test area consumer advertising materials | | | | | | X |
| Approve trade advertising materials | | | | X | | X |
| Determine merchandising plan and appropriation | | | | X | | X |
| Prepare media merchandising | | | | X | | X |
| Preparation of trade selling sheets | | | | X | | X |
| Determine educational plan and appropriation | | | | | | X |
| Prepare consumer educational materials | | | | | | X |
| Determine publicity plan and appropriation | | | | | | X |
| Prepare introductory publicity materials | | | | | | X |
| Determine sales promotion plan and appropriation | | | | X | | X |
| Devise consumer incentives, if required— premiums, contests, price offers, couponing, etc. | | | | X | | X |
| Consider multiple product tie-ins | | | | X | | X |
| Determine cooperative advertising policies | | | | X | | X |
| Prepare cooperative ads | | | | X | | X |
| Prepare point-of-purchase materials | | | | X | | X |
| Prepare product hang tags, boots, self-displays | | | X | X | | X |
| Decide on trade sampling appropriation | | | X | X | | X |
| Approve test area commercial plan and insertion schedule | | | | | | X |

**FIGURE 4–5**
(*concluded*)

| | Research & development | Finance | Production | Distribution | Legal | Communication |
|---|---|---|---|---|---|---|
| Product indemnity for field test | | | | | X | |
| Set sales quotas | | | | X | | |
| Sales force incentives, bonuses, premiums | | | | X | | |
| Trade incentives—buying allowances, contests | | | | X | | |
| Product printed material commitments | | | X | | | |
| Set up test area consumer sales audit panel | X | | | X | | |
| Trade sales kickoff | | | | X | | |
| Preintroductory measure of brand name awareness in test area | X | | | | | X |
| Advertising kickoff | | | | | | X |
| Survey trade performance in test area | | | | X | | |
| Test area user research | X | | | | | |
| Media coverage and intensity progress reports in test area—adjust to meet standards | | | | | | X |
| Post-introduction measure of brand name awareness in test area | X | | | | | X |
| Post-introductory new product profile study in test area | X | | | | | |
| Analyze factory sales data from test area | X | | | | | |
| Program performance reports in test area—adjust to meet standards | | | | | | X |
| Competitive media trend report of test area | | | | | | X |
| Evaluate sales and advertising, via progress reports throughout area test timetable | X | | | X | | X |
| Test area evaluation | X | | | X | | X |
| *Define special line management attention or policy changes required in large scale marketing | X | X | X | X | | X |
| *Recommendation for major expansion | New product committee | | | | | |

VI. **Marketing**
Turn over to appropriate product manager
and revenue division

*Action required by major officer of company.
SOURCE: Campbell-Mithern, Inc. Advertising, Minneapolis, Minn.

## FIGURE 4–6

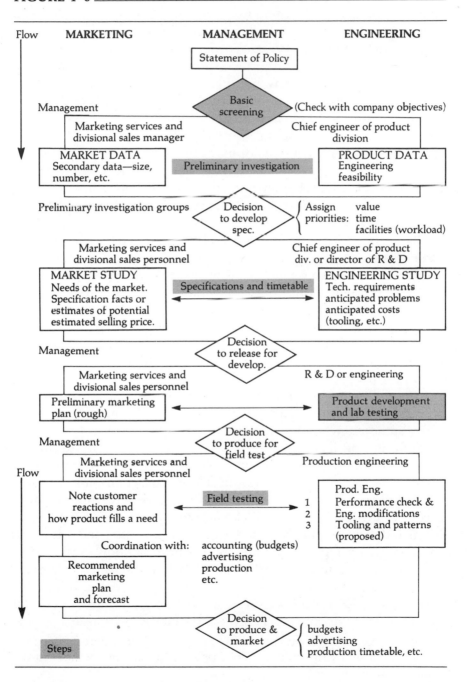

Although a structured process is needed to provide a disciplined approach to executing new product development, it should never become a bureaucratic process designed to kill projects. The step-by-step check and test approach is giving way to a more action-oriented posture in order to adapt to a more dynamic marketplace. Even a company like Procter & Gamble, for years the example of deliberate, painstakingly thorough product development, has started to streamline decision-making processes in order to more quickly respond to market opportunities. The key is assigning new product development responsibility to a person or team of intelligent, results-oriented people who can substitute judgment for facts when appropriate, who know when to eliminate steps in the process, and who are willing to assume the risks inherent in eliminating steps.

The turbulence and structural changes discussed in Chapter One (faster change of technology, stronger global competition) are forcing many companies to replace serial (step-by-step) product development with a more complex and risky parallel development for more rapid introduction. One technique for accelerating the process is building vertically integrated joint ventures to create "instant" new products, taking advantage of diverse strengths of the various partners, such as marketing, distribution, manufacturing, and R&D.

Regardless of how the process is structured, an axiom of successful product development is that there *must be* a product champion, someone who intensely believes in the product, is willing to fight for it, and has the stamina, energy, and creativity to push it through, around, or over the internal barriers that always exist in an organization. A classic example of a product champion who survived the best bureaucratic obstacles the U.S. government could erect was the late William B. McLean, who, along with a small team of men, developed the Sidewinder missile. The Sidewinder is about to celebrate its 30th anniversary as one of the nation's most effective and successful weapons. In an era when the Defense Department is plagued with criticism for buying $7,600 coffee pots, $400 hammers, and a number of trouble-prone, multibillion-dollar weapons systems, the story of the Sidewinder is unique.[3]

Weapons-development programs are rigidly generated from specifications set by the military. The specs set for the Sidewinder in the

---

[3] Excerpts from "Weapon of Choice," *The Wall Street Journal*, February 15, 1985, p. 1.

late 1940s were no exception. It had to perform in all weather conditions and had to be able to kill every aircraft by striking them head-on. In the early 1950s, one of the nation's most potent, most reliable, and simplest weapons was born under a cover of deepest secrecy at a Navy test facility in California's Mojave desert. Known by the code name Local Project 612, the Sidewinder missile-development program was so secret that its very existence was kept from meddlesome Navy and Pentagon officials in Washington who were financing it. And that, Sidewinder enthusiasts insist, is what made all the difference.

The Sidewinder was designed by a small team of men at the Navy's Naval Weapons Center at China Lake, Calif. The team, which included Mr. Laberge, an engineer who now is in charge of research for Lockheed Corp.'s missile and space program, was led by a physicist, the late William B. McLean. He scrounged money from other projects, scavenged spare parts from Pasadena junkyards, and was driven by a passion for making cheap, simple things that work. Current weapons-development programs, Mr. Laberge says, are rigidly generated from specifications set by the military-specifications, he says, that are "almost always asking for too much." "The way the world works," he adds, "once you get the specification you win the contract only by selling the customer what he wants. We set ourselves up by presuming we know the answer before we've done it."

That was not the way of Bill McLean, who sheltered the Sidewinder program from its critics and eventually forced the missile on a reluctant Pentagon. He ignored specifications and concentrated on concepts that his experiments told him would work. Working part of the time in his garage, Mr. McLean designed about 85 percent of the missile himself. It had a total of nine moving parts and its "brain" consisted of seven radio tubes. It used gas pressure from burning rocket fuel to move its control fins and to generate a small amount of electricity. There were no heavy batteries to wear down, no hydraulics systems to leak or freeze, no precision-machined tolerances. "It had the mechanical complexity of a small washing machine combined with a table radio." The first problem Mr. McLean ran into was money. China Lake, at the time, was operated by the Navy's Bureau of Ordnance. The Navy's Bureau of Aeronautics in Washington was in charge of all missile development, and it was devoting all of its money to the Sparrow. China Lake had a small amount of discretionary funds; and when those were exhausted, Mr. McLean's superiors in the Bureau of Ordnance—which had an intense rivalry with the Bureau of Aeronautics—found ways to siphon money from other programs to keep Sidewinder going.

Mr. McLean's next problem was testing. The first 13 shots of the Sidewinder failed. That, according to Mr. McLean's coworkers, would have also doomed a major development program. Officially, however, Sidewinder didn't exist. So Mr. McLean took what he had learned from the failures (caused by vibrations of the rocket interfering with electrical guidance) and applied that knowledge to a 14th shot, on September 11, 1953. It hit the target. Once the Sidewinder team demonstrated the missile could hit targets, the Navy's official interest was soon aroused. The Air Force, though, was resistant. Then Mr. McLean worked out a deal with an assistant secretary of the Air Force: If the Sidewinder could beat the Falcon in a shoot-out, the Air Force would consider buying some.

There are many stories about the shoot-out, which was staged by the Air Force at Holloman Air Force Base in New Mexico in 1956. Mr. McLean and a few people he had brought with him from China Lake found themselves up against a team of technicians from Hughes Aircraft Co., which was developing the Falcon. The Navy was given the corner of one hangar, an aging F-86 fighter, and a few wrenches. The Air Force assigned itself a newer fighter and tons of Hughes test equipment to monitor the more complex and delicate Falcons.

At one point, Mr. McLean decided to rattle the opposition by demanding that he be given some test equipment. What more did the Navy want? the Air Force asked. A stepladder and a flashlight, Mr. McLean responded. After a toss of a coin, the plane carrying the Sidewinder went up and knocked down the first target drone with one shot. For six straight days the Hughes team struggled with the Falcon, but it refused to leave the launcher.

For his efforts on the Sidewinder, Mr. McLean received a $25,000 award from the government and a plaque from President Eisenhower. He was later transferred from China Lake to the Navy's submarine-warfare research center in San Diego, where he served as technical director until retiring in 1974. He died four years later. To the end, he remained a maverick within the system. The Pentagon, he once complained before a Senate committee, has forgotten the need to experiment with prototypes.

There are at least three important messages in this example: make sure you have a product champion; keep your product concepts as simple as possible; and make a prototype as early as possible to see if the idea really makes sense.

How does an existing organization with all of its resistance to change and established policies and procedures create an environment for the Mr. McLeans of the world? By establishing the right leadership and spirit at the top of the organization. There is no substitute for top management's personal, day-to-day involvement in the new product development process for setting

**FIGURE 4–7** _____
New Product Management Scorecard
_____

Determine how well you are managing new products and the process.
Rate from 1 to 10 points for each question.
(10 = "Fully Meets," 5 = "Partially Meets," and 1 = "Does Not Meet")

*Score*

1. Our corporate growth plan includes an explicit strategic description on the role of internally developed new products over the next five years.

2. We have a well-defined new product strategy that identifies the financial gap and strategic roles new products must satisfy.

3. We establish different hurdle rates, based on associated risk.

4. We have had a systematic, yet adaptive, new product process in place for at least five years.

5. Idea generation for us begins *after* we have identified external market niches and assessed our internal competitive strengths.

6. We have a formalized monitoring and tracking system in place to measure cost per introduction and new product performance against established objectives.

7. We have compensation programs that encourage entrepreneurship reward risk-takers and reinforce innovative management.

8. We have a clear understanding of who is responsible for new product development.

9. Top management provides consistent commitment to new products in terms of funds and requisite managerial know-how.

10. We adapt our new products organization to match the requirements of our new products portfolio.

Total

*SCORE*

| | |
|---|---|
| 90–100 | We are one of the best! |
| 80–89 | Improvement areas exist, but we're in good shape. |
| 70–79 | We should consider making changes to our new products program. |
| Less than < 70 | We better get some assistance in managing new products. |

SOURCE: Booz Allen & Hamilton, Inc., 101 Park Avenue, New York, NY 10178

the example and the style of the organization. If the CEO believes new products are the lifeblood of an organization (and he should), and devotes time, attention, and rewards to the new product effort and the people who thrive on change, then the rest of the organization will follow.

If the CEO instead devotes the majority of his attention to financial monitoring and control, organization planning, information systems, manufacturing procedures, legal and public relations activities, or any of the other trappings of the chief executive role, new product development will suffer.

The best concepts, the greatest new products will not see the marketplace unless there is a marshaling of resources that capitalizes on the company's strengths and the opportunities in the market. Unless a company develops a management system that can take advantage of its strengths and make things happen, it will miss the opportunities that new products present. A company should not try to copy any other company's system, but rather try to develop a system that is right for it. It takes time, patience, money, leadership, and occasional expert assistance. The New Products Management Scorecard in Figure 4–7 rates how well a company is doing at new product development.

# 5

# Setting a Destination— Corporate Goals

When a company decides to be a pioneer in new products, it needs a clear idea of where it wants to go, or it may be destined to spend the proverbial "40 years wandering in the wilderness." The most debilitating activity a business can engage in, especially a small company, is a random and unfocused search for new products. Such a search can be an enormous drain on management as well as financial resources, and it can leave a company with nothing to take up the slack when the long-term mainstay product finally heads south.

A continuous introduction of line extensions, modifications, new styles, new models, or other variations of existing products can also destroy a business. The cost of management time, engineering resources, and capital and marketing investments devoted to products that primarily cannibalize current business without creating new customers and new market growth can gradually weaken the business.

The second abuse is more prevalent in larger organizations today. The blind belief in the theory of product life cycles and abuses in marketing segmentation and product differentiation have led to fractionated markets and unnecessary product proliferation. Product lines tend to be longer today, inventory dollars higher, brand cycles shorter, and return on assets lower. Does the world really need a banana-coconut flavored yogurt?

It may be time to adopt product strategies that reflect the financial and competitive realities. General Douglas MacArthur once said, when asked why he had the fewest casualties of any theater commander, "I will not take by sacrifice that which I can take by strategy."

In order to set a destination and develop a clear product strategy, the company must first conceive and articulate a mission. This term is a business extension of an old military term, and simply means a definition of the boundaries of the company's activity, and the ultimate goal (what type of war will you conduct, and in what theater of battle?). Although the concept is simple, the simplest things are often the most difficult in practice; and the thought process and discipline in developing and following a mission is a good example of this fact of business life.

The famous *Harvard Business Review* article by Theodore Levitt, "Marketing Myopia," best illustrated the need for creativity and vision in developing a business mission. It demonstrated the risk in defining a business too narrowly and missing opportunities for long-term growth. The inability of some railroads to view their business in broader terms of transportation, or real estate, or natural resource management, and eventually going out of business when the immediate market declined, is a classic example of a business boundary being set too narrow. Tom Peters illustrated the opposite problem of chasing diversification too far from current expertise in *In Search of Excellence* and developed the business principle of "sticking to your knitting."

The first step in setting a destination, then, is to define the boundaries of the business so they are large enough to allow and encourage significant new growth, but not so large as to go beyond the capabilities of the firm. This sounds simple, but it requires a creative vision from the CEO or top management team. It takes a sense of order about the traditional strengths of the company and a unique insight into the energizing trends in the marketplace.

Mission boundaries can be defined around a variety of business categories and can either restrict or stimulate visionary strategies:

**Trade Categories.** These tend to be narrow, nonconceptual, and consequently restrictive. An example is a broom and mop company that refuses to consider dustpans and other cleaning tools because it is in the "stick goods" business.

**Power Source or Material Categories.**   These categories are useful as a base for determining access to source materials and vertical integration, but do not define eventual businesses. The specialty steel companies that viewed their business as fast and flexible customer service versus steel managed to stay in business while the major steel manufacturers succumbed to Japanese competition.

**Distribution Categories.**   This is useful only in defining certain qualifications and requirements of products that pass through the categories. L'eggs built an entire business on the premise that panty hose could be successfully merchandised in grocery stores as well as traditional soft-goods retailers.

**Market Categories.**   These categories are expressed in a variety of terms, from demographics to psychographics to lifestyles. The terms have become cliches, unfortunately, but intelligently used are critical. Defining mission boundaries as the "over 55 population," "hard core exercise segment," or the "small business manager" has enabled many companies to achieve dramatic success with new products.

**Product Categories.**   These boundaries are determined only by the imagination of those who define them. Is Gerber's business baby food or babies? Is Levi Strauss & Co.'s business pants or clothing? Is General Motors' business automobiles or manufacturing technology? Is Philip Morris's business cigarettes or mass marketing of consumable packaged goods? Is it a lawn mower company or a lawn and garden marketer? Is it a paint sprayer company or a painting company?

Figure 5–1 shows a common matrix for defining mission boundaries or degrees of business diversification. This plus creative market vision can be used in setting boundaries.

Specific business goals within the mission, then, are an outgrowth of a strategic planning process. This process relies on understanding and evaluating the three "C's" of business strategy: Customers, Competitors, and Company.

**FIGURE 5–1**
Growth Vector Alternatives

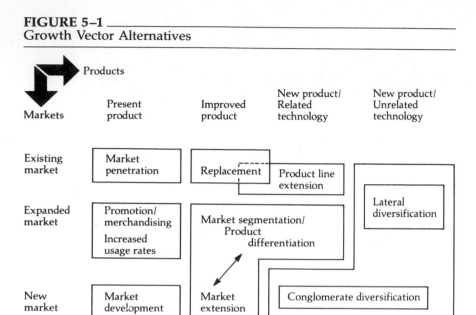

The customer analysis includes: segmenting into groups; determining customer perceptions of the products and company; mentally exploring unmet needs; and identifying potential future needs, including needs that can be created (more on this in Chapter Nine).

Understanding the competition is critical in developing products with a substantial competitive advantage: detail how each competitor attacks the market; locate any gaps competitors haven't filled; identify values the company can provide that competitors fail to provide; and predict reactions from competitors.

A company also needs to develop an unbiased appraisal of itself. It can do this by: carefully listing each strength and weakness being ruthless and objective; thinking of new ways to apply existing strengths to products or markets; and evaluating products and businesses as if they were a portfolio of investments and asking the question: Which would you bet your money on?

Peter Drucker, in his book *Innovation and Entrepreneurship* (Harper & Row), summarizes the innovation strategy process as: "Systematic abandonment, the business X-ray, and the definition of innovative gaps."

Having set boundaries and analyzed opportunities within them, the company is finally ready to commit to a destination or new product development goal and strategy statement. This statement must be committed to writing and be the outcome of a team process in order to obtain consistent management effort. The essential elements of the statement are the specifications of the product-market scope, the basic strategies to be used for growing within that scope, and some broad market and financial targets.

Too often, companies do not have stated goals. The owner or a small group of executives may think they know the company goals, but it is likely they would disagree. They might all agree on basic caveats, such as making money or reaching higher sales volume, but goals have to be carefully thought out and committed to paper to point to clear company strategies.

Goals, of course, are the ends toward which efforts are directed. Objectives relate to action or feeling, as well as something toward which effort is directed. An objective can be an aim or end action or even a goal. For many, the terms *goal* and *objective* are interchangeable. But there are subtle and important differences in individual interpretation. Most marketing people define goals as long-range aims and objectives as time-phased, short-range aims. Selling an important prospect can be classified as an objective, while increasing sales for the company is a goal. Usually, many objectives have to be met in order to meet the goals.

Distinguishing between goals or objectives is not as important as developing a system for establishing clear aims that includes committing them to writing. Developing a system should involve more than a few key executives locking themselves in a room and coming out with a list of goals. The approach must involve careful examination of internal and external factors that affect the company, as well as analysis of where the company has been, where it is now, and where it wants to go (which the goals will reflect).

Academicians as well as practitioners argue whether goals are set first and then strategies developed or whether goals are established during the process of developing strategies. Every company proceeds differently. Some small companies have the entrepreneur or key operating executives set the goals. In larger companies, corporate goals are handed down and from these the new product people develop their goals. Sometimes the goal setting is based strictly on an internal process, other times it takes into account analysis of external factors. Whichever way new product goals are developed, they should not be cast in stone. Working on the strategies helps make goals and objectives clearer.

The company's new product goals should not be confused with new product criteria, which are established later in the product development process. The goals are the end aim. The criteria will be the specific characteristics that the new product should embody in order to be considered by the company. Later in the book, we will fully discuss criteria.

Following is one process for using a team effort to establish common goals:

1. Appoint one person to lead the effort. This can be the CEO, strategic planner, or whoever is appropriate for the company.
2. Have every key decision maker in the company submit a one-page statement of suggested corporate goals or new product goals if corporate goals are known.
3. Have each key person list the company's strengths and weaknesses.
4. Have each indicate in a brief statement where they think the company has been, where it is now, and where they expect it to be in three and five years.
5. Have each person submit a suggested mission statement for the company and then for new product development and marketing.
6. Have each suggest the management system they believe is most appropriate for new product development and marketing.

The leader should then assemble these statements and others that are needed and compile all the suggestions into a list that is sent back for further consideration. A second revised set of documents should then be written by each person and returned to the leader. A meeting is then held and the revised and consolidated lists are discussed. The first draft of company goals is then developed. This first draft will be subject to revision as the strategies are developed.

If the do-it-yourself approach is not used, a consultant could be brought in to facilitate the process of developing goals, objectives, and strategies. (Facilitating means helping the company define its own goals, *not* doing it for the firm.) A good consultant will do exactly what a doctor does. It will work up a case history. The consultant will want to know the company's hopes, dreams, aspirations, previous marketing activities, and business history. From this kind of probing, the trained specialist will be able to determine what the opportunities are and, with the company's help, be able to establish practical goals.

As indicated earlier, the process of developing strategies will help in establishing goals and objectives. That is why goals should not be firmed up until the strategic planning is completed. Strategic planning is, as Chase and Barasch, authors of *Marketing Problem Solver*, wrote, "a complete plan of exactly how you would make the best use of your resources to achieve a goal."[1] They go on to list some examples:

Distinguish your product from that of competitors as viewed by your customers.

Offer only one product and try to attract all buyers (i.e., use an "undifferentiated strategy).

Develop separate products and marketing programs for each market segment (i.e., use a "differentiated" strategy).

Create new uses for existing products (through improved performance and/or exclusive features).

Diversify into new markets with new products, either through acquisition of companies or through internal development of new products.

Establish product leadership through development of quality products.

Develop _____ new products for commercialization consideration each year, beating competition to marketplace and establishing a reputation for innovation.

Broad business growth strategies can then be detailed with specific product-market strategies, which might include one or more of the following. Product-market strategies could include market opportunities, such as natural changes in the size of the market, new uses for the product or new user segments, innovative product differentiations, or new product lines. The strategy might be geared to product line gaps, such as filling out existing product lines or creating new product line elements. Distribution

---

[1] Chase, Cochrane & Kenneth L. Barasch, *Marketing Problem Solver*, 2nd ed. (New York: Chilton Book Company, 1977), pp. 78–79.

gaps can offer opportunities such as expanding distribution coverage, intensity, or exposure.

Or the marketer may choose a usage gap strategy to stimulate nonusers and light users or to increase the amount used on each occasion. Another strategy relates to competitive gaps, including penetrating the substitute's or direct competitor's position, or defending the firm's present position.

Strategies can be developed by being a careful "detective of change," looking for clues in outside trends. External factors that can affect the company or new products include economic conditions, government regulations, competition, customers, lifestyles, technology, markets, and demographics. In planning strategy, a company must decide which external factors will affect its efforts and to what degree. Sometimes the company can even shape or control these external factors to create opportunities (such as through lobbying or political action).

Internal factors also must be objectively analyzed. An internal audit can consider: management's mental set, personality, and personal objectives as they relate to the company objectives; the company's aggregate skills; resources available; capabilities; people; physical plant; management information system; geography; method of distribution; level of productivity; costs; and image. Other internal factors peculiar to a company's operation also need to be analyzed. From this analysis and the analysis of external factors, opportunities, problems, possibilities, and so on will become apparent, and from them, strategies are developed and goals firmed up. Figure 5–2 shows the flow in developing a product strategy or destination.

Following is one example of a strategy statement:

### New Product Development Strategy
#### Business Volume ($ millions)

|  | Year | | | |
|---|---|---|---|---|
|  | '84 | '85 | '86 | '87 |
| A. Financial Goal | $120 | $136 | $150 | $162 |
| Growth Rate |  | 13% | 10% | 8% |
| 1. Volume from current businesses | $109 | $113 | $118 | $123 |
| 2. Gap-volume required from acquisition, diversification, and new product development | $11 | $23 | $32 | $39 |

**FIGURE 5–2**

Highlighting Product Planning Activities in the Strategic
Planning Process

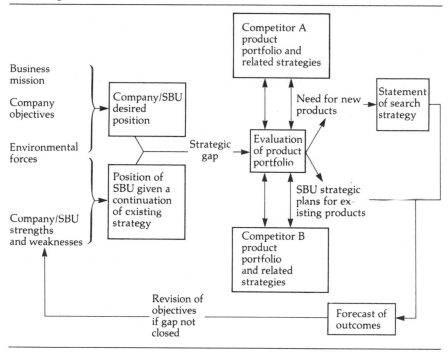

B. Market Position Statement

XYZ is the leader and innovator in the XXX industry. It has invented
a better way to XXX. Its products provide premium quality and performance and are a good value. XXX is the name millions of consumers should think of first when it comes to XXX.

C. Business Goals

1. Become the high-volume manufacturer generating greater margins through production efficiencies.
2. Leverage down the cost of sales as volume increases.
3. Continue to be the innovator, developing and marketing new
products.
4. Become the dominant company in the XXX market.

D. Strategy

Become a leader in the XXX industry through the development or
acquisition of unique, innovative, premium quality products. Build
and leverage distribution strength by establishing a permanent shelf
position in all major retailers; focus on products offering high-volume
manufacturing and mass marketing potential.

# 6

# Developing Product Objectives

In business, things seldom happen in a linear fashion. The sequence of events tends to vary, not only from business to business, but also from situation to situation. Sometimes new products develop in the sequence laid out in this book; other times, an activity may happen before or after logic would dictate. The important thing is not that each step always be taken sequentially, but that each step is taken somewhere in the process. Usually after the goals, objectives, and strategies for overall new product development have been established, criteria are set down for the specific product line being worked toward.

While overall new product goals and strategies tend to change slowly, the criteria for specific development should rarely be changed once established. Through adherence to the criteria for the development of the next innovation or invention, a product or product line can be systematically developed to fit the company's new product goals. The next new product and the one after may each have different criteria because each product will be building upon the other. Satisfying new product goals and strategies in turn satisfies the company's mission and overall corporate goals and objectives.

If specific criteria for developing new products are not set down, it becomes difficult to evaluate new product ideas and concepts. It is important to cull ideas early in the product development process because each step further into the process gets more costly. Success is also closely connected to careful elimination of ideas that do not fit into the corporate capabilities and market needs. Establishing specific criteria provides the first hard-nosed look at what the company wants as its new product.

Setting new product objectives forces identification and analysis of critical factors, raises issues, gets agreement and consensus from the management team, and helps to avoid "missing the obvious." Too often companies invest several years of R&D effort and expense only to discover the market isn't large enough to pay back the investment, or the product design concept forces a price beyond market acceptance, or the manufacturing process requires a tooling or machinery investment that would require a 20-year life cycle to generate an adequate return on investment, or, the ultimate omission, the CEO really had something else in mind.

A consumer goods company wanted to attack a new market segment to balance the volume of an existing product line. The product concept was revolutionary and required new design concepts. No criteria were established relative to the maximum tooling investment the company wanted to risk in the technology. The product gained immediate acceptance in the marketplace, orders increased much faster than anticipated, and duplicate tooling and other manufacturing investments had to be made to keep up with demand. The additional investments kept extending the payback period, however. In the meantime, competitors attacked the rapidly growing market with different technology. The company had lost its ability to react quickly because of the extensive fixed manufacturing investments, and it had to accept a lower market share rather than write off enormous tooling investments. A limit on manufacturing investments relative to the technology risk could have avoided much management anguish and maintained the company in a less vulnerable position.

Good product development objectives should include ranges and limits as well as specific results desired and should be established relative to the nature of the company and the industry it competes within. Look for inconsistencies and unrealistic expectations when setting criteria. Attacking a national market with a new product will require a much greater marketing investment and more time than a local or regional program and should generate a higher return on investment because of the greater degree of risk.

A company operating in an industry known for fast competitive reaction needs to set demanding criteria on payback time. It does not have the luxury of generating losses for three years while building the market. The company should consider the degree of concentration in the industry when establishing market share criteria. A 3 percent market share could be an attractive position in a fragmented market with 100 competitors and the top 3 owning a combined share of only 10 percent.

The rate of technology change in the industry also affects product objectives. Major breakthroughs do not occur monthly in industries such as farm machinery or hand tools, so a new product idea may have five years or more to earn a desired return. But in an industry like communications, information processing, or clothing, look for a return before the sun sets!

Product objectives and criteria need to relate to the overall company goals and mission discussed in the previous chapter. When building on an existing product category through model variations and line extensions, specific objectives should be modest. If set too high, the criteria may eliminate many ideas that, when introduced as a group of line extensions, could generate good growth and profitability. Major product breakthroughs, 50 percent market shares, 20 percent net after tax profit margins, and 25 percent return rates don't come often. If a company screens out all of the small ideas waiting for a few big hits, it may lose growth momentum, customer enthusiasm, and market position.

On the other hand, if the business mission is clearly designed to broaden activities into a major new category, the criteria should be set high enough to force true innovation. A company entering a totally new market or investing in a major R&D program should ensure that it accepts only a major idea before committing significant time and financial resources.

A good set of product objectives should flow directly from the introspection used in analyzing and defining the company mission and setting a destination. Start with a focus on key strategic issues before developing detailed quantitative criteria and checklists. For example, Signode Corporation wanted to step up growth and new product development within the general mission of packaging products. It successfully developed and introduced a line of plastic trays for frozen foods, usable in regular or microwave ovens, through venture teams operating within the following objectives and criteria:

1. Ventures must be business-to-business efforts. Signode is not ready to market to consumers.

2. The technology must be in place. The company does not wish to enter new areas that require long-term technical development.
3. The venture must make use of an area of manufacturing familiar to the company.
4. There must be strong evidence to show the company can attain a major market share within some reasonable time.
5. The investment in the new product cannot exceed $30 million.[1]

J. C. Penney Company, Inc., isn't a manufacturer, but it looks for new products that meet the following strategic criteria:

1. The new product must be an innovative solution to a problem, not simply a solution, but an innovative solution. It must clearly solve some problem better than any other solution.
2. The new product must be easily understood. Do not try to educate the consumer.
3. The new product must be obvious. Its attributes must be self evident. It cannot require marketing to distinguish it from its competition.
4. The new product must be low technology. It must sell without a warranty.
5. The product must utilize simple materials and processes. There must be low tooling investment and it can't not work.
6. The product must be at the right price point. It must qualify as an impulse purchase or gift and retail for $39.95 or less.
7. The new product must convey consumer satisfaction. It must not be too faddish or temporary.
8. The product must be positive. It cannot be destructive, unsafe, harmful to the environment, sexist, and such.
9. The product must be free-standing. It must be independent. It cannot be part of a system. It cannot be tied to the success of another product.
10. The new product must have an established distribution network. It must have a known retail or catalog source for availability.
11. The product must be desirable. It should be irresistible. It can be a "need," but must be a "want" as well.

---

[1] *New Product Development Newsletter*, 5 (November 1985), p. 2. © 1985 Point Publishing Co. Inc., Point Pleasant, N.J.

66

12. The new product should not appeal to everyone. If it does, there is danger that it will appeal to no one.[2]

Dun & Bradstreet wanted to reduce new product failures to nearly zero, so it adopted the following criteria to help screen out potential failures early in development:

- The idea is compatible with our corporate image.
- The product can be standardized.
- The idea has significant sales and profit potential.
- The market has repetitive functional need for more of the product.
- The product relies on managerial skills we have or can develop.
- The idea has a unique, distinctive benefit.
- The idea offers rapid startup to high velocity sales and early payback.
- There are no known legal or social (governmental) limitations.
- Developmental costs are not excessive.
- The product will not require intensive servicing.
- The product can be derived, at least in part, from existing production capability.
- The product should be sold by a sales force.[3]

General Mills, Inc., looks for a distinct competitive advantage that will last—either a unique design, a broad patent or license agreement, a strong brand, a low-cost manufacturing concept, or a high capital investment requirement locking out smaller competitors.

The following list of generic criteria was developed by Jack Loechner, president of The Associates Group, a consulting company specializing in new product marketing and development:

1. General program objectives in terms of number of items or lines, opportunities from which to select, size of opportunity sought.
2. Revenue or unit volume objectives within express period of time following commercialization.
3. Return on investment expressed in terms of dedicated assets employed.
4. Limitations on capital investment.

[2] Ibid.
[3] *Management Review,* January 1981.

5. Profitability objective in keeping with corporate standards and goals.
6. Development time for design, engineering, manufacturing, marketing plans.
7. Leveraging company assets: brand name, manufacturing, marketing, and so on.
8. Investment limitations in terms of development costs, tooling, inventory, distribution.
9. Technical or physical characteristics and/or limitations.
10. Marketing and distribution considerations: sales organization, customer base, served markets.
11. Specific introduction dates desired. Trade show requirements.
12. Proprietry or patent requirements for invention.
13. Overall corporate fit with current lines, services, business philosophy, integration plans.
14. Unit economics expressed in terms of base price, value added, price/volume relationship, labor versus material intensity.

New product objectives can be summarized in a strategic plan, or product innovation charter, a term used by Merle Crawford at the University of Michigan. A product innovation charter (PIC) is useful in documenting key strategic objectives, guiding the efforts of everyone involved in the development process, and keeping the critical issues visible throughout the development. A product development effort can get so immersed in technical and marketing detail that the team can lose sight of the proverbial "forest for the trees." A product development team can start with a very clear objective of improving the taste of a product through a new flavor/texture concept, and after nine months and 50 percent turnover in team members, find itself developing prototypes of a new convenience package. To make objectives stick, write them down.

A good PIC is developed through the corporate goal-setting process, an audit of strengths, weaknesses, and market opportunities, and probing discussions with management. Figure 6–1 illustrates the contents of a typical PIC.

The next step is to develop an evaluation system that measures the criteria. Any number of systems can be used. A simple system is to evaluate each criteria as vital, desirable, indifferent, or unnecessary.

## FIGURE 6–1
Product Innovation Charter

A. *The goal or objectives* for the product innovation activities.
   1. The *target business arena* that product innovation is to take the firm into, or keep it in. These arenas are defined in different ways, examples of which are:
      a. By product type (e.g. specialty chemicals, or cars and trucks).
      b. By end-user activity or function (e.g. data processing or food).
      c. By technology (e.g. fluidics or xerography).
      d. By customer or consumer group (e.g. service stations or state lotteries).

   2. The *position within those arenas* which the firm wishes to achieve. This position is usually stated in more than one way.
      a. Market share goal, or a position of relative leadership.
      b. Dollar goal, either sales volume, or profit level, total dollars, ROI, payback percent on sales, short-term/long-term.

   3. *Special goals, objectives, or conditions peculiar* to the firm's unique situation. Examples are:
      a. Image, to maintain or to seek.
      b. Smoothing out of various irregularities.
      c. Diversification.

B. *The program of activities* chosen to achieve the above goals.
   1. *Strengths to exploit:* Many exist, though usually one of three types:
      a. An *R&D* skill or capability, (e.g. glass technology).
      b. A *manufacturing* facility, process, skill, or material (e.g. food processing, or wood chips).
      c. A *marketing advantage* (e.g. strong sales force, an image, or a trade franchise).

   2. *Weaknesses to avoid:* Usually one or more of the same list as above, e.g., avoid relying on an R&D for a new product, or avoid new products which require unavailable market contacts.

   3. *Source of the innovation.* That is, will the new product's points of differentiation be developed:
      a. *Internally* (by R&D, marketing, etc.), or
      b. *Externally* (by acquiring companies, products, or processes), or by
      c. A deliberate *combination* of both, one variation of which is the joint venture.

   4. *Degree of innovativeness sought,* if any. Alternatives can include:
      a. *Inventive.* Technological leadership, wheter product, package, service, positioning, or whatever. Be "first to market" with it.
      b. *Adaptive.*Lay back, let others lead; adapt or modify; use "innovative imitation," be "second, but best."
      c. *Innovative applications.* Utilize established technology but apply it creatively to new uses (e.g., adhesives, or MOS technology). Essentially a special combination of the two above.
      d. *Economic.* Build strength by producing what others have created, but doing it more economically. The low-cost producer.
      (Note: As discussed in Chapter One, all of these approaches require innovation, just different types!)

**FIGURE 6–1** _____
(*concluded*)

5. *Special restrictions or directions*. Highly situational, but not miscellaneous or casual. Some examples are:
   a. *Level of risk* that is acceptable.
   b. *Sense of urgency* or criticalness.
   c. *Product quality level*—usually a stipulation of high quality, for protecting an image, or for trading one up.
   d. *Patentability*—sometimes absolutely critical.
   e. *Size or growth trends* in markets being considered, coming from the strategic planning matrices.
   f. *Line completeness*
   g. *Number of new items per year*, either a minimum or a maximum.
   h. Avoid certain competitors.
   i. Avoid environmental problem, or other social pressure.

If the evaluation turns up more "vitals" and "desirables" the criteria would seem to be indicating a go. This may not be so. Some factors may need to carry more weight than others. That is why many new product developers prefer an evaluation system that assigns numerical values. For example, a chemical company, after establishing general guidelines, set up an evaluation system based on "implication." First, the chemical company established the following guidelines:

- The primary focus should be consumer market oriented.
- The product formulation should contain chemical.
- The use of chemical should provide a real added value to the product performance.
- The degree of functional uniqueness should be significant, wherever possible.
- The product should be conducive to a premium pricing structure.
- A potential sales volume at the rate of $1 million or more should be feasible within 18 months after introduction.
- The product should have a lengthy expected life cycle.
- Although the use of existing sales and distribution channels is preferred, opportunities requiring distribution modification should be considered.
- Product improvements and product line extensions should be considered.

- Products should be "push" in nature, requiring minimum national consumer advertising support.
- Products need not be fully manufactured by the company; therefore, subcontracting would be permitted.

The generalized requirements were then developed by this chemical company into specific criteria. Each idea was evaluated in terms of the key "implications" of market acceptance and its relationship to the company's goals and objectives. The following evaluation measures were used to appraise each idea for its *relative potential value:* degree of product uniqueness, degree of product advantage, compatibility with present product line, availability of technology, competitive factors, effect on sales of existing product line, and distribution considerations.

A product criteria checklist would include newness, fit with existing facilities and skills, proprietary position, servicing requirements, technical feasibility, legal considerations, and organization support. On the financial checklist would be overall profit contribution, return on investment, total investment required, profit-risk ratios, effect on cash flow, and accessory income possibility. The market criteria include market size and expected company share, market growth, market positioning, effect on existing product line, competitive status, and distribution characteristics.

The procedure for establishing criteria includes the following steps:

1. Select primary evaluative criteria.
2. Weight criteria by their relative importance.
3. Establish range of rating scale.
4. Determine evaluators of proposal.
5. Calculate overall index for proposal.

An example illustrates the process. A home products company developed a combination weighting and evaluation scale system with ratings using a team approach, involving the division CEO, and getting a management consensus. Figure 6–2 illustrates the criteria and their relative weights, while Figure 6–3 shows the method of ranking each factor on a scale of zero to three.

Checklists and rating systems stimulate discussion, force analysis of facts, and get quick management consensus when trying to screen numerous ideas against an "opportunity profile" and "company fit" profile. Some positive aspects of checklists and

**FIGURE 6–2** _____

| | *Weighting–% of Total* | | |
|---|---|---|---|
| I. Market factors | 50% | | |
|   A. Size, growth, and seasonality | | 18% | |
|     1. Category size | | | 4% |
|     2. Historical growth | | | 2 |
|     3. Growth potential | | | 5 |
|     4. Seasonality | | | 7 |
|   B. Competition | | 15% | |
|     1. Degree of oligopoly control | | | 7% |
|     2. Competitive skill levels | | | 4 |
|     3. Marketing spending levels | | | 4 |
|   C. Composition | | 17% | |
|     1. Number of price points | | | 5% |
|     2. Breadth of distribution channel coverage | | | 5 |
|     3. Potential to establish/maintain marketable advantage | | | 7 |
| II. Fit-with company-factor | 50% | | |
|   A. Marketing, sales, and service | | 18% | |
|     1. Marketing skills required | | | 4% |
|     2. Sales capabilities required | | | 3 |
|     3. Fit with distribution channels used | | | 6 |
|     4. Importance of aftermarket service | | | 5 |
|   B. Financial | | 22% | |
|     1. Gross margins | | | 8% |
|     2. Tooling investment | | | 8 |
|     3. Marketing spending | | | 6 |
|   C. Product-related | | 10% | |
|     1. Manufacturing capability | | | 5% |
|     2. Product technology | | | 5 |
| | 100% | 100% | 100% |

rating systems are they create systematic reviews, force consideration of important issues, force corporate planning and establish objectives, and reduce complex decisions to manageable size. But on the negative side of ratings systems, the evaluations may be intuitive and not reflect thought, the proposals may not lend themselves to scoring, each evaluator will not be equally able to judge all critical areas, and the composite score may not show the variability of ratings and dimensions.

**FIGURE 6–3**
Factor Evaluation Scales

| Market Factors | 3 Pts. | 2 Pts. | 1 Pts. | 0 Pts. |
|---|---|---|---|---|
| 1. Category size | Large ------------------------- Small | | | |
| 2. Historical growth | Dramatic---------------------- Negative | | | |
| 3. Growth potential | Dramatic---------------------- Negative | | | |
| 4. Seasonality | Nonseasonal---------------- Highly seasonal | | | |
| 5. Oligopoly control | Fractionalized --------------- Controlled | | | |
| 6. Competitive skills | Poor--------------------------- Excellent | | | |
| 7. Category marketing spending | Nonexistent------------------ Intense | | | |
| 8. Number of price points | High & Low ---High only Low only | | | |
| 9. Distribution channel coverage | Broad ------------------------- Limited | | | |
| 10. Marketable advantage | Achieveable------------------ Unachieveable | | | |
| **Fit with Company** | | | | |
| 1. Marketing skills | Full owned------------------- No experience | | | |
| 2. Sales capabilities | Complete-------------------- None related | | | |
| 3. Distribution channels | Identical --------------------- Dissimilar | | | |
| 4. Importance of after-market service | Very important ------------- Unimportant | | | |
| 5. Profitability | Above criteria--------------- Below criteria | | | |
| 6. Tooling investment | Zero--------------------------- Substantial | | | |
| 7. Marketing spending | Zero--------------------------- Substantial | | | |
| 8. Manufacturing capability | Complete-------------------- None related | | | |
| 9. Product technology | Complete knowledge----- None related | | | |

Other methods for measuring criteria exist and can be found in the textbooks mentioned in previous chapters. It is necessary to develop the questions or criteria important to the company's situation; establish a system that is consistent in measuring the criteria so systematic evaluation can be made; and involve the company decision makers.

Keep in mind that the establishment of criteria and their evaluation is not static. In this chapter, the criteria we refer to are the first measure of new ideas and concepts. Additional measurements will be made throughout the development process in the ever-wandering trail of new product pioneering.

# 7

# Getting Creative

Creativity: an arbitrary harmony, an expected astonishment, a habitual revelation, a familiar surprise, a generous selfishness, an unexpected certainty, a formable stubbornness, a vital triviality, a disciplined freedom, an intoxicating steadiness, a repeated initiation, a difficult delight, a predictable gamble, an ephemeral solidity, a unifying difference, a demanding satisfier, a miraculous expectation, an accustomed amazement.[1]

All of these conflicting emotions describe the combination of efforts required to achieve creative success in new product pioneering. A product pioneer needs to get an idea *and then do something with it.*

History is full of examples of individuals who were able to both conceive ideas and develop them. The Renaissance period witnessed an explosion of creativity in the arts and sciences with pioneering geniuses like Da Vinci, Newton, Mozart, Bach, Van Gogh, Rembrandt, and others. More recent examples coincided with the birth of America and included pioneers like Ben Franklin, Thomas Jefferson (as the first secretary of state, he was also the first director of the U.S. Patent Office, which traces its roots to Article One of the Constitution), and the most famous inventor of the Industrial Revolution, Thomas Edison.

---

[1] George M. Prince, *The Practice of Creativity* (New York: Macmillan Publishing Co., 1970), p. xii. © 1970 George M. Prince.

All of these great creative individuals were endowed with brilliance, but they also had something else in common: They worked hard and were sometimes driven by sheer economic need. Mozart was nearly destitute from squandering his fortunes and worked around the clock to complete enough compositions to support his needs. When George Frederick Handel was close to broke, he closeted himself for 21 days and emerged with a complete score of the *Messiah* (few of the themes were original, incidentally; Handel dredged them up from his unconscious where they had been stored from earlier works or hearing other composers). At the end of a concert at Carnegie Hall, Walter Damrosch asked Rachmaninoff what sublime thoughts had passed through his head as he stared out into the audience during the playing of his concerto. "I was counting the house," Rachmaninoff said.[2]

Thomas Edison was characterized by the press of his day as "The Wizard of Menlo Park," but he admitted that, in his case, invention was 1 percent inspiration, 99 percent perspiration. Peter Drucker in his book *Innovation and Entrepreneurship* points out that innovation isn't mysterious, doesn't depend on inspiration, and isn't an activity confined to a special class of geniuses. Just as systematic research can result in the invention of a new product, innovation can result from a purposeful pursuit. So don't waste too much time sitting around in an executive retreat waiting for divine inspiration and a spark of genius to strike—it probably won't. With more than 4.5 million patents issued to date in the United States alone, one can imagine that not all occurred through sparks of intuition.

Occasionally an inspired idea seems to just pop into someone's mind. The idea may or may not relate to the business the person is in. It may be practical to develop the idea, or the idea may be lost to the marketplace because the wrong person thought of it or it was thought of at the wrong time. Pioneering new products in a systematic way requires directing and *working* the creative process. It starts with certain types of products or concepts that can help meet company goals. It isn't likely that a chemical company dedicated to expansion by developing new chemical products that can be manufactured in its factories would accept an idea for a steel-fabricated product even if the idea was the greatest in the world. Steel fabrication probably would be a new business to the chemical company, and unless it wanted to undertake a new business, the best the chemical company could do would be to sell the idea.

Simply having an idea in today's marketplace is not enough. Even Edison turned fewer than 100 of his 1,000 patents into salable products. The idea must be related to the goals and resources of the business the new product developer is in or wants to be in. The object of this book is to provide a systematic approach to the pioneering of new products that serves individual and company goals. This means knowing the desired business and the desired direction of business growth.

The idea that creativity could be induced in others and systematically developed got its start in the 1930s when Alex Osborne of the advertising agency Batten, Barton, Durstine, and Osborne developed a technique he called brainstorming. Process knowledge has expanded rapidly since then and now includes several psychological and group dynamics techniques. Following is a description of some of the more common methods:

## BRAINSTORMING

Brainstorming is an unstructured process where judgment is deferred and quantity of ideas is sought. A group or groups of from 6 to 12 individuals sit down to a freewheeling, fast-paced session. Criticism is not permitted. The goal is listing as many "wild" ideas as possible. A strong group leader is needed to restrict judgments and criticism, to keep the pace moving, and, most important, to encourage each person to listen to the other's idea and to move each idea ahead by adding to it. The leader must be able to stimulate discussion and control behavior.

As unstructured as brainstorming seems to be, it is more than six people getting into a room together and tossing out ideas. Preparation is necessary. A statement of the problem should be prepared, group members chosen carefully so a variety of knowledge is represented in the group, and ground rules (no judgment, not even the flick of an eyebrow, quantity of ideas, no idea being too ridiculous) spelled out. Someone needs to take notes so no idea is lost. Using a tape recorder doesn't work well because it results in a lot of conversation to review and may restrain participants.

Robert Hisrich and Michael Peters list six states of brainstorming[3]:

1. State the problem and discuss it for familiarity and background.
2. Restate the problem.
3. Write down the restatement responses for all to see.
4. Start a warmup session to get participants freewheeling, laughing, and in the mood for brainstorming.
5. Conduct the actual brainstorming session.
6. Come up with the "wildest idea."

Many brainstorming variations have been developed. Will Gordon, the man who wrote the book on Synectics®, did not tell the problem to the group but directed the conversation toward the problem without divulging it. Another variation is called reverse brainstorming; the weaknesses are thought of and listed instead of solutions. Later every weakness is addressed as to improvement or elimination. Sometimes it is useful to break the group into subgroups, have them brainstorm for short, intensive periods, and then reappraise the subgroups a number of times to illuminate subliminal personalities and use new combinations of people as stimulants. These are sometimes called buzz groups.

There are many proponents of many different brainstorming systems. It doesn't matter which variation is used as long as the results are there.

## CHECKLIST

The checklist technique of idea generation simply amounts to examining some kind of list that could suggest solutions for a given problem. The theory behind checklists is based on new combinations of unrelated elements, using an idea checklist to force nonobvious and nonhabitual combinations. Checklists can

---

[3] Robert D. Hisrich and Michael Peters, *Marketing Decisions for New and Mature Products: Planning Development and Control* (Columbus, Ohio: Charles E. Merrill Publishing Co., 1984).

extend the intuitive idea supply, first, by directly providing solution possibilities, and second, by indirectly stimulating the production of new ideas beyond the list itself.

A. F. Osborn devised a list of 73 idea-spurring questions to inspire product idea generation sessions.[4] Following are some of the key question categories:

- *Put to other uses?* New ways to use the product as is or if modified?
- *Adapt?* What else is like this? What other place or thing does this suggest?
- *Modify?* Change meaning, color, motion, sound, odor, form, shape?
- *Magnify?* More time? Greater frequency? Stronger? Higher? Longer? Thicker? Plus ingredient? Multiply?
- *Minify?* Smaller? Lower? Shorter? Lighter? Split up? Understate?
- *Substitute?* Who or what else instead?
- *Rearrange?* Interchange components? Other layout? Other sequence? Transpose cause and effect?
- *Reverse?* Transpose opposites? Turn it backward? Upside down? Inside out?
- *Combine?* How about a blend? An assortment? Combine units? Purposes? Appeals?

## ATTRIBUTE LISTING

This technique involves listing the basic characteristics of a product or product concept and then using brainstorming to generate quantities of ideas for providing different consumer benefits. The technique consists of several basic steps: list the attributes/characteristics, specifications, or even the limitations of the object or problem under consideration; develop a list of modifications or changes that would make the product more desirable; and evaluate the suggestions, selecting those ideas that are consistent with the original objectives.[5]

---

[4] Gary A. Davis, *Psychology of Problem Solving* (New York: Basic Books, 1972) © 1972 Gary A. Davis.

[5] Angelo M. Biondi, ed., *Have an Affair with Your Mind* (Great Neck, N.Y.: Creative Synergetic Associates, Ltd., 1974) pp. 24–29. © 1974 Synergetic Associates, Ltd.

An attribute idea generation process used on a camera might look like this:

| Component Part | Attributes or Specifications | Ideas Generated |
|---|---|---|
| Camera Body | weight? | Wafer-size and shape, imitation of clothing or accessories, expansion size. |
| Lens | size? | All-in-one, interchangeable built-in filters, automatic lens, expansion hood. |
| Film | shape? color? | Interchangeable preloaded camera backs, multitype dial yourself film. |
| Viewfinder | material? | Periscope, bright contrasting colors for focus. |
| Case | purpose? | Integral part of the camera, waterproof, shockproof, pocketbook, magnetic, contains a tripod. |
| Strap | flexibility? | Multiple length, variable functions—wrist, arm, neck—theftproof, personally identifiable. |

## MORPHOLOGICAL ANALYSIS

This more complex, multidimensional form of attribute listing enables a creative session to visualize and analyze all possible combinations of the variables relating to a product concept. It is basically a technique for combining two or more variables in multiple ways to look for unique product ideas. A simple example would be a three-dimensional analysis of a wall paneling product line where new varieties could be based on at least three variables: material: hardboard, plywood, wallboard, plastic; color: birch, oak, walnut, maple; and surface: knotty, large open grained, close grained, flecked.

These variables would generate 64 combinations. This concept has been expanded to allow the analysis of an almost unlimited number of variables and combinations with the aid of computers and a research technique called conjoint analysis.

## TRIGGER RESPONSE

Trigger response is a technique developed by George Muller, director of design at Ford Motor Company.

A group or groups of 8 to 12 people are established. Each group defines the problem it's working on. All groups may work on the same problem or on separate problems, sometimes with a large group of people. The entire group can decide on the problem to solve, then break into teams of 8 to 12 people.

Once the problem is defined and the desired solution clearly stated, each group draws two lines down a piece of paper. This gives three columns. Each group lists in the first column all the solutions to the problem group members can think of. Each group gets 8 to 10 minutes to write down solutions. A feeling of pressure needs to be created to encourage quick solutions.

Someone is picked at random from one of the groups to read the list. All other groups strike out duplications and at the same time write down in column two any new ideas triggered. The process is repeated once again to fill column three.

After each group has completed the process, the lists are collected and discussed with all participants to see if any other thoughts occur. The final lists are then given to an interdisciplinary group of executives to discuss and evaluate. This is basically a form of "forced relationship" brainstorming and can be executed in various ways to stimulate creativity.

## SYNECTICS

In 1961 William J. J. Gorden wrote *Synectics, The Development of Creative Capability*, published by Harper & Row Publishers, Inc.[6] Synectics, from the Greek, means the joining of different and apparently irrelevant elements. Synectics theory applies to the integration of diverse individuals into a problem-stating problem-

---

[6] William J. J. Gorden, *Synectics, The Development of Creative Capacity* (London: Collier Books, Collier-Maxmillian Ltd., 1968). Permission for the use of the word *Synectics* (to Williams) given by Synectics, Inc., Cambridge, Mass.

solving group. It is difficult for a company to employ synectics as a creative technique without a trained leader.

The synectics approach is based on four key concepts:

**1.** *Listen:* Unstructured meetings are often long on talking and very short on "active listening." Synectics encourages listening through a skilled moderator writing on a flip chart, reinforcing to make sure no ideas are lost, and controlling the discussion so all members can express their views fully.

**2.** *Spectrum Policy:* This is the concept that most ideas may be bad but can be moved along a spectrum by identifying and building on good points until an acceptable solution is reached.

**3.** *Common Understanding:* The process uses role playing between the leader, the group, and someone designated as the "client" with the problem or need. This forces a common understanding and attention on a central issue.

**4.** *Group Leader:* As mentioned previously, a skilled group leader is critical to facilitate the process and avoid the usual jockeying for leadership that subconsciously or consciously occurs in group dynamics.

A typical synectics session runs for two or three days and the basic flow is repeated many times. The group is usually composed of personnel from inside the organization, but outsiders, including consumers, can be useful group members. One of the major benefits of a good synectics session is its ability to integrate marketing, R&D, engineering, and manufacturing points of view.

## THINK TANKS

This concept is based on the use of a panel of uninvolved experts from a variety of fields in a brainstorming type of process, and it is often used in government, defense, and advanced research projects. Innotech, Trumbull, Conn., has extended the concept to general business new product development.[7]

Innotech maintains a data base called BrainBank® consisting of several thousand scientists, industrialists, academics, magazine writers, and other experts from around the country, who, when

---

[7] *Inc. Magazine,* October 1985, pp. 108–109.

asked, travel to Trumbull for a half-day thinking session on behalf of Innotech clients. Innotech selects through a computer search five to seven group members, purposely including representatives from disparate disciplines. For a construction equipment manufacturer, Innotech included an entomologist to steer engineers away from predictable nuts-and-bolts themes. His analysis of strength-to-weight ratios in ants turned out to contribute significantly to the development of a new earth mover.

All of these group creativity techniques have some common elements that seem to work. They establish openness and participation; encourage many and diverse ideas; build on each others' ideas; orient toward problems; and use a leader to guide the discussion.

Two other elements key to idea generation success are "thinking big . . . then little," and "working a program." Thinking big means starting with the business framework or mission established in corporate goal setting, looking for business opportunity ideas within the mission, and finally generating product or service ideas within a business concept. Creativity and idea generation are essential at all three levels, but usually are applied only at the product level and too early in the process.

Working a program means a commitment to treat idea generation as a formal, structured, continuous process of creativity sessions, research activity, expanding, discarding, and reviewing ideas. It takes time, money, inside and outside people who know the business, and accountability for producing results.

A company in the hardware industry used a task force approach with quarterly meetings and research and analysis "homework" between meetings. The sessions were held in conjunction with company or industry events to bring outside, real-world stimulation and to avoid the idea drought that often occurs in extended sessions held at executive retreats. Examples of meeting sites included a consumer focus group research session with a creativity meeting immediately following, a "field day" event where all task force members used all products in a live setting, a major industry trade show where everyone was exposed to all the latest new ideas in the industry, and even a session held in conjunction with a sales meeting in Las Vegas to get some risk-taking ideas flowing.

Each session resulted in decisions to discard or expand on ideas and in assignments such as vendor, distributor, or customer visits, market research projects, engineering prototypes, financial analysis, or followup brainstorming sessions.

Despite the best efforts at group creativity techniques, major breakthroughs are often solely individual experiences or visions and are usually a result of the three S's of creativity: sensitivity, synergy, and serendipity.[8]

Serendipity relies on an awareness of relevancy in accidental happenings.

> The stethoscope was first thought of when Laennec noticed some children playing with a rod of wood. The gramophone was invented because Edison, playing about with Morse dots on a string of waxed paper, noticed a hum when the paper passed rapidly beneath a needle. The process of vulcanization, which turned rubber into a useful material, was the result of some random experimentation by Charles Goodyear. A chance observation by Niepce in 1816 created the invention of the camera. He noticed that a piece of silver chloride paper on the lab bench retained the image of a spoon after the spoon had been removed. From that observation came the use of silver chloride paper to react to light and give a permanent record.[9]

Synergy is the association of two or more elements in a new way resulting in something more than the sum of the parts.

> Concrete was known by the Romans and used by them, but then the knowledge was lost or at least dormant for many centuries. A crucial invention made by an Englishman in 1854—reinforcing the concrete with iron bars—changed the entire nature of concrete. It could now be used for large spans, as well as pillar-type support. It acquired a tensile strength which bricks and stone could never have had (Actually, what really made concrete the favored building material was a combination of other synergistic occurrences including higher labor costs, the style and size of modern buildings, prefabrication, and steel skeleton support concepts).[10]

Sensitivity involves *awareness*, the use of the senses to spot opportunities, incongruities, deficiencies. Goethe said the greatest genius would never be worth much if he pretends to draw only from his own resources. "What is genius," he said, "but the fac-

---

[8] Sidney J. Parnes, *Creativity: Unlocking Human Potential* (Buffalo, N.Y.: D.O.K. Publishers, Inc., 1972), p. 34.

[9] Edward DeBono, ed., *Eureka!* (New York: Holt, Rinehart & Winston, 1979), p. 155. © 1974 Thames and Hudson Ltd.

[10] Ibid., p. 86.

ulty of seizing and turning to account everything that strikes us—every one of my writings has been furnished to me by a thousand different persons, a thousand different things."

The most important way to improve and develop personal creativity skills is to intensify and hone perceptions. Read constantly, be an observer of trends, discard biases. Perceptive people are constantly scanning for clues and facts, "reality testing" by paying attention to the outside world. They tend to have varied interests, are intensely involved in the world around them, are self-confident, and are always open to new experiences.

Most people see what they want to see and hear what they want to hear. That subjectivity determines the level of accuracy with which we view things around us. Children are enormously creative. As they become adults, they develop expectations or mental blocks. These blocks can be perceptual, cultural and environmental, emotional, intellectual, or expressive blocks. We encounter them in the business world through common statements like: "It won't work!" "Let's form a committee." "We've never done it before." "Don't be ridiculous." "It isn't in the budget." "We're not ready for that." "Has anyone else tried it?" and the enduring "Our business is different." These blocks can be overcome by consciously identifying them and by adopting a questioning and inquisitive attitude and a fluency and flexibility of thinking.

Following are several guidelines for improving personal creativity and eliminating mental blocks:[11]

1. Give yourself plenty of dream space.
2. Enhance your environment for maximum creativity—look for variety in life and working environment.
3. Seek out idea-oriented people.
4. Draw out people's creativity at every opportunity.
5. Break out of your everyday routines.
6. Impose deadlines on yourself.
7. Become an expert in your area of innovation—read, listen, make connections.
8. Focus on where other "idea people" get ideas.
9. Look for ideas by studying problems.
10. Protect your ideas from negative people.

---

[11] *Republic Magazine*, October 1985.

The common thread running through personal and group creativity is a *disciplined, determined pursuit* of ideas. Discipline can actually stimulate creativity rather than restrict it. Shakespeare wrote his sonnets within a strict discipline, 14 lines of iambic pentameter, rhyming in three quatrains and a couplet. Mozart wrote his sonatas within an equally rigid discipline—exposition, development, and recapitulation. Were these gentlemen dull?

Determination and pressure can be powerful stimulators of creativity. The most productive, prolific creativity in business occurs in a typical advertising agency creative group three days before a client campaign presentation, and the agency director has just suggested they start over again. Contrary to some beliefs, the creative process doesn't end with an idea; it *begins* with an idea. Ideas must be implemented in order to be useful. Pursue ideas with determination and creativity, and someday they may show up on the list of other great ideas in Figure 7–1.

## FIGURE 7–1
## Chronological Table

| | Contemporary Events | Man Moving | Man Taking |
|---|---|---|---|
| **1500** | 1492 Columbus lands in America | Pencil<br>Dredger | |
| | 1534 Henry VIII founds Church of England | | |
| | 1571 Battle of Lepanto | 1580 Newspaper | |
| | 1588 Spanish Armada | | |
| **1600** | | | |
| | 1616 Pocahontas comes to London | | |
| | 1649 Beheading of Charles I | | |
| | 1660 Louis XIV assumes power | | |
| **1700** | 1693 Last witch burnt at Salem | 1709 Piano | 1712 Steam engine |
| | | 1716 Diving bell | |
| | 1720 South Sea Bubble | 1731 Sextant | |
| | | | 1772 Papier mâché |
| | 1776 Declaration of American Independence | | |
| | 1789 Storming of the Bastille | 1783 Balloon | |
| | | 1792 Semaphore | |
| | | 1797 Parachute | |
| | | 1798 Lithography    Steamship | |
| **1800** | | | 1800 Battery |
| | | 1812 Printing technology | |
| | 1815 Battle of Waterloo | 1816 Camera | |

| Man Living | Man Working | Key Devices | |
|---|---|---|---|
| 1509 Wallpaper<br>Naval mine | Rolling mill   Theodolite<br>Vice and spanner | | |
| 1560 False limbs | | | |
| | | 1588 Pendulum | |
| 1589 Knitting frame | | | |
| | 1590 Microscope<br>1592 Thermometer<br>1600 Foot rule<br>1608 Telescope<br>1614 Logarithms | | |
| | 1621 Slide rule<br>1640 Micrometer<br>1642 Calculating machine<br>1643 Barometer | | |
| | 1658 Balance spring | | |
| | | 1659 Air pump | |
| | 1666 Calculus | | |
| Cigarette | | 1676 Universal joint | |
| 1679 Pressure cooker | 1679 Binary arithmetic | | |
| 1733 Flying shuttle   Seed-<br>drill<br>1752 Lightning conductor<br>1770 Spinning jenny<br>1771 Factory farming | 1735 Marine chronometer | | |
| 1775 Water closet | | | |
| 1779 Crompton's mule | | Screw and<br>screwdriver | |
| 1789 Beehive<br>1790 Dental drill | | 1789 Governor | |
| | 1791 Metric system | | |
| 1792 Cotton gin | | | |
| | | 1794 Ball-bearings | |
| 1796 Vaccination | | | |
| 1799 Bleaching powder<br>Anesthetics<br>1801 Gas lighting<br>1810 Ultra-violet lamp | | | |
| | 1812 Hydraulic jack<br>1814 Spectroscope | | |
| 1815 Miner's safety lamp<br>1816 Fire extinguisher<br>Stethoscope | | | |

**FIGURE 7–1** _____
Chronological Table (*continued*)

| | Contemporary Events | Man Moving | Man Taking |
|---|---|---|---|
| 1800 (cont.) | | | 1820 Elastic<br>1821 Electric motor<br><br>1827 Matches |
| | | 1829 Braille<br>1830 Railways | |
| | | | 1831 Dynamo  Transformer |
| | | 1832 Tram and trolleybus | |
| | | | 1833 Water turbine |
| | 1837 Accession of Queen Victoria | 1837 Screw propeller<br>    Diving apparatus<br>1837 Electric telegraph<br>1839 Bicycle | |
| | | | 1841 Vulcanized rubber |
| | | | 1850 Paraffin |
| | | | 1856 Bessemer steel<br>1860 Internal combustion engine |
| | 1863 Battle of Gettysburg | 1863 Underground railway<br>1864 Driving chains | |
| | | | 1866 Dynamite<br>1868 Plastics |
| | 1871 Germany becomes a State | 1873 Typewriter<br>1875 Submarine<br>1876 Telephone<br>1877 Gramophone | |
| | | 1880 Half-tone block<br>1881 Stereophony | |
| | | 1884 Motor-car   Airship<br>    Fountain-pen<br>1885 Motor-cycle | 1884 Steam turbine |
| | | | 1886 Aluminium |
| | | 1888 Pneumatic tyre<br>    Glider<br>1893 Carburettor<br>1895 Cinematograph<br>1896 Radio | 1893 Diesel engine |

| Man Living | Man Working | Key Devices | |
|---|---|---|---|
| 1818 Blood transfusion | | | |
| 1826 Corn-reaper | 1821 Thermocouple | | |
| 1830 Food canning<br>　　　Sewing machine<br>1830 Lawn mower<br>　　　Plywood<br>1830 Treshing machine<br>　　　Crop rotation<br>　　　Artesian well | | | |
| 1834 Refrigeration | 1832 Galvanometer<br>Steam hammer | | |
| 1840 Postage stamp | | | |
| 1844 Paper patterns<br>1847 Ophthalmoscope<br>1848 Rifle   Camouflage<br>Weedkillers and pesticides | | | |
| 1853 Safety lift<br>1856 Aniline dyes<br>1860 Can opener<br>　　　Linoleum<br>　　　Pasteurization | | Telegraph cable<br>1852 Gyroscope | |
| 1869 Torpedo<br>1870 Lister's spray | 1869 Metal plane | | |
| 1873 Barbed wire<br>1875 Gas mantle<br>1876 Carpet sweeper | | | |
| 1879 Filament lamp<br>　　　Cream separator<br>1880 Inoculation | 1880 Artificial languages   Blowlamp<br>Ultrasonics | | |
| 1883 Machine-gun   Man-made fibers | | | |
| 1887 Combine harvester | | | |
| 1889 One-armed bandit | | | |
| 1895 X-ray | | | |

90

## FIGURE 7-1
Chronological Table (*concluded*)

| | | Contemporary Events | Man Moving | Man Taking |
|---|---|---|---|---|
| **1900** | | 1901 Death of Queen Victoria | 1897 Teleprinter<br>1899 Magnetic tape-recorder<br><br>Silk-screen printing<br><br>1904 Caterpillar track<br>1905 Hydrofoil   Aeroplane<br>1907 Helicopter | 1902 Synthetic minerals |
| | | | | 1912 Stainless steel |
| | | 1914 First World War | 1914 Traffic lights | |
| | | | 1926 Rocket | |
| | | | | 1930 Gas turbine |
| | | | 1932 Parking meter<br>1934 Catseye   Television<br>1935 Hearing aid<br>      Juke box<br>1937 Xerography<br>1938 Ballpoint pen<br>1939 Jet engine | 1938 Stirling engine |
| | | 1939 Second World War | | 1942 Nuclear reactor |
| | | | 1943 Aqualung | |
| | | | 1947 Polaroid camera<br>1948 Long-playing records<br>      Music synthesizer<br>1955 Hovercraft<br>1956 Videotape recorder<br>1957 Spacecraft | 1952 Float glass |
| | | | | 1959 Fuel cell |
| | | | 1962 Communications satellite | |

(Reprinted with permission from *Eureka!*, edited by Edward De Bono, Holt, Rinehart and Winston, New York, 1974.)

| Man Living | Man Working | Key Devices | |
|---|---|---|---|
| 1897 Breakfast cereals<br>1899 Aspirin<br>1901 Vacuum cleaner<br>1902 Safety razor   Surgical<br>transplants<br>1903 Electrocardiograph<br>1904 Vacuum flask | 1903 Oxy-acetylene welding | 1902 Photoelectric cell | |
| 1908 Conveyor belt<br>1910 Therapeutic drugs | 1910 Geiger counter<br>1911 Cloud chamber<br>1912 IQ tests | | |
| 1913 Zip fastener<br>1914 Brassière<br>1915 Tank   Gas mask<br>   Synthetic fertilizers<br>   Washing machine | 1916 Sonar<br>1921 Lie detector | | |
| 1929 Iron lung<br>1930 Supermarket<br>   Cloud-seeding<br>1934 Fluorescent lamp | Teaching machines<br>1930 Cyclotron<br>1931 Radio telescope   Electron<br>   microscope<br>1935 Radar | | |
| 1937 Electric blanket | | | |
| 1939 Insecticies | | | |
| 1942 Napalm | | 1941 Aerosol spray | |
| 1944 Ballistic missile<br>   Kidney machine<br>1945 Nuclear bomb<br>1946 Automation | 1946 Computer | | |
| 1948 Microwave cooking | 1952 Bubble chamber | 1948 Transistor | |
| 1955 Non-stick pans<br>   Contraceptive pill | Fibrescope | | |
| | | 1960 Laser | |
| 1966 'Miracle' rice | | | |

# 8

## Prospecting for Gold—Sources of New Product Ideas

Once personal and group creativity skills have been developed, the next step is to look for the start of an idea or several unrelated things that can be put together in a new way. The world is cluttered with veins of golden idea material; the key is to prospect for the ideas in a targeted way rather than randomly searching the hills. That is the reason for defining goals and new product criteria as discussed in earlier chapters.

Aware observation of the business world can generate many ideas. Peter Drucker, in *Innovation and Entrepreneurship*, defines seven "macro" sources for innovation opportunity as:

1. The unexpected—unexpected success, unexpected failure, unexpected outside event.
2. The incongruity—between reality as it actually is and reality as it is assumed to be.
3. Innovation based on process need.
4. Changes in industry structure or market structure that catch everyone unaware.
5. Demographics—basic population changes.
6. Changes in perception, mood, and meaning.
7. New knowledge, both scientific and nonscientific.[1]

---

[1] Peter F. Drucker, *Innovation and Entrepreneurship* (New York: Harper & Row, 1985), p. 35. © 1985 Peter F. Drucker.

He focused on these sources based on the belief that the over-whelming majority of successful innovations *exploit change*. And monitoring change will lead to ideas for innovation and new products.

Open-minded and intense reading of general business liter-ature helps create a good detective of change. Michael Kami, a business consultant and strategic planning professional, recom-mends a regular process of reading, looking for "clues" and clip-ping ideas from publications. Following is a sampling of a reading list for keeping aware of the business world:

## PUBLICATIONS

| Period | Title | Subscription |
| --- | --- | --- |
| Daily | *The Wall Street Journal* | 200 Burnett Rd., Chicopee, MA 01021 |
| Weekly | *Business Week* | McGraw Hill, 1221 Ave. of Americas, New York, NY 10020 |
| | *U.S. News & World Report* | P.O. Box 2860, Greenwich, CT 06830 |
| Bi-Weekly | *Fortune* | 541 N. Fairbanks Ct., Chicago, IL 60611 |
| | *Forbes* | 60 Fifth Ave., New York, NY 10011 |

| Period | Title | Subscription |
|--------|-------|--------------|
| Quarterly | *Society and Innovation* | Warren, Gorham & Lamont, 210 South St., Boston, MA 02111 |
| | *Economic Outlook, USA* | Survey Res. Center, University of Michigan, P.O. Box 1248, Ann Arbor, MI 48106 |

## REFERENCES

Monthly   *Economic Indicators* (Council of Economic Advisors)*
*Survey of Current Business* (U.S. Department of Commerce)*
*Business Conditions Digest* (U.S. Department of Commerce)*
*Monthly Labor Review* (U.S. Department of Labor)*
*International Financial Statistics IMF*, Washington, DC 20402
*OECD Observer and Economic Outlook*, OECD Publications Center,
1750 Pennsylvania Ave. NW, Washington, DC 20006

Annually   *U.S. Statistical Abstract* (U.S. Department of Commerce)*
Economic Report of the President*
U.S. (Federal) Budget*

*U.S. Government publications from Superintendent of Documents, Government Printing Office, Washington, DC 20402.

## SPECIALIZED MATERIAL

Trade and technical publications pertinent to the lines of business of the organization.

Functional publications (personnel, marketing, procurement) relating to your main responsibilities.

Primary and secondary research can be used to generate ideas in various business situations. Primary research is developing data from the source, or from scratch. Secondary research is using research conducted by others, such as trade organizations, trade journals, other companies, and the government.

## PRIMARY RESEARCH SOURCES

Internal sources are the most obvious origin of new product ideas but are not always fully utilized. Most companies will gather ideas from the R&D department, their executives, engineers, and others who are close to the new product development process; but too often the salespeople, clerks, foremen, operators, and so on are not solicited for new ideas. Company personnel can be a rich source of ideas if the company sets up a means of communication. Suggestion boxes are helpful in soliciting new ideas, but a more proactive approach will get better results.

A company should advise all employees of the search for new ideas. Give them some criteria or a mission statement for the new product effort so they will have a clear idea of new product developments thrusts. More new product ideas can be generated by making it easy for employees to submit ideas. This can be done by providing forms or incorporating a place on forms such as on salesperson's call report to put down new product ideas. The company newsletter or newspaper could be used periodically. Companies also need to make it clear who new ideas should go to, and then it should be sure every idea is acknowledged and thanks given even if the idea is not used. Employees also need to know what or how much the reward will be if the idea is used.

External sources such as customers, vendors, competitors, venture capital companies, investors, banks, patent attorneys, trademark and patent offices, consultants, patent brokers, advertising agencies, research companies, designers, universities, research laboratories, trade magazine editors, trade shows, and so on all are viable sources of new product ideas for some companies but are not necessary for all companies. One external source will prove more valuable than another for a specific concern.

Customers are close to their needs, and through proper research these needs usually can be identified. It is also very worthwhile to pursue not just the customers, buyers, engineers, and key executives, but also their sales force and, where appropriate, the users of the product. If the ultimate customer is the consumer, then the consumer becomes the key target of the search for new product ideas or concepts. In addition to the many research techniques used to elicit ideas from consumers, a few ongoing techniques give rise to new product ideas.

Monitoring consumer correspondence is an excellent source of ideas as is having a toll-free telephone number on all packages. Scrutinizing warranty cards and planting selected questions on the warranty card can also elicit ideas. Contests, such as the bake-off contest Pillsbury has been running annually since 1949, may produce new product ideas. Eric Von Hippel, writing for the March/April 1982 *Harvard Business Review,* discusses how a computer software company and a bakery products company get new product ideas from customers. Hippel agrees with us that customers are a readily available, low-cost source of new product ideas.

Sources of raw material systems and parts can often suggest innovation and new product ideas. Sometimes it's a new material that can lead to the new product, such as a new type of plastic or a formula for a type of metal that will perform in new ways. A new system for manufacturing or handling materials can also affect a product or bring about innovations that make the product different and therefore new. A constant search of suppliers, not just a casual "what's new," is called for on an ongoing basis. Buyers, engineers, and anyone who deals with suppliers should be constantly on the alert for opportunities. Management must keep them abreast of new product efforts so they are motivated to pursue their suppliers and, in some cases, pursue them with specific new product objectives.

Competition should be constantly screened for products that can be made and marketed with a competitive advantage or innovated upon. Often, a competitor product review can suggest something that can be improved, manufactured more economically, or innovated upon.

The three external sources (customers, resources, and competition) all require an ongoing systematic approach to get the most out of them. They cannot be just added to the list of potential resources and then looked at periodically. A program in each area should advise people of the company's new product goals as well as provide feedback. A communication system that makes a complete circuit of sending a message, having it heard, and receiving a response combined with a motivator to fuel the action will start and maintain the cycle of feedback. Some key points of such a system are:

1. Establish clear goals.
2. Determine who will be responsible for this ongoing effort.
3. Identify the targets from whom feedback is desired.
4. Choose vehicles, such as newsletter, personal interview, questionnaires, carefully and with an eye to their being ongoing devices.
5. Know what will be done with the information.
6. Spell out the reward and recognition system.

In order to solicit ideas from the other external sources of new product ideas (venture capitalists, patent brokers, inventors, and so on), people need to be assigned to contact these sources and know for what purpose. Clear criteria for the search, even if broad and general, have to be spelled out in order to avoid being inundated with nonrelated opportunities. It is good to get a lot of new product ideas, but they have to be channeled into areas of interest and be manageable bits of information. By knowing in general what a company is looking for, having the responsibility assigned, and devising a system for collecting and evaluating the data, resources can be made to work for the company.

## SECONDARY RESEARCH SOURCES

Secondary resource sources can also be of help in searching for new products. There are many newsletters, trade publications, government agencies, and so forth that supply new product idea opportunities. The following is a list of secondary sources:

- Official Gazette of United States Patent & Trademark; Office of Commissioner of Patents and Trademarks, Washington, DC 20231.
- Foreign trade patents such as: Institut National De La Propriete Industrielle, 26 Bis Rue De Leingrad 75008 Paris.
- *New Product New Business Digest,* General Electric Co., 120 Erie Boulevard, Schenectady, NY 12305.
- New Products and Processes, Newsweek, 444 Madison Avenue, New York, NY 10022.
- Prestwick International Inc. has a number of newsletters such as *New From Us.* The address is P.O. Box 205, Burnt Hills, New York, NY 12027.

- Predicasts Inc. "Technical Survey" published weekly and other industry reports and studies can be obtained from Predicasts, 1101 Cedar Avenue, Cleveland, OH 44106.
- NASA Tech Briefs from National Aeronautics and Space Administration, Director Technology Transfer Division, P.O. Box 8757, Baltimore/Washington International Airport, MD 21240.
- *New Product Development Newsletter,* published monthly by Point Publishing Co., Inc., P.O. Box 1309, Point Pleasant, NJ 08742.
- Dancer Fitzgerald Sample, Inc. *New Product News* newsletter, New Food and Drug Products, 405 Lexington Avenue, New York, NY.
- Inventors Shows: write to local Chamber of Commerce for schedule of shows, or to the Office of Inventions and Innovations, National Bureau of Standards, Washington, DC 20234.
- The *International Commerce Magazine* contains a "licensing opportunities section." It is published by the U.S. Department of Commerce and is available upon subscription through a local Department of Commerce office.

Ideas that come from outside the company can cause legal problems. An idea might be submitted that the company has already thought of, or the idea might not belong to the person who sent it in. Claims and counterclaims can ensue from the most innocent of encounters. For example, one executive from outside the company, Mr. Smith, suggests an idea to his friend Mr. Jones. It is used. Nothing passes in writing. Mr. Smith wants to be paid for the idea, but the company wasn't even aware it was his idea. The company thought the idea belonged to company executive Mr. Jones, who presented it as his. To make it even worse, the idea was proprietary to Mr. Smith's company. What a tangle for the courts to unravel, and a costly one, too.

Companies need a procedure for handling outside ideas. The procedure should be set up by the legal resource, and product development personnel should be briefed on how it works. Unfortunately, there is no one way or best way to handle outside ideas. Some companies virtually refuse to consider any outside unsolicited ideas. Others have every idea go to the legal department and a release is sent to the sender. If the release is not signed, the idea is returned and no company executives ever see it. Some companies welcome ideas and have an active program of assignment of the ideas tied to a release. This is done in case the company is already working on or has previously documented the idea. Unfortunately, no system can be suggested, but the following points are offered for consideration.

**1.** Any verbal ideas should be put in writing.

**2.** Any unsolicited ideas should go to the legal department or to an especially assigned "reader." If the envelope gives no indication that it contains a new idea, whoever opens it should stop reading as soon as he knows it is an idea and forward it to legal or to the reader, who then will give it a number or some sort of identification and send a waiver and thank-you letter to the sender. The conditions for considering the idea should also be spelled out for the submitter.

**3.** Only if a waiver is signed is the idea sent to the new product development people for consideration.

**4.** Be sure no one in the company takes it on himself to answer, correspond, acknowledge new ideas, or seek waivers.

**5.** If the submitter has a patent and it accompanies the idea, it can be freely considered and evaluated.

Another basic and very important source of ideas is a thorough examination of the company's existing products, looking for opportunities to adapt, eliminate, combine, add, reduce, or otherwise change to meet a new market opportunity. Start by turning the traditional new product idea "funnel" upside down, beginning with an existing product and generating as many expansion ideas as possible. *New Product Development Newsletter*[2] suggests the following questions for generating new ideas from existing products: Can the product do better with a new person or team? Can we expand the product's potential with a change in design? Could it grow in new and different markets (including foreign)? Can we find new uses for it? Can we find new potential customers?

The newsletter also suggests looking for elimination possibilities—the "donut hole" approach, or "don't invent a better mousetrap; just get rid of the mice!" Examples include: Gutters carry away water from your roof. A new device called "Weather-

---

[2] *New Product Development Newsletter*, 5 (October 1985), pp. 2–3. © 1985 Point Publishing Co. Inc., Point Pleasant, N.J.

Foil" replaces gutters with a slotted device that causes water to break into droplets and scatter over a wide area. Or, don't make spare tires; get rid of flats. Tires go flat because the air gets out. Get rid of the air. Major tire company looks at sponge-rubber filled tire. No air; no flat.

The engineering and marketing group can undertake a thorough technical evaluation of the product, looking for opportunities to change design and provide new customer benefits in any of these areas: serviceability, human factors or "ergonomics," safety, cost, reliability, durability, performance, versatility, and producibility. A conscious effort to analyze the design relative to each of these factors can often result in a new product concept.

Revitalizing tired products can also create major new growth opportunities[3]:

- Does the worn-out product have new uses? Arm & Hammer baking soda sales rose sharply after the product was promoted for freshening refrigerators.
- Is there a broader target market? Procter & Gamble reversed Ivory soap's declining sales by advertising it for adults, rather than just for babies.
- Is there a trend to exploit? Dannon yogurt sales exploded after the product was linked to consumers' interest in improving their health.
- Can the product's distribution channels be expanded. Hanes did this when it packaged L'eggs panty hose in containers resembling ostrich eggs and displayed them on tall revolving stands in supermarkets.

Repackaging for added convenience can also breathe new life into a product. Examples include: Felt-tip pen with insecticide (D-Con); brush shaving cream dispenser (Gillette); toothpaste pump dispenser (12 percent of toothpaste market); cardboard juice boxes (Tetra-Pak); nail polish pen (Aziza); drip-proof spout and bottle cap-measuring cup (Liquid Tide). (Many of these packaging concepts were being used in Europe long before they were "invented" in the United States. Don't reinvent the wheel—take a trip to Europe instead.)

Looking for product-service "crossover" opportunities for an existing business can also be productive. If a company produces

---

[3] Carter Henderson, *Winners* (New York: Holt, Rinehart & Winston, 1985), p. 148. © 1985 Carter Henderson.

tangible products, it can look for ways to add services to them (also a good technique for staying competitive in a world marketplace). Add a unique training service, a computer-based delivery system, a state-of-the-art parts supply system, or a custom design and installation service. If a company provides a service, it can look for ways to add "hard technology" to the business; automatic tellers in banking, CAT scanners in medicine, precooked or preprocessed foods in the fast food business, computer-based information systems in financial services and travel, self-service computer terminals in grocery and department stores, and so on.

A current manufacturing investment or process may lead to some new product ideas. The Pillsbury Toaster Strudel became a major success with some 360 million servings annually, but it was born out of sheer fear. The company was concerned when Totino's Crisp Crust pizza was introduced in 1979 that if volume fell short of projections, Pillsbury would be sitting on a new multimillion-dollar production facility in Murfreesboro, Tenn. So it looked for other products with crust material requiring the same production process. Those Toaster Strudels are now zipping off a production line in Murfreesboro at the rate of 2,000 per minute.

Benetton, the Italian producer of knit goods and rapidly growing franchise chain of retail stores, took a look at the way sweaters were manufactured, made some changes, and built a world-wide business success out of it. Benetton changed the process to allow dyeing after production versus dyeing yarns before knitting, allowing outlets to delay color commitments until later in the selling season. Fashion color trends change rapidly, and Benetton's reaction capability gives it a major competitive edge.

Finally, once a company finds an idea and begins developing it, it should consider getting a patent on the idea (or at least checking its patent status). Since 1980, Congress has strengthened patent laws and courts are enforcing them more vigorously. The antitrust fervor of the 1960s and 1970s caused many patents to be viewed as a 17-year monopoly by the court, and executives came to look at the process and possible infringement as something for lawyers to worry about when and if their companies were sued. Recent damage awards such as $120 million to Hughes Tool for infringement of its drill-bit patent and $45 million to Pfizer/Shiley Inc. with $143 million in sales infringing on its blood-oxygenator patent show the peril of viewing patents as a minor issue. The United States issues 66,000 patents each year—if you have a good idea, make sure you stake your claim with the rest of them.

# 9

# Market Research . . .
# Fact or Fiction?

Market research has many similarities to product research: it involves a search into the unknown, and it may lead to many wrong answers, excursions down wrong paths, misinterpretation of results, occasional surprises, and a few dramatic discoveries. Yet many managers view market research as a science, perhaps because of its extensive use of statistics (much like the design engineer who uses formulas to guarantee results on the production line).

David Ogilvy noted an increasing reluctance on the part of marketing executives to use judgment and commented, "They are coming to rely too much on research, and they use it as a drunkard uses a lamppost, for support rather than for illumination."[1] A few companies and executives subscribe to the opposite viewpoint that market research is inherently a useless activity and a waste of money. The Sony Corporation has seldom conducted market research. It believes that market research cannot identify needs people don't realize they have or determine interest in a unique product concept for which people have no reference point. Sony has certainly succeeded without research when introducing breakthrough concepts such as the Walkman; but its consistency of

---

[1] David Ogilvy, *Confessions of an Advertising Man* (New York: Atheneum, 1980), p. 100. © 1963 David Ogilvy Trustee.

earnings growth has suffered, possibly because of the lack of a managed market research program to maintain a steady pace of product development between breakthroughs.

History has verified that breakthrough developments probably would not have been identified through any structured market research:

> In Mexico, wheels have been found on a child's toy from the pre-Columbian period, but there is no evidence of their practical use. Toy helicopters were in use in Europe in the 14th century, but the adult helicopter had to wait many centuries for a suitable power unit. It took 700 years from the development of the saddle to the invention of the stirrup in Western Europe. The advantage of the stirrup is that it gives the rider the same sort of stability he would have if both his feet were on the ground . . . a great advantage in warfare. No one doubts the importance of aircraft in modern war, and yet some years after the Wright brothers had flown a plane, the U.S. Congress actually passed a bill preventing the Army from wasting its money experimenting with flying machines.[2]

These advances didn't take so long because of official opposition or lack of support; the slow advances simply reflect the feeling of people throughout history. *Most people are happy with things as they are.* When people are happy with things as they are, they see no need for change and no advantage in it. The advantages can often be seen only after the change has occurred. And even then, many developments linger in obscurity because no one other than the inventor recognizes a problem needing a solution.

Gerald Schoenfeld, a new product idea generation consultant in New York, recalls that Church & Dwight Company, maker of Arm & Hammer baking soda, plodded through questionnaires with 5,000 consumers to ask them what their "refrigerator needs" were. The consumers couldn't really think of any. But at one of his idea sessions, the concept of baking soda as a refrigerator air freshener occurred.[3]

We were involved with several "problem detection" studies in the home improvement industry in which we listened to hundreds of homeowners describe how generally satisfied they

---

[2] Edward DeBono, ed., *Eureka!* (New York: Holt, Rinehart & Winston, 1974), p. 12. © 1974 Thames and Hudson, Ltd., London.

[3] *Fortune*, February 7, 1983, p. 61.

were with life. We conducted a telephone survey once to identify categories of dissatisfaction with house painters and had to probe more than four times to get a glimpse of marketable problem solutions. Yet when an improved service was offered and promoted, the phones rang off the hook. We asked hundreds of people what they didn't like about their lawn mowers and found a high degree of satisfaction. Yet, after an easier starting engine was developed and promoted, sales increased dramatically.

So what is the hapless marketing executive to do? What he's being paid for—think. Market research is an input and diagnostics tool, *not* a magic answer. Like any other tool, it can be used properly or misused. Following are some guidelines to using market research properly.

**Determine When to Use and When to Forgo.**   If the new product concept is so unusual or such a breakthrough that the customer cannot easily see the benefit or relate it to his current situation (Sony Walkman), or if the concept depends on an infrastructure of supporting elements (cable TV), or if the concept is so broad it allows the customer to do new things in new ways (personal computers), don't bother spending research dollars to identify the size of the market.

**Balance the Cost of Research with the Risk of Mistakes.** Executives are paid to take risks using good judgment and to preserve corporate viability; if the decision is critical and difficult to change or retract from, it should be backed up with research.

**Develop a Set of Business Norms to Analyze New Research Findings Against.**   Look at likes/dislikes scores, purchase intentions, price sensitivity, and other research data relative to past successes and failures, not in absolute terms.

**Test and Offer Alternative Solutions.**   Use research as a diagnostic tool, testing several alternative concepts, pricing strategies, and product positionings, and use the results as an input to refine and develop an optimal solution.

**Make Market Research Actionable.**   Probably two thirds of all market research is reviewed, provokes responses like "isn't that interesting," and then lies on a shelf or is filed away to gather dust. Before initiating or approving any market research project, insist that the possible outcomes are defined ahead of time and what decisions and action will occur as a result.

**Use Research to Stimulate Creativity.**   Any time money is spent to talk to customers or prospects (directly or indirectly), look at it as a great chance to identify new opportunities. Involve key people throughout the product development team, and spend some time in the research review generating ideas.

**Use It, But Don't Believe It.**   Consider market research for what it is—a model of real life, but not reality.

If used wisely, market research can provide help throughout the new product development process: idea generation, screening, product design and development, product evaluation, and new product marketing. Research International, a London-based market research firm, has a proprietary system that organizes common research techniques into a progressive sequence of activities starting with "Conceptor," an idea generation process;

**FIGURE 9–1a**
Conceptor (The Conceptor System for Understanding Markets and Creating New Product Concepts)

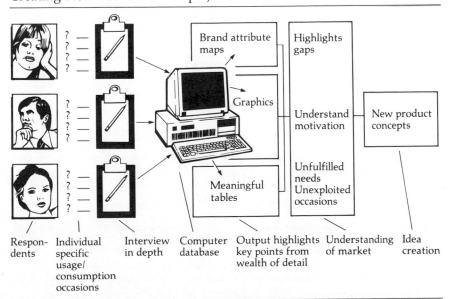

| Respondents | Individual specific usage/consumption occasions | Interview in depth | Computer database | Output highlights key points from wealth of detail | Understanding of market | Idea creation |

SOURCE: Research International, 23 East 22nd Street, New York, NY 10010.

**FIGURE 9–1b** _____
Locator (The new procedure for developing new products from initial concepts to finished brands)

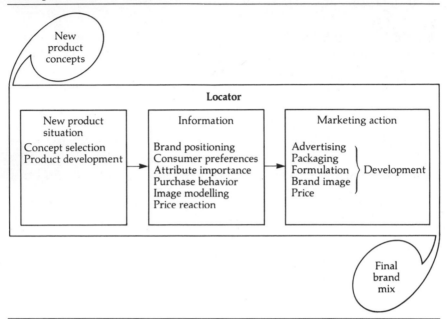

**FIGURE 9–1c** _____
Sensor (Combines advantages of)

Key measures produced for new brand

| | |
|---|---|
| Cumulative trial | Market share |
| Long-term repeat purchase | Source of share |
| Price elasticities | Diagnostics |

Predictions based on three models of consumer behavior

Simulated purchasing (trial/repeat model)
Consumer preferences (brand preference model)
Trade-off (brand/price trade-off model)

**Sensor** is a Trademark.

"Locator," a product positioning process; and "Sensor," a product marketing analysis. Figure 9–1 illustrates the system and lists the most frequently used market research techniques.

The following is a summary of the typical key questions and techniques used in each phase of new product development.

## IDEA GENERATION

Key questions include: What segments of need exist in the market? What gaps exist in the competitive need fulfillment? What are the dynamics of the need segments? What bothers customers? What benefits are desired? What are the strengths/weaknesses?

Several research techniques can be used. In a focus group, a skilled moderator leads small groups of consumers/customers from the target market in a discussion of problems, needs, product concepts, competitive brands, and new ideas.

For market structure analysis/gap analysis, quantitative research is designed to cluster product attributes/benefit perceptions into basic dimensions, determine distance between basic groups, and identify groups where needs are not being satisfied. It is multidimensional research that structures a market on the basis of products, needs, and usage occasions with the objective of defining and understanding the *dynamics* of a market beyond traditional secondary data sources. It answers questions such as: What are the products in the market and how do consumers react to them? How are the products used, by whom, when? Which products compete/substitute for each other? What product attributes lead consumers to use the products in the way they do?

Problem detection studies are quantitative surveys to define problems in a category and rank them based on *intensity* (how bothersome are they?), *frequency* (how often do they occur—and for how long?), *preemptibility* (the extent to which products/services already on the market can handle the problem).

Task analysis is a technique involving actual observation or recall to identify steps involved in a project (baking bread, selecting and opening a bank account, mowing the yard, painting the house) and problems encountered. A consumer might be asked to list all tasks involved in a project (with an incentive to get a quantity of tasks), whether it was a pleasant or unpleasant task, why they feel that way, and whether they would like to see it simplified or changed.

**FIGURE 9–2** _____

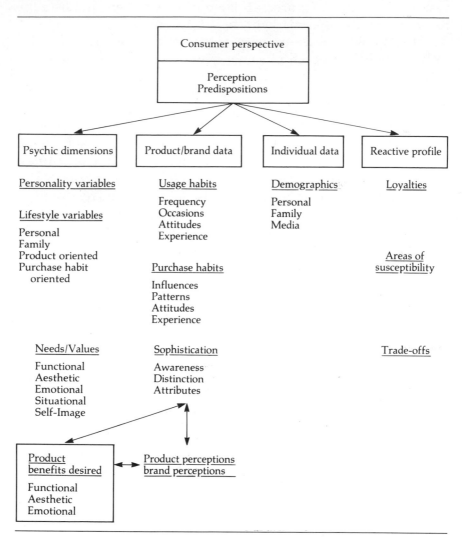

SOURCE: Rabin Research Co., Chicago, IL.

Figure 9–2 illustrates the range of consumer attributes and segments that might be identified and quantified in any of the idea generation techniques. The basic issue remains: How does the new product developer really get from data to new product ideas? Can an understanding of the market and consumers' problems/needs generate product concepts? At some point the developer must still take a *creative leap,* and that's when market research becomes marketing art.

## CONCEPT SCREENING

Key questions are: How large is the potential market (or estimated trial purchases)? What are the important concept attributes? What is the best positioning for the product? Is the market segmented? How? What are the demographic, psychographic, and product class usage characteristics of target market segments?

Research techniques include: focus groups, small group discussions and reactions to concepts described verbally, visually, or in a three-dimensional model; quantitative surveys, either shopping mall intercepts, field survey office interviews, or mail surveys, all using concept illustrations, descriptions, or samples to elicit large sample responses; Design Inquiry ®. King-Casey Inc., a New Canaan, Conn., industrial design and new product development company, has developed a proprietary technique that falls somewhere between qualitative focus groups and large sample techniques. The Design Inquiry process includes the following techniques and philosophy:

- Falls between qualitative and quantitative research.
- Utilizes large enough samples to yield limited quantitative data.
- Employs in-depth interviews—personal and/or groups.
- Involves open-ended questions for maximum consumer input.
- Gets at nuances and subtleties that might be missed in ordinary quantitative research.
- Involves entire team of design, marketing, and research personnel.
- Brings creative and design perspective to marketing and research interpretations.
- Marries intuitive creative talents and pragmatic business disciplines.
- Generates responses that can be acted on visually by the designers.
- Results in products and designs that are in tune with consumer needs and fulfills their expectations, and are the "right" solutions because they will sell the most merchandise at the best profit possible.

Regardless of which technique is used, the way the concept is illustrated and defined to the consumer is critical in generating usable results. The concept statement should clearly state the problem being solved, a definition of the type of solution the product provides, and the necessary supporting attributes that lend credibility to the product. Following are some guidelines:

Use normal language. Often the concept board will be used when no one is around to explain what a word or term means. Also, make sure the sentences are short. You're not writing a traditional English composition. You are writing more in the style of advertising without attempting to interject creative twists (there are no slogans).

The verbal section of the concept board should have a number of paragraphs. Avoid long, involved paragraphs, particularly when referring to several kinds of supporting attributes. It is better to break them into paragraphs that contain one, or at most, a few kinds of supporting attributes.

It is best to avoid catchy names in concept statements, unless the name is an integral part of the product concept or aids in the communication of the concept. It is best if the name indicates the function of the product. For example "A SAFE TRICYCLE" will be better than "HEAVY WHEELS" if talking to mothers who are prospective purchasers of a tricycle type toy that will not tip over. Ultimately, you might want to call it something like "HEAVY WHEELS." But that would be a result of what you learned in your positioning research. It almost never is a good idea to use names in concept statements. In some areas, though this may be tempered. In the area of cosmetics, the name often becomes a part of the total package. Therefore, in areas like cosmetics and toiletries sometimes a name has to be part of the concept statement. It is an area in which good judgment is needed.

Finally, the concept should have a one- or two-sentence summary that puts the concept in perspective.[4]

Figure 9–3 shows an example of a "concept board" sketch and a verbal description.

## PRODUCT DESIGN AND DEVELOPMENT

Key questions include, Which design features should be included? Which are not important? How should the product be packaged/presented to the customer? How will the product be used? What

---

[4] Eugene J. Cafarelli, *Developing New Products and Repositioning Mature Brands* (New York: John Wiley & Sons, 1980), p. 111. © 1980 John Wiley & Sons, Inc.

# FIGURE 9–3

**Sixteen-Hour Facial Lotion**

Today's active woman demands a lot from her cosmetics because she is often on the go from morning till night. Unfortunately, in her busy day there's often not a chance to change make-up. And the kind of make-up that you like to use in the morning is not always right as the day goes on, or when you sit down for an evening meeting. For different times of the day, your needs are different and there isn't one cosmetic that will do everything you want.

That's the reason a well-known cosmetics company developed *SIXTEEN-HOUR FACIAL LOTION*. You can apply it in the morning and feel comfortable that you're doing the right thing for your face and making it look good all through the day and evening.

It has cleansers to remove dry skin early in the morning, a sun screen to protect your face throughout the day and an emolient to make your skin soft and attractive all day long. It is a clear lotion and acts as a perfect base for whatever cosmetics you want to put over it. You won't have to worry. You will look good all day and your face will be protected all day.

And *SIXTEEN-HOUR* cosmetics are safe too, because they're made of natural ingredients. In fact, these are the same ingredients you probably would use if you had the time and expertise to formulate a facial lotion that's just right for you.

*SIXTEEN-HOUR FACIAL LOTION.* An answer to a question today's woman has raised.

SOURCE: *Developing New Products and Repositioning Brands,* Eugene J. Cafarelli. © 1980 by John Wiley & Sons. Reprinted by permission of John Wiley & Sons, Inc.

are the durability/reliability expectations? How will the product be maintained? What are the service support needs, expectations?

Research techniques include multidimensional feature/benefit analysis (often using computer techniques to analyze large data bases and combinations of alternatives)—conjoint analysis, multidimensional scaling, multivariate analysis; trade-off analysis—placing a monetary cost on each product feature and analyzing consumer reactions and value interpretations; prototype use tests—in-home/business or laboratory use of prototypes, customer feedback on likes/dislikes, problems experienced; extended field tests—1- to 12-month or longer actual use by a small sample of customers to analyze likes/dislikes, reliability, durability, and performance in an extended, live environment.

Product samples are often used in these research techniques and can be three-dimensional mockups out of foam board, clay models, painted appearance models, "bread board" functional models (no attempt to create final appearance), or complete working/appearance models. A key issue is to be aware that *no model* will completely represent a final manufactured product in appearance, performance, reliability, or durability, and research results should be considered accordingly.

## PRODUCT EVALUATION

Key questions include, Does the final design meet target customer expectations? Are enough customers willing to pay the price necessary to generate an adequate return? How many can be sold? Over what period of time? If a consumable product, what will trial and repeat purchase rates be? Does the product and package appearance communicate the right visual signals, generate a high perceived value?

Research could be attained through a large sample concept test using photographs with comprehensive descriptions or shopping mall, on-site, or mail surveys; an extended large sample in-house or field use test from pilot manufacturing runs; a simulated test market—economical concept created by Yankelovich, Skelly & White, Inc., and others to simulate buying behavior in a store "laboratory" (good predictive norms have been established for many packaged goods categories, but is still developing for consumer durables); a panel of "experts" or personal interviews for commercial/industrial products or services with limited market size.

## MARKETING PLAN

There are two key questions in the new product marketing phase: What is the best positioning for the product (how to best communicate the most important benefit to the most important target market segment)? What is the optimum price, promotion technique, advertising strategy, distribution channel, marketing investment?

Research techniques include quantitative customer studies using conjoint analysis and other multivariate procedures to optimize the marketing mix and simulated test markets. Another technique is the live test market—the traditional "final check" in the consumer packaged goods industry, requiring a major investment and a period of at least six months to one year. Figure 9–4 shows cities commonly used as test markets and a variety of test market service organizations. Although new technology such as electronic scanners at checkout counters has made test market evaluation faster and easier, there are any number of things that can

**FIGURE 9–4** _____

| | | | |
|---|---|---|---|
| **Standard Test markets** | Peoria | South Bend, Ind. | *Portland, Me. |
| | Phoenix | | *Savannah, Ga. |
| Albany- | Portland, Ore. | Spokane | *Tucson |
| Schenectady- | Providence, R.I. | Tucson | **Telesis Group** |
| Troy | Quad Cities: | _Micro Markets:_ | *Albany, Ga. |
| Atlanta | Rock Island | Augusta, Ga. | *Austin, Texas |
| Boston | & Moline, Ill.; | Austin, Texas | *Boise,Idaho |
| Buffalo | Davenport & | Chattanooga | *Burlington, Vt. |
| Cincinnati | Bettendorf, | Duluth- | *Eugene, Ore. |
| Cleveland | Iowa | Superior | *Santa Barbara, |
| Columbus, | (Davenport- | Green Bay | Cal. |
| Ohio | Rock Island- | Savannah, | *Sioux Falls, |
| Dallas-Fort | Moline | Ga. | S.D. |
| Worth | SMSA) | **Marketest,** | **ParaTest** |
| Dayton | Rochester, N.Y. | division of | **Marketing** |
| Denver | Sacramento- | Market Facts | Binghamton, |
| Des Moines | Stockton | *Binghamton, | N.Y. |
| Fort Wayne | St. Louis | N.Y. | Chattanooga |
| Grand Rapids- | Salt Lake City | Erie, Pa. | Evansville, Ind. |
| Kalamazoo- | San Diego | *Fort Wayne | Fresno |
| Battle Creek | Seattle-Tacoma | *Fresno | Lexington, Ky. |
| Houston | Syracuse | *Little Rock | Madison |
| Indianapolis | Tampa-St. | *Spokane | Omaha |
| Jacksonville | Petersburg | *Syracuse | Peoria |
| Kansas City | Tucson | *Wichita | Spokane |

**FIGURE 9–4**
*(concluded)*

| Louisville | Control | Nielsen Data | Wilkes-Barre, |
|---|---|---|---|
| Minneapolis- | markets | Markets | Pa. |
| St. Paul | (Forced | *Boise, Idaho | |
| New Orleans | Distribution) | *Green Bay | |
| Oklahoma City | Burgoyne, Inc. | *Peoria | |
| Omaha | *Mini Markets:* | | |
| Orlando- | Binghamton, | | |
| Daytona | N.Y. | | |
| Beach | Erie, Pa. | *Indicates cities in which the company | |
| | Peoria | maintains permanent distribution, | |
| | Portland, Me. | merchandising, and auditing services. | |

## Guide to test market services

If you're looking for help with test market auditing or control-market testing, the following are leaders in those fields.

For names of other research companies, consult such publications as the American Marketing Assn.'s 1979 *International Directory of Marketing Research Houses and Services (Greenbook)*, AMA-New York Chapter, 420 Lexington Ave., New York, N.Y. 10017, or *Bradford's Directory of Marketing Research Agencies and Management Consultants in the U.S. and the World*, P.O. Box 276, Dept. A, Fairfax, Va. 22030.

**Store/warehouse auditing services**

**Audits & Surveys, Inc.,** 1 Park Ave., New York, NY 10016 (212-689-9400)

**Burgoyne, Inc.,** 309 Vine St., Central Trust Bldg., Cincinnati, Ohio 45202 (513-621-8940)

**Ehrhart-Babic Associates, Inc.,** Metropolitan City, 120 Rte. 9W, Englewood Cliffs, NJ 07632 (201-461-6700)

**Market Audits, Inc.,** 4000 Executive Park Dr., Cincinnati, OH 45241 (513-563-9550)

**Market Facts, Inc.,** 100 S. Wacker Dr., Chicago, IL 60606 (312-641-5200)

**A.C. Nielsen Co.,** Nielsen Plaza, Northbrook, IL 60062 (312-498-6300)

**ParaTest Marketing, Inc.,** 707 Westchester, White Plains, NY 10604 (212-490-1360)

**Selling Areas-Marketing, Inc.** (SAMI), 1271 Ave. of the Americas, New York, NY 10020 (212-556-4206)

**Store Audits, Inc.,** 580 Sylvan Ave., Englewood Cliffs, NJ 07632 (201-569-0903)

**Consumer diary panels**

**Consumer Mail Panels,** division of Market Facts, 605 Third Ave., New York, NY 10016 (212-953-9444)

**Home Testing Institute, Inc.,** 2 Sixth St., P.O. Box 5020, Garden City Park, NY 11040 (516-741-1460)

**Market Research Corp. of America (MRCA),** 4 Landmark Sq., Stamford, CT 06901 (203-324-9600)

**National Family Opinion, Inc.,** P.O. Box 315, Toledo, Ohio 43691 (419-666-8800)

**National Purchase Diary Panel, Inc.,** 15 Verbena Ave., Floral Park, NY 11001 (516-328-3941)

ParaTest Marketing (see Fig. 9–4)

**Telesis Group,** Butler Sq. 851W, 100 N. Sixth St., Minneapolis, MN 55403 (612-371-5550)

**Control market tests**

Audits & Surveys (see Fig. 9–4)

Burgoyne, Inc. (see Fig. 9–4)

Ehrhart-Babic (see Fig. 9–4)

Market Audits (see Fig. 9–4)

**Marketest,** division of Market Facts, 605 Third Ave., New York, NY 10016 (212-953-9444)

**Nielsen Data Markets** (see A.C. Nielsen)

ParaTest Marketing (see above)

Store Audits (see above)

Telesis Group (see above)

SOURCE: *1980 Portfolio Sales & Marketing Plans* by Sales & Marketing Management, a division of Bill Communications, Inc., New York, N.Y.

still go wrong and mess up the findings. Competitors can distort results by slashing prices in test cities, shipments may be delayed resulting in stock-outs, new competitive products may be introduced simultaneously, etc. Because of this and the expense, many companies are forgoing test markets and, instead, rolling out new products regionally in such a way that the marketing mix can be fine-tuned over time.

Regardless of which research techniques are used at which stage of product development, they all have advantages and disadvantages. Focus group research is a very controversial technique but has the attraction of being economical and less time consuming than large quantitative studies. The cost can be as low as $2,000 to $5,000, and results can be available in two weeks. In contrast, a quantitative survey can easily run between $10,000 and $100,000 and requires a minimum of five to six weeks. The key to getting results out of focus groups is to use a skilled moderator; use the groups for idea generation, *not* decision making; and involve all members of a new product development team for maximum creativity.

Concept tests are a valuable technique. They permit testing before prototype development, allow early product modifications at lower cost, are relatively inexpensive compared with physical product testing, reduce danger of premature disclosure to competitors, and help define target market characteristics and needs.

Their limitations include: uncertainty of what is being measured: ad copy, product position, or product idea; imperfect prediction of market share or test market performance: product must deliver promises of concept description, and product and target may shift between concept and introduction.

Quantitative surveys have the distinct advantage of the laws of statistics, which provides a degree of assurance in the projectability of results. The greatest drawback in many quantitative techniques is the lack of *direct* exposure to the product, the difficulty in describing the product in terms large samples perceive identically, and the cost of large samples.

The selection of a specific research technique is often based on the importance of various information categories and project requirements. Figure 9–5 lists a range of techniques in increasing cost order and rates their effectiveness in measuring certain market characteristics and meeting project needs.

Market research, like many functions of management, is a specialty where outside resources working with company per-

**FIGURE 9–5**
Comparison of Methods

| Consumer acceptance | Trade acceptance | Competitive effects | Cannibalization | Promotion effects | Price effects | Estimate demand | Realism | Control | Quick results | Low costs | |
|---|---|---|---|---|---|---|---|---|---|---|---|
| • | | | | | | | | •• | •• | •• | Focus groups |
| • | | | | | | | | •• | •• | •• | Employee panels |
| • | | | | | • | | | •• | •• | •• | Central location testing |
| •• | | | | | | •• | • | • | •• | • | In-home consumer testing |
| •• | | • | • | • | •• | •• | • | •• | • | • | Controlled distribution tests |
| •• | •• | •• | •• | •• | •• | •• | •• | • | | | Test markets |

sonnel can add synergy and produce imaginative and effective results. It is also a field full of suppliers with a wide range of competence. Consider the following questions when evaluating market research suppliers:

1. Has the supplier had prior experience with the technique being used?
2. What is the extent of this past experience? The quality?
3. Is the supplier able to conduct both the qualitative and quantitative phases of the project?
4. Is the proposed methodology tied to the overall goal and specific objectives of the study?
5. How detailed and thought out is the analytical plan?
6. Has the supplier outlined hypothetical outcomes?
7. Are cost and timing requirements realistic?
8. Check references.

Despite correct research techniques applied at the right phases in product development and with the help of the best research suppliers, disaster can still strike. Witness Coca-Cola Co., which spent two years testing its new Coke on 200,000 people. Unfortunately, it asked the wrong people the wrong questions and came up with the wrong conclusions. Instead of talking to the hard-core Coke drinker, Coca-Cola checked out casual users in blind taste tests. Instead of being upfront with the plan to drop the old favorite, the company never mentioned it. It measured attitudes (what people say or think) but did not gauge behavior (what people really do).

Hindsight is easy and offers 20/20 vision. Coca-Cola managers deserve an A+ rating, however, for turning disaster into an unprecedented market success. They recognized their mistake quickly, reacted extremely fast for a large corporation playing with the "family jewels," and flooded grocery shelves with an updated Coca-Cola Classic within 12 weeks. Not only did Coca-Cola breathe life into an old product, but it also ended up with twice the shelf space as before and millions of dollars worth of free publicity. A "Classic" marketing example.

Common executive errors that might have occurred in the Coke case and certainly occur frequently in many corporate offices include:

**1.** Only reading the executive summary, ignoring the detailed data, or the questions asked, or the descriptions on concept boards. Kenneth Roman, president of advertising agency Ogilvy & Mather, speaking on the subject of why brands fail (May 1985), recollected a research report that said diet positioning beat taste positioning for a new beverage—something that didn't make sense to him. On looking at the concept boards, he saw huge, refreshing illustrations of icy pitchers . . . and tiny headlines: taste on one, diet on the other. What *both* concept boards said to the consumer was refreshment; diet was strictly a secondary point.

**2.** Letting psychographics and lifestyle trend publicity override tradition and imagination. A Michelob campaign, apparently a product of lifestyle research run wild, portrayed imitation yuppies and left distributors cold. Henry Weinhard's Private Reserve with the concept of limited bottlings and western heritage moved it to a position as the leading superpremium beer in the Pacific Northwest.

**3.** Trying to put everything from research into one marketing campaign. The essence of positioning is sacrifice. Something must be sacrificed so the advertising can concentrate on one big idea.

**4.** Assuming "average" represents "majority." Coca-Cola executives might have assumed that New Coke offered the preferred taste to the majority of the market. If so, they suffered from the "majority" fallacy. Go to the detail and check the *distribution* of responses. An average preference may represent a hole in the

FIGURE 9–6 _____

| Where Do You Get Your Information? | When's the last time you sat in the bleachers? When's the last time you heard a Jefferson Starship record? (More than a million were sold last year.) Did you see Superman II? (It did $14 million its first weekend.) Do you read Reader's Digest? (The circulation is 31 million worldwide.) Have you seen the top 10 TV shows? When's the last time you took a trip on a Greyhound bus? How many times each month do you shop in a supermarket? Have you seen evangelists on TV? (Viewers send them millions of dollars.) Have you browsed through a card shop? (Hallmark sells one billion cards a year.) Have you stood on an assembly line? Gone down into a coal mine? Spent time on a farm? If you don't know what's happening in other people's worlds, you can't make good decisions in the business world. |
|---|---|

A message as published in the *Wall Street Journal* by United Technologies Corporation, Hartford, Connecticut 06101, © United Technologies Corporation, 1982.

middle of two distinctly different market segments, such as hard-core Classic Coke drinkers and innovators with an appreciation for a new Coke taste.

5. Killing great ideas because research says consumers don't like it without verifying and coming to grips with personal judgment. In the 1920s, 80 percent of consumers told General Electric they wouldn't want an electric ice box—too noisy and dangerous.

6. Believing in enthusiastic reactions to concept research without having the product to back up the claims. Make sure the product is superior first, then research the positioning.

7. Believing what consumers say, rather than what they do. When a consumer is asked if he likes his potato chips groovy, slightly burned, and highly salted, he will say, "of course not."

But offer him a few fixed that way, and it may be exactly what he likes.

**8.** Believing that because you are a consumer or have worked in your industry 20 years you know everything there is to know about your customer or prospect. The diversity of human characteristics is immense. See and remember Figure 9–6 when considering the next market research proposal.

Market research is a vital part of new product development. The $1.3 billion industry is growing 12 percent a year and employs more than 21,000 dedicated professionals. When it comes to delving into the muddled mind of the customer, however, consider research an art as well as a science and back it up with experienced management and good judgment.

# 10

## Is It Worth It?
## The Business Review

During the course of new product pioneering, emotions can range from wild enthusiasm to frustration and discouragement. Development team members can view their projects and ideas as exciting breakthroughs one day and the next day wonder why anyone would be interested in the product.

Changing conditions, both inside and outside the company, can also influence day-to-day perceptions of an idea's potential. Changes in team members and management can bring in new opinions. Yesterday's pet project can become today's sinkhole for wasting money. Product design and test results may indicate performance or durability far removed from original targets. Competitors may introduce new products with similar benefits. The economy may shift gears, enhancing certain market and industry segments and hurting others.

A consistent evaluation process used in various phases of product development is a way to add some stability to the emotions and changing business conditions. There are at least four stages of evaluation in a typical product pioneering effort—preliminary screening, market/business evaluation, product evaluation, and final business review.

Preliminary screening is generally based on secondary research data (information available from publications and historical surveys), technical feasibility review (R&D judgment), and management judgment (formal or informal group consensus, ranking, or rating). The goal at this stage should be to eliminate obvious losers quickly, *not* to kill ideas that may have potential. The people involved in a screening evaluation should be thoroughly familiar with the company mission or goal, the product development criteria or charter, and the reasoning behind both. In addition, they must have a broad business viewpoint, a flexible attitude, and a degree of creativity. A good policy at this stage is to require unanimous or at least a majority consensus before eliminating ideas.

If an idea passes a preliminary screening review, it means that management is willing to invest some time and money to explore the idea in greater detail. A market/business evaluation is a detailed review of external market and internal business factors to determine the magnitude of the opportunity and the degree of risk associated with it. This review can include comprehensive market research as discussed in Chapter Nine, and it attempts to evaluate two key variables: How attractive is the market opportunity? How compatible is the idea with the business, goals, and criteria?

Product evaluation is needed because the R&D process of new product pioneering can be just as much an art as marketing is. Product characteristics will change during the development process, and a variety of technical evaluations must be made to determine the potential success of the idea in meeting or creating market needs. These evaluations can include prototype reviews, cost studies, consumer use tests, or simply technical, judgmental assessment of probabilities.

The final business review can include a detailed sales forecast, pricing analysis, expense and investment projections, probability and sensitivity analysis, and final check against company goals and project criteria. It should provide a "go/no go" decision on market introduction.

Each stage of evaluation should include both qualitative and quantitative thinking and should combine objectives and criteria with experience, past benchmarks, and good judgment. To avoid getting lost in detail and losing sight of vital issues, it helps to keep in mind a few common elements of any new product success: market size and need, competition, and the uniqueness of the idea. The Forum Corp., a leader in management development and marketing and sales training, utilizes an evaluation system built around three simple questions: Is it *real*? Can we *win*? Is it *worth* it?

Figure 10–1 shows the decision-free framework utilized by The Forum Corp. in product planning seminars designed to help a company adapt unique considerations for evaluating and managing a product development project.[1] Regardless of which detail factors are analyzed and evaluated, if these three questions are kept in mind throughout a project, the chances of success will increase dramatically.

A. David Silver, a widely known venture capitalist, has developed a disciplined method of reviewing business deals that might also apply to new product evaluation. He suggests there are three laws of venture capital that should be committed to memory:

1. Accept no more than two risks per investment.
2. $V = P \times S \times E$, where $V$ = valuation, $P$ = the size of the problem, $S$ = the elegance of the solution, and $E$ = the quality of the entrepreneurial team.
3. Invest in big $P$ companies, because the public market will accord to them unreasonably high $V$'s, irrespective of $S$ and $E$.[2]

We would add a fourth law: Invest in businesses where there is an opportunity to capture a dominant market share—either a unique niche or an industry with fragmented competition. Silver considers a startup company to be exposed to five risks (and the same probably applies to new products):

1. The development risk: Can we develop the product?
2. The manufacturing risk: If we can develop it, can we produce it?
3. The marketing risk: If we can make it, can we sell it?
4. The management risk: If we can sell it, can we sell it at a profit?
5. The growth risk: If we can manage the company, can we grow it?[3]

---

[1] The Forum Corp., "Product Evaluation and Planning Program (PEP)," © 1977 Schrello Associates, Inc. Reprinted by permission from The Forum Corp. of North America.

[2] A. David Silver, *Venture Capital* (New York: John Wiley & Sons, Inc., 1985), p. 88.

[3] Ibid., p. 89.

# FIGURE 10-1
## Decision Considerations

**DECISION FACTORS**

**CONSIDERATIONS**
Developed and specialized for each company, product area and market by their experts.

| Decision Factor | Sub-factor | Considerations |
|---|---|---|
| Is it real? | Is the market real? | Is there a need/want? — Kind of need/want; Timing of need/want; Alternate ways to define need/want |
| | | Can the customer buy? — Structure of the market; Market size & potential; Availability of funds |
| | | Will the customer buy? — Priority; Product awareness; Perceived benefits/risks; Future expectations; Price vs. benefits |
| | Is the product real? | Is there a product idea? — Ways to satisfy identified market; Feasibility; Acceptability; State-of-the-art |
| | | Can it be made? — Designed; Developed; Tested; Produced; Inspected; Distributed; Installed; Serviced |
| | | Will it satisfy the market? — Design/Performance features; Cost; Unit cost versus volume; Availability |
| Can we win? | Can our product be competitive? | On design/performance features? — Quality; Utility; Convenience; Reliability; Serviceability; Style; Color; Safety; Uniqueness |
| | | On promotion? — Customer and trade advertising; Packaging; Technical Services; Sales promotion |
| | | Is the price right? — Cost; Pricing policies; Terms and conditions; Competition; Other price considerations |
| | | Is the timing right? — Introduction; Design changes; Sales campaigns; Price changes; Competitor reaction |
| | Can our company be competitive? | In engineering/production? — Experience; Capabilities; Plant locations; Processes/Patents; Unique ideas |
| | | In sales/distribution? — Relation to present customers; Distributor/Dealer network; New marketing techniques |
| | | In management? — Experience; Organization; Financial strength; New management approaches; Commitment |
| | | In other considerations? — Past performance; General reputation; Present market position; Geopolitical |
| Is it worth it? | Will it be profitable? | Can we afford it? — Cash flow; Investment and timing; Sales and timing; Net cash flow |
| | | Is the return adequate? — Absolute profit; Relative return on investment; Compared to other investments |
| | | Is the risk acceptable? — What can go wrong; How likely; How serious; What can be done; Uncertainties |
| | Does it satisfy other company needs? | Does it support company objectives? — Future business; Relation to present products/markets; Use of resources; Company desires |
| | | Are external relations improved? — Distributors; Dealers; Customers; Local communities; General public; Governments |
| | | Is there an overriding factor? — Labor; Legal; Political; Stockholders/owners; Company image; Executive judgment |

SOURCE: © 1977 Schrello Associates, Inc. Reprinted by permission from The Forum Corp. of North America.

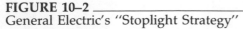

**FIGURE 10–2**
General Electric's "Stoplight Strategy"

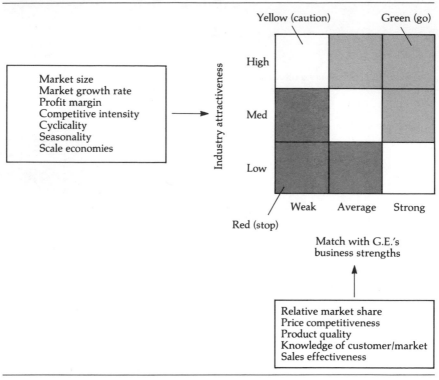

SOURCE: General Electric Company

The strategic questions and guidelines posed by Schrello and Silver are good to keep in mind as a project progresses and more detailed analysis is conducted. These common sense guidelines could have prevented numerous new product failures. Examples of low-problem or nonproblem solvers in the 1970s include feminine deodorant sprays, safer automobiles, automated voting systems, windpower, electric cars, and a variety of food products that appear on the shelves one month and vanish the next.

A comprehensive business review addresses two primary subjects: How attractive is the market? and How well does the concept match current business strengths? Figure 10–2 shows a matrix of these dimensions used by General Electric as a quick screening method. Boundaries on market size can be established by a quick check of Department of Commerce statistics on annual factory sales of the business category within which the new product would compete. The Standard Industrial Classification (S.I.C.) code sys-

**FIGURE 10–3**
The Standard Industrial Classification (S.I.C.)

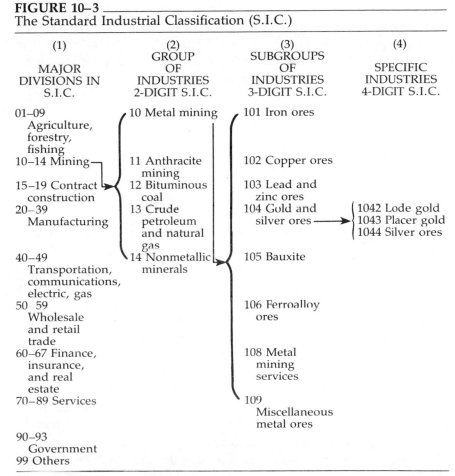

| (1)<br>MAJOR<br>DIVISIONS IN<br>S.I.C. | (2)<br>GROUP<br>OF<br>INDUSTRIES<br>2-DIGIT S.I.C. | (3)<br>SUBGROUPS<br>OF<br>INDUSTRIES<br>3-DIGIT S.I.C. | (4)<br>SPECIFIC<br>INDUSTRIES<br>4-DIGIT S.I.C. |
|---|---|---|---|
| 01–09<br>Agriculture,<br>forestry,<br>fishing | 10 Metal mining | 101 Iron ores | |
| 10–14 Mining | 11 Anthracite<br>mining | 102 Copper ores | |
| 15–19 Contract<br>construction | 12 Bituminous<br>coal | 103 Lead and<br>zinc ores | |
| 20–39<br>Manufacturing | 13 Crude<br>petroleum<br>and natural<br>gas | 104 Gold and<br>silver ores | 1042 Lode gold<br>1043 Placer gold<br>1044 Silver ores |
| 40–49<br>Transportation,<br>communications,<br>electric, gas | 14 Nonmetallic<br>minerals | 105 Bauxite | |
| 50–59<br>Wholesale<br>and retail<br>trade | | 106 Ferroalloy<br>ores | |
| 60–67 Finance,<br>insurance,<br>and real<br>estate | | 108 Metal<br>mining<br>services | |
| 70–89 Services | | 109<br>Miscellaneous<br>metal ores | |
| 90–93<br>Government | | | |
| 99 Others | | | |

SOURCE: U.S. Department of Commerce

tem breaks business activity into industrial segments as illustrated in Figure 10–3. This will usually provide only a gross indicator of market size because of broad category statistics, or a product concept that overlaps several categories, or a major breakthrough concept that doesn't easily fit into the S.I.C. system. Predicasts, Inc., is another good library source of market size and growth rate projections based on S.I.C. code. Department of Commerce and Bureau of Census publications can also provide data on industry profit margins, employment, value added by manufacturer, and competitive concentration.

Another approach to quickly gauging market size is to estimate the number of ultimate potential customers and an annual penetration or usage rate. If a business is related to certain types of consumers, Census Bureau data will reveal information about consumers, such as that there are 85 million households in the country, 60 million single-family households, 65 percent of females work outside the home, 24.1 million people in California, and more. A.C. Nielsen Co. and other consumer polling organizations can provide a variety of segment statistics on households or consumers, including current ownership or usage of products and services by demographic segment. Penetration rates can be estimated by historical growth of similar categories, and annual usage of consumable products or services can be projected based on frequency of use of similar items (such figures are often available from industry trade journals).

An example will help illustrate this approach. A company was considering developing an automotive accessory product for older consumers living in urban areas. The product would offer benefits related to safety and protection, but it would definitely not be essential for automobile usage. A check of *Merchandising Week*, a retailing trade journal, indicated current annual sales of safety items as follows: smoke detectors, $153 million; CB radios, $283 million; auto radar detection, $68 million; and home security systems, $94 million.

A further check of what might be considered nonessential consumer equipment products showed the following volumes: circular saws, $59 million; toaster ovens, $58 million; floor polishers, $23 million; and trash compactors, $72 million.

Commerce Department and Census Bureau data indicated that the total number of persons 40 years or older living in urban areas and owning automobiles was 7.4 million. If half of these people owned the product and replaced it every 10 years (at $79 each), a mature market would be $29 million annually (100 percent target market ownership would equal a $58 million annual market). A quick evaluation based on this information would say that the ultimate market size was probably somewhere between $10 million and $50 million and would grow at a rate proportionate to automobile sales and the 40 and older population segment—possibly close enough to make a preliminary go/no go decision and proceed to the next step (but certainly not close enough to "take to the bank").

A similar approach can be used with industrial products or even services. A company intended to establish a network of diagnostic radiology centers in 25 leading markets. A rough approximation of the market potential is realized by multiplying the number of radiologists times their average annual gross income. A telephone call to the American Society of Radiologists (check the library for directories of associations) or reference to published indexes will indicate 18,000 radiologists at an average gross annual income of $100,000, or a $1.8 billion annual market. A check of census data would reveal that the 25 target cities represent 60 percent of the population, or $1.1 billion. The company thinks its concept could capture at least a 10 percent market share resulting in about $100 million in annual revenues. This may be enough to proceed to the next phase of business development, but a variety of additional secondary and primary research techniques should be used to verify that the company could, in fact, capture the 10 percent share. (This research should include demographic usage of radiology, segments of providers such as university hospitals with their own equipment, direct personal interviews with radiologists, and so on.)

The general procedure for a market size analysis could be summarized as:

1. Define the primary target market in demographic terms—age, income, place of residence, occupation, and so on—if consumers; S.I.C. codes, volumes of business, number of employees, geographic location if industrial customers; and revenues of existing providers if services.
2. Estimate the percent of the target market likely to eventually own or use the product or service.
3. Estimate a product life if a durable, an annual usage rate per user if a consumable or service product.
4. Estimate a market share factor based on the uniqueness of the product and the degree of competition in the market.
5. Do a "sanity" check based on the annual market size of similar product categories, services, or industries.

The growth rate of a category can be estimated in a number of simplistic ways based on industry projections, growth of similar categories, and historical data. Judgment plays a critical role in projecting growth, however, and can be aided by being a "detective of change" as discussed in Chapter Seven and Eight and by using a "chained relationship" thought process. For example: 35-to-44-year-olds make up the fastest growing population segment, increasing 38 percent from 1983 to 1993. The age group represents the greatest purchasing segment of household furnishings. The do-it-yourself industry has grown at a more than 10 percent annual rate for the past decade. The physical size of new houses is shrinking because of cost and affordability. Home furnishings are rapidly adopting a European look in reaction to consumer demand generated by extensive European travel during high dollar exchange rate periods. The company has a new product concept for a line of knocked-down, easily assembled case goods furniture with a European styling.

The "chained relationships" indicate that the company could rightly expect that whatever its estimated share of the case goods industry is, its market *potential* should grow at 8 percent to 10 percent or greater annual rates (until these conditions change).

Numerous other tangible and intangible market conditions and relationships can affect the attractiveness and potential of a market for a specific company. The degree these factors are quantified and evaluated can vary with the size of the development project and the magnitude of the risk to the company (and sometimes vary with the number of product managers on staff and the size of the budget available). Figure 10–4 is a consolidated list of market attractiveness and business compatibility factors from a variety of sources. Each factor can be simply rated by management judgment (high, medium, low, 1 to 5 scale) or analyzed with extensive research. The end result should be an index or evaluation rating that supports a management decision to invest limited additional time and money resources in one project versus others.

**FIGURE 10–4**
Market Attractiveness Factors

| | Market Attractiveness | | | | | |
|---|---|---|---|---|---|---|
| | Current | | | 5 Years Ahead | | |
| | Hi | Med | Lo | Hi | Med | Lo |
| **Market Factors** | | | | | | |
| Size | | | | | | |
| Growth rate | | | | | | |
| Diversity (opportunity to segment) | | | | | | |
| Stage of life cycle | | | | | | |
| Demand cyclicality/seasonality | | | | | | |

**FIGURE 10–4**
(*continued*)

| | Market Attractiveness | | | | | |
| | Current | | | 5 Years Ahead | | |
| | Hi | Med | Lo | Hi | Med | Lo |
|---|---|---|---|---|---|---|
| Pricing sensitivity/stability | | | | | | |
| Distribution requirements | | | | | | |
| **Service requirements** | | | | | | |
| Level of technology | | | | | | |
| Potential for functional substitution | | | | | | |
| Captive customers | | | | | | |
| Customer concentration | | | | | | |
| Customer bargaining power | | | | | | |
| Stability in recessions | | | | | | |
| Foreign market opportunity | | | | | | |
| Overall Market Factors | | | | | | |
| **Competitive Factors** | | | | | | |
| Degree of concentration | | | | | | |
| Attitude—passive? aggressive? | | | | | | |
| Changes in type/mix | | | | | | |
| Leader's position—importance? changing? | | | | | | |
| Sensitivity of shares and market size to price, service, etc. | | | | | | |
| Extent of "captive" business | | | | | | |
| Vertical threats/opportunities | | | | | | |
| Overall Competitive Factors | | | | | | |
| **Financial/Economic Factors** | | | | | | |
| Industry profitability | | | | | | |
| Level and trend of leaders | | | | | | |
| Leveraging potential, e.g, economies of scale | | | | | | |
| Investment intensity | | | | | | |
| Industry capacity utilization | | | | | | |
| Raw material availability | | | | | | |
| Barriers to entry | | | | | | |
| Changes/threats on key leverage factors (e.g., scale economics, pricing, etc.) | | | | | | |
| Overall Financial/Economic Factors | | | | | | |
| **Social/Political Factors** | | | | | | |
| Social attitudes/trends | | | | | | |
| Environmental aspects | | | | | | |
| Regulatory exposure/ vulnerability | | | | | | |
| Unions | | | | | | |
| Overall Social/Political Factors | | | | | | |

**FIGURE 10–4**
(*continued*)

| | Market Attractiveness | | | | | |
| | Current | | | 5 Years Ahead | | |
| | Hi | Med | Lo | Hi | Med | Lo |
|---|---|---|---|---|---|---|
| **Technology** | | | | | | |
| Maturity/volatility | | | | | | |
| Complexity | | | | | | |
| Patent protection | | | | | | |
| Product/process opportunities | | | | | | |
| Overall Technology Factors | | | | | | |
| Overall Market Attractiveness | | | | | | |

## Business Compatibility Factors

| | Business Strength | | | | | |
| | Current | | | 5 Years Ahead | | |
| | Hi | Med | Lo | Hi | Med | Lo |
|---|---|---|---|---|---|---|
| **Marketing factors** | | | | | | |
| Share of served market | | | | | | |
| Coverage | | | | | | |
| Breadth of product line | | | | | | |
| Product differentiation | | | | | | |
| Product quality | | | | | | |
| Pricing | | | | | | |
| Sales service/effectiveness | | | | | | |
| Distribution | | | | | | |
| Advertising/promotion | | | | | | |
| Company image/reputation | | | | | | |
| Customer satisfaction | | | | | | |
| Others | | | | | | |
| Overall market factors | | | | | | |
| **Technical factors** | | | | | | |
| Technical service | | | | | | |
| Patent position/technology protection | | | | | | |
| Technology position/proprietary advantages | | | | | | |
| Others | | | | | | |
| Overall technical factors | | | | | | |
| **Production factors** | | | | | | |
| Capability | | | | | | |
| Cost/efficiency | | | | | | |
| Integration/flexibility | | | | | | |
| Available capacity/location | | | | | | |
| Others | | | | | | |
| Overall production factors | | | | | | |

**FIGURE 10–4**
(*concluded*)

| | Business Strength | | | | | |
| | Current | | | 5 Years Ahead | | |
| | Hi | Med | Lo | Hi | Med | Lo |
| --- | --- | --- | --- | --- | --- | --- |
| **Financial/economic factors** | | | | | | |
| Investment intensity | | | | | | |
| Vertical integration | | | | | | |
| Raw material security | | | | | | |
| Ability to protect economics as business matures | | | | | | |
| Others | | | | | | |
|   Overall financial/economic factors | | | | | | |
| Overall business strength | | | | | | |

After a company has determined that a market opportunity exists, it must still evaluate the product concept to ensure that it provides a benefit to the market. It's easy to get a good market reaction to a product concept described in glowing terms, but it's sometimes more difficult for the engineers and product development team to execute. Conversely, drawings, sketches, mock-up prototypes, and breadboard prototypes may elicit negative market research reactions because they give off negative quality signals or don't seem real. To avoid these biases, the product must be continuously evaluated against objectives and design parameters.

The first step in product evaluation can be a technology feasibility assessment by R&D and manufacturing or operations personnel. Idea generation, discussed in Chapters Seven and Eight, has created a concept. Key market needs have been identified through market research, as reviewed in Chapter Nine. The concept and needs should be documented in a project summary that would include a verbal description of the concept, size of the opportunity, and key design parameters or objectives, plus a timetable or schedule for the first phase of activity.

The design parameters would be specific to the industry but might include characteristics such as the following for durable goods: size, weight, speed, strength, versatility, reliability (mean time to first failure), durability (failure rate per 1,000 hours), cost/performance ratio; for nondurables: taste, color, texture, smell, size, weight, ingredients, shelf life; for services: transaction speed, se-

**FIGURE 10–5**
Project Rating and Probability

Project: _____
Objective: _____
Major market segments: _____
Concept description: _____
_____
_____
_____
_____

Target introduction date: _____

| Key Design Parameters | Weight | Probability (0 to 1) |
|---|---|---|
| 1. _____ | | |
| 2. _____ | | |
| 3. _____ | | |
| 4. _____ | | |
| 5. _____ | | |

Total weighted technical probability _____
Market success probability _____

Financial summary:

| | YEAR | | | | | |
|---|---|---|---|---|---|---|
| | 1 | 2 | 3 | 4 | 5 | Total |
| Unit volume | | | | | | |
| Revenue | | | | | | |
| Profit contribution | | | | | | |
| Development cost | | | | | | |
| Capital investment | | | | | | |

Project rating* _____

*(Total profit contribution) ÷ ([Development cost + Capital investment]
× Technical Probability
× Market Probability)

lection (versatility), reliability (time, performance, call-backs), quality level, frequency, flexibility.

A weighting factor could be assigned based on the parameter's relative importance to the market, and then each parameter could be given a probability of success rating by a design group. A preliminary screening evaluation, including technical feasibility and market feasibility, might be summarized in a form similar to Figure 10–5. This is only a first screen type of evaluation based on rough estimates and management consensus and is an attempt to rank projects rather than project financial results. A more comprehensive evaluation, discussed later in this chapter, would include a more detailed financial analysis considering the time value of money (net present value of cash flows, internal rate of return, and so on).

Additional product evaluation can involve prototype test data, consumer or field use test data, and further internal feasibility and probability assessments. Focus is critical during technical development. Designers can easily get absorbed by all of the detailed technical issues and challenges and lose sight of the most critical objectives.

Projects where the elegance of the design overshadows critical performance elements during the course of 6- or 12-month timetables occur in every business. Examples of such projects include a unique cooling system for a machine without providing any performance boost; the use of new, exotic materials requiring extensive testing, with no real strength or reliability advantage; extensive design of a new, compact power transmission system for a product where the major objective is versatility; a long search for a low-salt ingredient for a food product, when the key objective is quick preparation. An example in a service industry is an expensive development of a customer information tracking system, when the major objective of a new service is high-quality performance.

More innovative product concepts have longer lists of design objectives and an even greater chance of diluted effort. To avoid this, identify the one or two *most important* parameters for market success and evaluate them closely at every review meeting.

If there is one common variance in every design project, it is unit cost. We have yet to see a major new product concept that meets or beats its cost target in the first manufacturing run. This variance can be reduced (but probably never eliminated) by thorough and frequent cost estimating throughout the design process. The best opportunity to reduce product cost is while the product is being designed. Take advantage of the opportunity by establishing a discipline of "value engineering" within every new product development project.

The second common variance in every project is sales forecasts versus actual results. This should be expected because statistical forecasting depends on large amounts of historical data and a relatively stable situation. Neither of these exists in new product pioneering. Good evaluation of products and commitment of major company resources depends on sales projections, however, so an intelligent, rational attempt must be made. Three techniques for developing volume forecasts are: top-down, based on market segmentation techniques; bottom-up, based on distribution and sales force analysis of likely customer purchases, or detailed count of prospective customers meeting certain criteria; and cross-sectional analysis, based on volumes, buying habits, and time series history of similar products or similar situations.

In addition, there are both quantitative and qualitative techniques for projecting the annual rate of sales. Before committing the company to a market introduction, all of these methods should be used. Each method can be supported with greater or lesser amounts of market research and statistical analysis depending on the investment and business risk.

The top-down approach attempts to segment "total potential" to arrive at "company market demand." In its most comprehensive format, segmenting total potential would consider the following: company market demand for a *product* is the *total industry volume* that would be *bought* by a *defined customer group* in a *defined geographic area* in a *defined time period* in a *defined market environment* under a *defined marketing program* resulting in a *defined market share*.

Following are some examples of top-down segment forecasting:

In a geographic approach, demand for a new pharmaceutical could be projected as the national market for the category times the percentage of total national *buying power* in target markets (disposable income factored by retail sales factored by population) times percentage of retail sales accounted for by target distribution channels or stores (drug only, no grocery, convenience, or department stores) times company estimated share of store volume (two leading brands already on shelves with maximum share for third brand of 10 percent) equals demand for a new pharmaceutical.

In the category spending approach, demand for a new light beer could be estimated as population times personal discretionary income per capita times average percentage of discretionary income spent on food times average percentage of amount spent on food that is spent on beverages times average percentage of amount spent on beverages that is spent on alcoholic beverages times average percentage of amount spent on alcoholic beverages that is spent on beer times expected percentage of amount spent on beer that will be spent on light beer equals demand for a new light beer.

In demographic segmentation, a new cross-country ski product demand might be total population times percentage in the snow belt times percentage over 16 years times percentage with household income greater than $20,000 times percentage active in outdoor sports times market share estimate.

If detailed category sales data is already available, demand forecasts can still be generated by segmenting the category volume by specific product attributes. For example, market demand for stereo TV systems might be a function of total unit volume color TVs times percentage greater than $300 retail price times percentage of homeowners owning audio stereo systems greater than $500 retail.

Bottom-up forecasting is critical because, sooner or later, a prospect has to purchase the product. And a grass-roots forecast of who will actually buy helps balance the variances that exist in top-down gross numbers. It also helps generate a specific sales plan and gets a sales force involved and committed. Examples of bottom-up forecasting include: General Electric directly surveying nuclear reactor customers to determine buying interest in a new heat dissipation system; a lathe manufacturer asking its sales force and distributors to project sales of a new model by customer within S.I.C. code; a garden tool manufacturer asking its leading retail customers how many stock keeping units of a new line they would stock and their expected turnover rate.

Cross-sectional analysis involves collecting sales data on products providing similar customer benefits but in totally unrelated categories. The concept was discussed earlier in this chapter related to market size analysis and can be refined for more detailed forecasting. For example, a company is introducing a product with the following characteristics: home maintenance product, outdoor maintenance, used infrequently (once per year), substitutes either not available or tedious, retails for $100 to $200, low service and high durability important, and speed of result important.

The company considers power chain saws, gas-powered string weed trimmers, and portable water pumps to share similar attributes. Based on Simmons Market Research Bureau data for those items, the company projects a peak annual volume range of 300,000 to 500,000 for its new product.

An example of a forecasting model incorporating both top-down and cross-sectional techniques is the following hypothetical volume model of a powered snow shovel for use as an emergency automobile accessory:

136

A. *Older persons (40 and older) living in large urban areas*
1. Estimate of total persons 40-plus living in urban areas of more than 175,000 (Projection From U.S. Census Data) = 10,618,000.
2. Percentage persons in 40+ age group owning at least one car = 74.5%.
   Percentage persons in urban SMSA owning at least one car = 67%.
   Weighted average = 70%.
3. Total number of persons 40+ in urban areas with automobiles (.70 × 10,618) = 7,433,000.
4. Percentage garaged cars (estimate) = 35%.
5. # persons in target audience with ungaraged cars = 4,831,000.

Assume an ultimate penetration of 3 percent[1] (144,930 units) obtained over three years as follows:

|  | Percent | Number units sold |
|---|---|---|
| Year 1 | 45 | 65,219 |
| Year 2 | 35 | 50,726 |
| Year 3 | 20 | 28,985 |
|  | 100% | 144,930 |

[1]Based on assumption that penetration would be approximately half the level of snow chains.

B. *Gadget freaks*
Assume that the auto-powered shovel achieves ultimate penetration of 15 percent* of all persons who bought radar detectors for their cars (850,000). Over a three-year period, the volume generated would be as follows:

| Year | Percent | Number units |
|---|---|---|
| 1 | 45 | 57,375 |
| 2 | 35 | 44,625 |
| 3 | 20 | 25,500 |
|  | 100% | 127,500 |

*Estimate based on consensus judgment.

C. *Physically handicapped persons*
   Number of persons with heart conditions that necessitate physical limitations (per U.S. National Center for Health Statistics) = 4,741,400.
   Percent in snow belt (estimated 50 percent) = 2,370,700.

Assume ultimate penetration of 2 percent[2] over a three-year period. The volume that would be generated by year is as follows:

| Year | Percent | Number units |
|------|---------|--------------|
| 1 | 47 | 21,337 |
| 2 | 32 | 14,224 |
| 3 | 21 | 9,484 |
|   | 100% | 45,045 |

[2]Assumed to be less than the penetration of the target audience.

D. *Volume summary*
   Based on the volume estimates from the individual target segments, the following provides the topside volume potential:

| Target group | Year 1 | Year 2 | Year 3 |
|--------------|--------|--------|--------|
| Older persons | 65,219 | 50,726 | 28,985 |
| Gadget freaks | 57,375 | 44,625 | 25,500 |
| Physically handicapped | 21,337 | 14,224 | 9,484 |
| Total | 143,931 | 109,575 | 63,969 |

A key part of cross-sectional analysis is obtaining data on similar products. If this is not readily available, a relatively quick (four weeks) technique is a mail survey using a variety of homeowner panel group research organizations (such as National Family Opinion Poll, Datagauge by Market Facts.) Figure 10–6 illustrates a $5,000 to $10,000 quick panel survey used to support cross-sectional analysis of a consumer durable like an auto power snow shovel.

Regardless of which technique or combination is used, an aggregate market potential must be broken down into annual sales. Several techniques are used to determine sales.

## FIGURE 10–6

Panel Member:

Today, I'm concerned about what, if any, safety devices you keep in your family cars(s).

1. Please indicate which, if any, of the prelisted safety devices you or other family members usually have in your car(s).

| | Car #1 | | Car #2 | |
|---|---|---|---|---|
| | Keep in car | Do not keep in car | Keep in car | Do not keep in car |
| | (13–14) | (16–17) | (20–21) | (23–24) |
| Flashlight | ☐1 | ☐1 | ☐1 | ☐1 |
| Flares | ☐2 | ☐2 | ☐2 | ☐2 |
| First aid kit | ☐3 | ☐3 | ☐3 | ☐3 |
| Blanket | ☐4 | ☐4 | ☐4 | ☐4 |
| Extra water for battery | ☐5 | ☐5 | ☐5 | ☐5 |
| Hazard reflector | ☐6 | ☐6 | ☐6 | ☐6 |
| Air for flat tires | ☐7 | ☐7 | ☐7 | ☐7 |
| Extra antifreeze/coolant | ☐8 | ☐8 | ☐8 | ☐8 |
| Tool kit | ☐9 | ☐9 | ☐9 | ☐9 |
| Jumper cables | ☐0 | ☐0 | ☐0 | ☐0 |
| Fire extinguisher | ☐X | ☐X | ☐X | ☐X |
| Extra windshield washer fluid | ☐R | ☐R | ☐R | ☐R |
| Dry gas (in winter) | ☐–1 | ☐–1 | ☐–1 | ☐–1 |
| Snow shovel (in winter) | ☐–2 | ☐–2 | ☐–2 | ☐–2 |
| Sand/salt (in winter) | ☐–3 | ☐–3 | ☐–3 | ☐–3 |
| Aerosol de-icer (in winter) | ☐–4 | ☐–4 | ☐–4 | ☐–4 |
| Extra weight for traction (in winter) | ☐–5 | ☐–5 | ☐–5 | ☐–5 |
| Winter tires (in winter) | ☐–6 | ☐–6 | ☐–6 | ☐–6 |
| Traction mats (in winter) | ☐–7 | ☐–7 | ☐–7 | ☐–7 |
| Ice scraper (in winter) | ☐–8 | ☐–8 | ☐–8 | ☐–8 |
| Chains (in winter) | ☐–9 | ☐–9 | ☐–9 | ☐–9 |

Do *not* own second car              ☐1   (19)

2. Please indicate which, if any, of the prelisted items you currently have in your home.

| | Have in home | Do not have in home | |
|---|---|---|---|
| Snow shovel | ☐1 | ☐2 | (26) |
| Power snow blower/thrower | ☐1 | ☐2 | (27) |

**FIGURE 10–6**
(*concluded*)

|  | Have in home | Do not have in home |  |
|---|---|---|---|
| Power push lawn mower | □1 | □2 | (28) |
| Rider lawn mower | □1 | □2 | (29) |
| Gas chain saw | □1 | □2 | (30) |
| Electric chain saw | □1 | □2 | (31) |

3. Have you, or another member of your family bought any shares of common stock. . .

|  | Yes | No |  |
|---|---|---|---|
| Within the past 6 months | □1 | □2 | (32) |
| Within the past 12 months | □1 | □2 | (33) |

4. Do you or another member of your family own any real estate other than your home?

Yes ⊔1     No □2

Thank you.

---

Many diffusion models for consumer durable goods have been developed and tested for correlation against historical product history and provide a means of quantifying the traditional "S" curve most new durable products follow for initial purchases. The models all rely on the assumption that the probability of purchase at any time is related to the number of previous buyers. The behavior rationale is that consumers include early adopters, who provide initial growth for a new product, and followers, who depend on broader distribution, more industry advertising, and word-of-mouth exposure before they are confident enough to make a purchase decision. These models are primarily useful in predicting an approximate peak annual volume, and the time to reach peak. Figure 10–7 shows the accuracy of diffusion models used in major categories of consumer durables.

A variety of models for consumer nondurables have also been developed similar to durable goods diffusion, but are based on initial trial rates and repeat purchase rates as two interdependent variables.

**FIGURE 10–7** _____

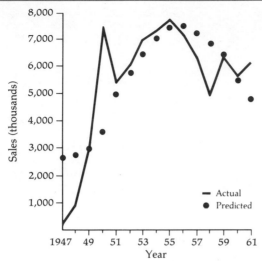

Actual sales and sales predicted by regression equation (black & white television)

*Comparison of predicted time and magnitude of peak with actual values*
*for eleven consumer durable products*

| Product | $q/p$ | Predicted time of peak $T^* = (1/(p + q))$ Ln $(q/p)$ | Actual time of peak* | Predicted magnitude of peak $S(T^*) = m(p + q)^2/4q$ $(10^6)$ | Actual magnitude of peak $(10^6)$ |
|---|---|---|---|---|---|
| Electric refrigerators | 82.4 | 20.1 | † | 2.20 | † |
| Home freezers | 9.4 | 11.6 | 13 | 1.2 | 1.2 |
| Black & white television | 9.0 | 7.8 | 7 | 7.5 | 7.8 |
| Water softeners | 16.7 | 8.9 | 9 | .5 | .5 |
| Room air conditioners | 40.2 | 8.6 | 7 | 1.8 | 1.7 |
| Clothes dryers | 20.7 | 8.1 | 7 | 1.5 | 1.5 |
| Power lawnmowers | 36.7 | 10.3 | 11 | 4.0 | 4.2 |
| Electric bed coverings | 41.6 | 14.9 | 14 | 4.8 | 4.5 |
| Automatic coffee makers | 18.1 | 9.0 | 10 | 4.8 | 4.9 |
| Steam irons | 11.4 | 6.8 | 7 | 5.5 | 5.9 |
| Recover players | 26.3 | 4.8 | 5 | 3.8 | 3.7 |

*Time period one is defined as that period for which sales equal or exceed $p\,m$ for the first time.
†Interrupted by war. Prewar peak in year 16 (1940) at $2.6 \times 10^6$ units.

SOURCE: Frank M. Bass, "Management Science," 15, No. 5, (January 1969), p. 221.

Although models have been developed for industrial goods and services, penetration and growth is more related to sales and distribution techniques and marketing investment, and a group qualitative forecasting technique may be best.

A final technique for forecasting is to develop probability estimates for each range of possible volumes and develop a weighted probability forecast or a risk analysis. Figure 10–8 shows what a

**FIGURE 10–8** _____

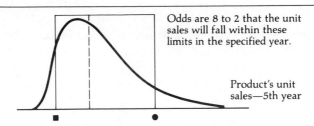

Odds are 8 to 2 that the unit sales will fall within these limits in the specified year.

Product's unit sales—5th year

■ Lower 10th percentile:

That low estimate such that there is only one chance in ten that the actual outcome will be below this figure.

● Upper 90th percentile:

That high estimate such that there is only one chance in ten that the actual outcome will be above this figure.

probability distribution curve might look like for a long-range new product forecast.

A general guideline for new product forecasting, however, is do it, but don't believe it. It provides some ranges to plan around, but the key to business success is the ability to react to changes and deviations. Oversophistication in forecasting can lead to an assumption of accuracy that doesn't exist. Successive layers of assumptions quickly compound error probability. For example:

|  | *Probability of Forecasted Volume* |
|---|---|
| Total Market | 90% (10% error factor) |
|  | × |
| Segment Volume | 80 (20% error factor) |
|  | × |
| Company Peak Share | 80 (20% error factor) |
|  | × |
| Years to Peak | 70 (30% error factor) |
|  | 40% compound probability (i.e., +/− 60% error factor!) |

Tracking corporate earnings forecasts in *The Wall Street Journal* versus actual results verifies that errors of this magnitude occur. And that presumably involves forecasting an entire business with some ability to manipulate actual results through management decisions.

A final business review of a new product concept must include not only projected volume, but also a reasonable expectation of profits, cash flow, investments, and ultimate returns. A complete marketing plan needs to be completed (as discussed later) to estimate all expenses, but some assumptions need to be made early in development and updated and tracked all the way through introduction and commercialization.

A company needs to make marketing estimates that include unit prices, unit sales (based on marketing strategy to be followed and competitive reaction), promotional expenditures, and effect on existing products. Investment estimates should include depreciation estimates based on expected value of capital expenditures, timing of capital investment and working capital outlays, and associated production capacities. Cost estimates should involve allocation of administrative overhead, annual fixed costs, and unit costs as a function of volume.

Numerous spread sheets and financial planning software programs are available for analyzing business projections and should be used as an evaluation tool. Following are some guidelines for using versus misusing financial software:

1. Clearly list assumptions versus facts.
2. Run cash flows as well as income statements and balance sheets (the purpose of any new product is to generate cash, not accounting-format income).
3. Test and document the spread sheet to ensure accuracy and visibility of assumptions.
4. Calculate NPV (net present value) or IRR (internal rate of return) considering a realistic capital or opportunity cost. The company should certainly do better than municipal bonds on a return rate, and the higher the risk, the higher the return.
5. Utilize the spread sheet for sensitivity analysis and "what if" questions. This is the greatest value of a new product evaluation process (what if unit cost increases 30 percent; what if volume is half, double; what if advertising cost is 15 percent versus 10 percent).
6. Rerun the analysis every three months *after* introduction to track against original assumptions, take corrective action, and improve assumptions on future projects.

7. Don't let the power of the computer in number generation lead you to believe that the outcome is any more certain—its's not.

After generating a great idea that meets corporate objectives and fits new product charter criteria, and a thorough evaluation says "go," stop for a moment and ask two soul-searching questions: Will the end customer say "Hey! This really works"? Will others believe him and try it?

If the answer is yes to both, then become a product champion and push it through the many obstacles yet to be encountered. Don't kill a good idea too soon if your heart says it's right and the data say it won't fly. And don't support something you know is a loser, even if analytical evaluations all say go. Facts *and* judgment—that's what product evaluation *and* management is all about.

# 11

# Getting to the Market

The United States is home to nearly 2 million consumer goods retail establishments, spread across 22 industrial classifications, and some 300,000 wholesale establishments in both consumer and industrial categories. With such a range of choices, the alternatives and challenges facing a new product marketer are a little greater than those faced by the American pioneer. Fortunately, the problem can be simplified by focusing on the larger segments of the distribution system and the channels unique to the product category (but keeping an open mind on creative opportunities—more on that later).

Retail outlets can be simply classified into categories based on products sold—general merchandise ("department" stores) or specialty retailers. They can be further classified by their pricing-service mix—full-service department store, discount department store, full-service or discount specialty store. Type of organization—chain, independent, or group—is a final category. Distributors can be classified similarly based on their breadth of merchandise, price-service mix, and organization structure (independent, group, co-op organization). The channels can be reached and sold through a company sales organization or independent sales agents. Finally, a company can forgo retail store distribution channels and focus on either direct marketing (phone, mail) or contract sales directly to other manufacturers. Each industry has its traditional segments and terminology (off-price rack store, box store, warehouse store, value-added retailer, cash and carry, installer, regional discounter, co-op member), and numerous books and publications about distribution are available. The objective of this chapter is to help analyze and define distribution strategies and programs specifically for new products. The various categories will be reviewed as they relate to new product considerations.

The first step in selecting a path to the market is to fully understand the target customer in terms of:

1. What are their shopping habits?
2. Where do they currently buy similar products?
3. How frequently do they shop?
4. How many different stores do they shop? Which types?
5. How long does the purchase decision last (how many days spent shopping)?
6. How many competitive products do they consider?
7. How much information do they need to make a purchase decision?
8. How important is a product demonstration in the purchase decision?
9. How important is retailer service?
10. How important is location convenience?
11. How important are warehousing, delivery, installation, reorder services?
12. How critical is price?
13. How important is parts and service support?
14. How important are credit terms?
15. How important are full choice selection and options and accessories?
16. How important are retailer guarantee and credibility?

These questions can be answered through primary or secondary research as discussed in Chapter Nine, but the new product developer should pay more attention to what the customers *do* versus what they *say*. If research data say convenient location and helpful sales clerks are more important than price, but industry sales data indicate 76 percent of the category volume is sold through discount stores, believe that consumers will pass up service for price, given a choice. If consumers or industrial users are analyzed in mass terms, their habits will always follow general retailing and industrial distribution patterns and won't provide any help

**FIGURE 11–1**
Channels of Distribution—Paint

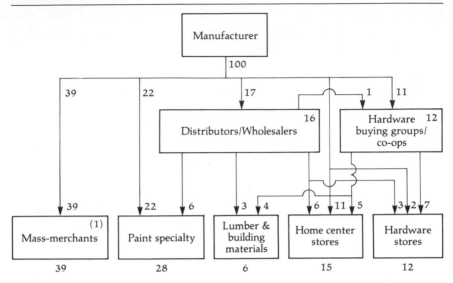

Note:

Figures represent percent of sales estimated to pass through each channel at a given level in the distribution system.

(1) Mass merchandisers and discount department stores have been aggregated into one box labeled mass merchants.

on new product strategy. The key is to identify a *target segment* of users and answer the above questions relative to the target.

A company in the do-it-yourself (DIY) hardware industry profiled five categories of consumers using a quantitative research survey. The five segments were based on psychographic and lifestyle factors relative to DIY activities, but the survey also identified price orientation and retailer service requirements. The survey helped prioritize distribution channel focus for a new product introduction. When targeting active, confident do-it-yourselfers, the primary retail outlet should be general department stores, such as Sears or Wards. The information-hungry DIY researcher prefers hardware store outlets.

A second step in distribution channel selection is to analyze and understand the current structure of the industry in terms of channels and share of the industry. Figure 11–1 shows a diagram of the distribution system for paint, and Figure 11–2 shows an

**FIGURE 11–2**
Channels of Distribution—Electrical Products Manufacturer to
Consumer

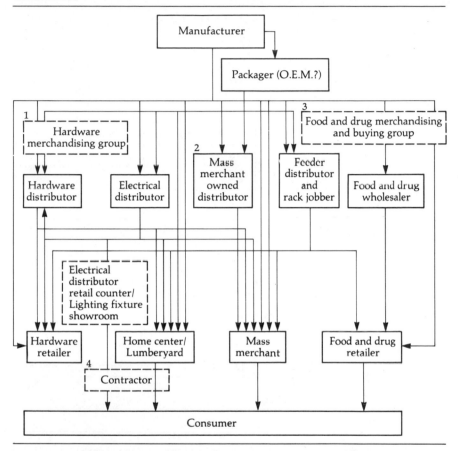

example of electrical products. Figure 11–3 is a combined analysis
of paint and power tools designed to support a channel decision
on the introduction of a powered painting tool. This type of data
can be gathered from many of the sources reviewed in Chapter
Nine, including the Department of Commerce, industry trade
journals, and discussions with retailers and salespeople. Even if
it's only a management estimate, an industry distribution structure diagram should be documented to help organize and clarify
thinking. For example, if the business objective includes a specific
market share, a structure analysis helps determine what share of
which channels may be required to achieve the objective.

**FIGURE 11–3** _____
U.S. Distribution Channels for Painting and Power Tool Products
(Estimated share of $ volume and estimated number of stores or
companies)

| Estimated 1980 factory shipments: (consumer only) | Paint | $3.0 billion |
|---|---|---|
| | Painting products | $1.0 billion |
| | Power tools | $4.0 billion |

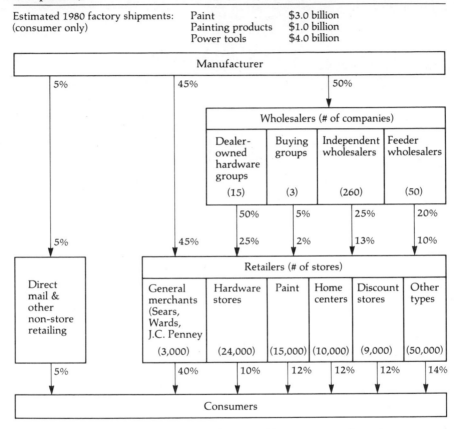

58 million single-family households (including second homes, vacation homes).
29 million multi-family apartments, condominiums, duplexes, etc.
87 million total households

223 million people

As retailing becomes more concentrated and more competitive, retailers keep looking for ways to further differentiate themselves. Matching the target customer profile to appropriate distribution outlets may be more complex than a choice between high price-full service versus discount-limited service. Figure 11–4, for example, shows a matrix analysis of retail offerings in the hardware industry.

**FIGURE 11–4** _____
D.I.Y. Distribution: Retail Differentiation within the Consumer Market

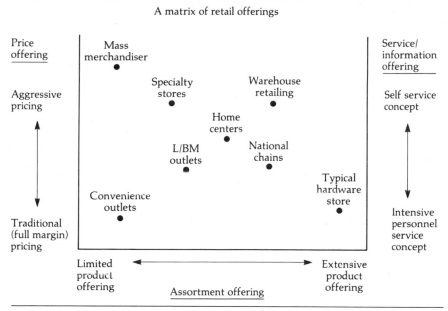

A matrix of retail offerings

SOURCE: National Retail Hardware Association and Home Center Institute.

A third step in the analysis is to review the new product carefully in terms of which distribution services may be necessary, important, or helpful in getting the product to the ultimate user: For example, if the product has a limited shelf life, fast delivery and inventory replenishment are required. Special transportation requirements, accounting for speed, bulk, freshness, fragility, and so on, may be necessary. Parts and repair service may need to be considered, and installation or training may be needed. The product may call for retailer advertising and promotion support or retailer credit. If it's a new concept, retailer sales assistance may be needed.

After defining the target customer shopping habits and needs, analyzing the industry distribution structure and the new product distribution requirements, the company can begin to develop a distribution strategy that relates to the product goals and objectives. Some strategic considerations are profit/volume objectives, geographic objectives, timing, market share, and product risk.

**Profit/Volume Objectives.**   High volume goals for the new product (relative to the industry category) may require broad distribution including many different channels. If the product strategy is to occupy a premium-quality, high-margin niche, then narrow specialty channels may be more appropriate.

**Geographic Objectives.** Quick national distribution will require chain store and multiple-step distribution channels, where a regional or local geographic market can sometimes be reached with direct sales efforts to individual stores.

**Timing.** If the new product plan requires high-volume distribution in the first year, the company will probably have to target direct sales to regional chain organizations large enough to generate significant volume, but small enough to act fast on a new item.

**Market Share.** If the objective is to secure a small, but unique position in a category, the company might target distribution channels and retail outlets not currently handling the category. If it seeks a dominant position, the company must attack and attempt to displace competitors in most channels.

**Product Risk.** If the technology or market acceptance is still uncertain (because of fast time schedules, limited research resources, or major concept breakthrough), the company may want to restrict initial distribution to channels capable of providing strong customer service and support or even restrict to direct mail marketing initially to prevent negative retailer reaction.

Each distribution channel segment has certain advantages and disadvantages related to new products. Following is a summary of pros and cons to consider when formulating channel strategy.

The positive aspects of distribution through department stores, such as Sears, Wards, J. C. Penney, include national coverage with centralized buying, extensive and cost-efficient advertising support, consumer loyalty, consumer credit, convenient locations, and high-volume opportunity through more than 1,400 stores. The drawbacks include slow to add/change lines, extensive product testing procedures (could be helpful in verifying product performance), sales support at regional level occasionally required, extensive commitments from the manufacturer, such as capacity, delivery capability, unique products, could be disastrous if dropped later.

Distribution through discount department stores, such as K Mart and WalMart, means lower retail price to the consumer and faster market penetration; regional or national coverage, strong central buying and control; aggressive advertising; high store traffic, consumer visibility; convenient locations; and high-volume opportunity. But discount store distribution also may prohibit or limit use of other competing channels because of pricing; tends to "cherry pick" fastest moving items in a line; may not give a new product time to develop market awareness (demand fast turnover); means no sales or service support is provided, although point-of-sale literature, samples, and signage are getting better all the time.

Specialty outlet stores such as hardware, drug, appliance, sporting goods, clothing, lawn and garden, automotive, and stationery, want a broad selection so it's easier to get trial on new products; provide extensive sales support to help explain new products; offer personal contact with customer to get feedback on new product reaction and help get attention and add credibility for new product; and can provide demonstration, set up, and service support. But these same outlets are usually expensive and time-consuming to reach, requiring multiple distribution steps and heavy manufacturer sales support on a new product; generally have low traffic, meaning slow exposure to new products; require strong advertising support from manufacturer to develop awareness and consumer interest in new items; and have high margin requirements, resulting in high retail prices that may slow market penetration for a new product.

The direct marketing distribution channel is fast and easy to test and develop customer interest; can reach best prospects and get quicker momentum in a new product; provides unrestricted geographic coverage; offers high margins and/or low price by eliminating traditional distribution margins; and can reduce risk of new product introductions such as timing and credibility with distribution channel. On the negative side, direct marketing makes it expensive to reach large market; has high startup fixed marketing expense, such as printing and processing; provides no retailer advertising or sales support; the customer can't "touch and feel" the product; and this form of distribution is impractical for some categories.

Industrial products generally have a more limited choice of distribution channels, and the basic trade-off for new product introductions usually involves deciding between factory direct sales or a distributor/dealer organization.

Using a factory direct sales channel means time allocated to a new product can be controlled; if sales organization already exists, new items can often be introduced without incremental cost; and immediate feedback of customer reactions to the new product is provided. But if the organization doesn't exist, it adds an extremely expensive fixed costs. Also, the sales force may be reluctant to take time away from "bread and butter" products to introduce a new item.

Industrial distributors provide quick geographic and S.I.C. category coverage. The distributor can add benefits to the product, such as local inventory and service, special installation or use expertise, financing, combine as part of a system sale, and exchange obsolete product or inventory. This channel also offers variable versus fixed expense. But the negative aspects include difficulty in getting distributors to promote new items; the manufacturer may still have to back up the products with a "missionary" sales effort from the factory. If a competitive line exists, it may be difficult to get the distributor to add a second line or change vendors. Also, the distributor may protect some customers and refuse to sell to competitive users.

A distribution alternative for consumer goods or industrial products manufacturers is to forgo the distribution function in part or altogether on a new product. This means selling direct to another company or several accounts that perform the distribution function. This can be in the form of an exclusive joint venture; an original equipment manufacturer (OEM) program to several manufacturers; a private brand program to a manufacturer, distributor, or retailer; or a "national account" program with several large wholesalers or retailers. All of these alternatives involve delegating control of a portion of the distribution function and providing some degree of exclusivity— receiving, in turn, some form of longer term or higher volume contract. The programs can be designed in a variety of ways to meet the needs of the parties, but generally have the following advantages: volume commitment reduces manufacturing risk on a new product with uncertain demand; manufacturer or retailer will stock and promote more heavily if given some exclusivity and committed to large volumes; manufacturer or retailer may be able to add value not possible from the source, such as brand name, advertising or distribution and sales power, credibility, or package with other products, systems, or services.

The disadvantages to such programs include losing the ability to add value to the product through distribution, thus operating at lower margins; dependence on the OEM or exclusive account to introduce the product to the right prospects in the right way, featuring the right benefits, at the optimum speed; dependence on a few key people in a few key accounts; and being one step further removed from end user feedback.

All of the distribution channels share one factor when it comes to new products: *resistance to change.* The new product developer is extremely close to the new concept, having lived with it through months of frustrating failures and design obstacles. When the developer starts presenting the new product to salespeople, distributors, and buyers, he might be met with doubt, suspicion, and apathy. Most of these individuals will perceive the idea as a problem rather than an opportunity.

For them it means systems and bureaucracy to contend with. It means 10 new item numbers to get assigned, three product and advertising committees to present to, getting the warehouse and the operations department set up to handle it, more ad materials to get to the ad department, and so on and so on. A new product means increased risks for the buyer, who may be nine months from early retirement or the next promotion, new to the job, under pressure from the boss to increase department turnover performance, or in the middle of a political battle between the field organization and merchandising headquarters. And distributors, retailers, and even sales agents and company sales forces have limited time to devote to new products. To give attention to new products, they have to sacrifice time spent on managing their day-to-day on-going business (the same problem that exists trying to push a new product through an internal organization—see Chapter 15). Retail buyers often have inventory commitment limitations ("open to buy" limits) they cannot exceed. Distributors, especially industrial distributors, can have an extensive investment in parts and accessories inventories, literature, and sales know-how; if the new product replaces existing lines, the new product developer has to justify a major investment write-off, not just inventory investment in a new item.

The key way to overcome these obstacles with most distribution channel segments is to sell *business opportunity*, not just product technology. Show why the product will appeal to large numbers of customers (backed up with research if possible), show why end users will want the product versus competitive items, gain credibility by referring to other retail success stories or test market data, show how the product will help distributors or retailers *increase their business and profit*, and create a perception that the risk for them is not in changing, but in the failure to change if other distributors and retailers get behind the product first.

Other key factors that appeal to retailers when reviewing a new product are: quality, competitive price, merchandising and advertising support, sales rep support, financial stability, full line—not just an item, and flexible programs.

Figure 11–5 shows the results of a survey in the hardware industry indicating general buyer rating of the importance of 40 different factors. Although "satisfactory turnover" is rated fourth, it's obvious that if it doesn't happen, the new product won't last long, and all the other issues become nonissues. The buyer must be convinced that the product will move off the shelf. To accomplish this, use product knowledge, market knowledge, market research, effective product demonstration, and industry success stories. Following is a summary of other major issues covered in the survey data, as related to either retail or wholesale buyers:

- The *honesty and integrity* of the salesperson must be established before any further progress can be made with either category of buyer.
- *Price advantage* is the major issue with both retail and wholesale buyers unless the seller can show the consumer will readily see an advantage to purchasing a higher priced item.
- *Turnover* is becoming increasingly important to buyers. The wholesaler needs to be certain that any new product will not add to his already long list of slow-moving products. His is a particularly acute problem as he cannot convince his customer, the retailer, to run ads to assist him in moving such items. One of his major concerns is his dead inventory caused by slow turnover and compounded when retailers discontinue these slow turning items.

**FIGURE 11–5** _____
How Buyers Rate 40 Basic Marketing Considerations

|  | Buyer Rating % |
|---|---|
| Honesty and integrity | 100 |
| Importance of followup (doing what one promises and says they are going to do) | 98.6 |
| Honesty and candidness in relation to foul-ups | 96.8 |
| Satisfactory turnover on an item or line | 95.6 |
| Knowledge of product in the line | 94.8 |
| Accurate information on delivery schedules | 93.6 |
| Being thoroughly prepared for the call | 92.9 |
| Reputation of the company | 90.2 |
| Proper supporting literature—catalog pages, repro art for catalogs, etc. | 89.7 |
| Service level—performance expected and received | 89.3 |
| Competitive pricing | 89.3 |
| Respect for buyer's time/seller's time | 88.7 |
| Consumer advertising | 88.0 |
| Return on investment | 84.6 |
| Genuine interest in helping the movement and sell-through of the merchandise | 87.5 |
| Knowledge of the industry | 85.4 |
| Markup or margin on the product line | 84.6 |
| Availability of smart sales-making packaging | 79.4 |
| Breadth of line (complete assortment) | 74.3 |
| The desire to receive constructive criticism | 74.2 |
| The monitoring and feedback of information on local promotions | 74.0 |
| Ability to communicate changes in corporate programs and objectives | 70.2 |
| Familiarity with the customer's or the vendor's operation | 72.7 |
| Providing data and information on competition at the retail level | 70.6 |
| Trade advertising—supporting the product | 69.0 |
| Frequent personal contact | 67.2 |
| Attending national trade shows | 66.3 |
| Availability of factory-produced displays | 66.2 |
| Dealing with a direct factory sales force | 64.3 |
| Attending trade shows on a local level | 63.6 |
| Contact at the top executive level | 63.6 |
| Liking the individuals that you deal with | 61.5 |
| Cooperative ad programs | 59.1 |
| Dealing with an independent rep sales force | 58.1 |
| Providing data on the competition at the manufacturing level | 57.6 |
| The need for written presentations | 56.1 |
| The need for written summary of what is discussed at various meetings between the parties | 53.8 |
| Having lunch meetings | 26.3 |
| Socializing | 22.5 |
| Having dinner meetings | 21.1 |

SOURCE: _Hardware Retailing,_ August 1981.

- Turnover is also extremely important to retailers. They are concerned about turnover because of its impact on return on investment (R.O.I.) and by its ability to create store traffic and departmental sales volume.
- *R.O.I.* is a very key element to retail buyers. Most retail buyers are now evaluated based on their department's R.O.I. and will, therefore, carefully examine any element that contributes to it. Unfortunately, most wholesalers are not as sophisticated and do not consider R.O.I. Wholesale buyers tend to look only at price advantage and/or available markup.
- *Available markup* or gross margin is important to both retail and wholesale buyers, however, it tends to be viewed only as one element of R.O.I. to retail buyers. Wholesale buyers continue to consider available markup as extremely critical in itself. This may contribute to a typical wholesaler problem of excess inventory.
- *Consumer advertising* is extremely important because it creates awareness, value, and demand. Retail buyers are very sophisticated when evaluating an advertising package. They can readily evaluate the effectiveness of a program and can usually separate a carefully planned creative and media program aimed at consumers from one designed only to impress buyers; they can separate loader and puller advertising approaches. Again, wholesale buyers tend to attach much less importance to consumer advertising. Their reaction will be in response to excitement generated by their retail buyer.
- *Company reputation and service levels* are becoming more important to both types of buyers. Current trends in the economy have forced many manufacturers to reduce inventories to very low levels, thereby making it impossible to react quickly to customer requirements. Buyers are being burned more than ever before and are much more wary.
- *Co-op advertising* is critical to retail buyers and nearly meaningless to wholesale buyers. Co-op is less a guarantee of retailer support than it was in previous years. This is true as more buyers look at R.O.I., and almost all factories offer good co-op programs. However, only a few manufacturers can offer a full package of turnover and store traffic created by national advertising plus an effective co-op advertising program.

- *Factory displays* are important to retail buyers in those rare instances where a manufacturer accomplishes a unique fixture that can truly influence consumer purchase intent. Wholesalers attach little importance to most displays. Most wholesalers consider displays as a real problem as they consume nonprofit space in their warehouses and are expensive to distribute because of bulk and weight.
- *Support material* in the form of consumer literature and catalog sheets is considered a very important element to both retail and wholesale buyers; however, as a general rule neither can use support material effectively.
- *Breadth of line* is a feature to which many manufacturers attach a great deal of importance. Retailers know that most lines have "heroes" and "dogs." They face a great deal of pressure to control inventories and know that "dogs" can quickly affect R.O.I. More than ever before, a manufacturer is forced to sell each item in his line as every stock keeping unit is reviewed separately.

Today's buyer is much more sophisticated and much more cautious. Noticeable differences exist in this sophistication between retailers and wholesalers as groups and even more noticeable differences among particular customers in either group. It is vital to understand and appreciate how each customer views each element that influences purchase decisions in order to effectively sell a new product. Various techniques and marketing mix decisions to support these program elements will be reviewed in Chapter 13.

Selecting the right distribution channel is a matter of knowing target customer, industry distribution structure, product requirements, and characteristics, attitudes, and purchase influences of the distribution buyer and matching these against company goals and new product objectives. But add a bit of creativity to a structured analysis before finalizing a selection. It could turn into another gold mine in the form of a distribution innovation.

L'eggs panty hose became a clothing institution by using a "crossover" distribution strategy— selling its product in the grocery channel, a first for the panty hose industry—combined with some unique packaging and intensive in-store support. Chipwich became an ice cream institution by introducing its product not in traditional distribution channels, but by blanketing Manhattan with street vendors. Frito Lay dominates the potato chip market by focusing on a comprehensive physical distribution system providing daily delivery to ensure fresh taste. Avon and Mary Kay Cosmetics created institutions by developing a distribution channel composed of door-to-door salespeople and unique incentive programs. Other entrepreneurs are creating winning products every day by using innovative forms of distribution such as vending machines, telephone marketing, cable TV direct marketing, shopping mall kiosks, and industrial supply "supermarkets."

Consider using the opportunity presented by a major new product introduction to also try a new form of distribution. It could be a faster and more effective route to the market.

# 12

## Pricing for Survival and Success

Other than "Hello" and "Good-bye," the most frequently spoken words have to be "how much?" If you've ever traveled in a non-English-speaking country, you've probably taken the time to learn that phrase. If you ever spent any time in an auto dealership, browsed through a gift shop, talked with a salesman, or looked at a new home for sale, you've heard or used that phrase. It is no surprise, then, that price tends to become a fundamental issue in many business discussions, especially when planning a new product introduction.

A term that is unfortunately used far too infrequently in business and is probably misunderstood by many business people is *value*. Dictionaries define it: "worth as measured in usefulness or importance; merit." It can be defined simply in business terms as the *benefit* a customer receives in a product or service *as viewed by* the customer, *relative to* the price paid. Pricing cannot be considered in a vacuum. It becomes a part of the marketing mix and the product design.

Some examples illustrate the complexity of the "value" offering versus the "price" of a product. In 1946, Reavis Cox wrote a one-sentence description of the marketing mix elements that became part of the price of a ton of iron ore. Ray Culley, a member of the Market Research Division at Republic Steel, updated that classic item as follows:[1]

> A price for steel becomes not merely $39.50 a hundred pounds but $39.50 per hundred weight of Hot Rolled Alloy Bars produced in an electric furnace to American Iron and Steel Institute (AISI) specifications for E 52100 containing the following chemical composition limits based on standard heat analysis ranges and limits for open hearth, basic oxygen and electric furnace processes subject to standard variations for product analyses: carbon .98/1.10 percent, manganese .25/.45 percent, phosphorus .025 percent maximum, sulfur .025 percent maximum, silicon .15/.30 percent and chromium 1.30/1.60 percent with small quantities of certain elements present which are not specified or required and are considered incidental to the following maximum percentages: copper .35, nickel .25, and molybdenum, produced to a rockwell "B" maximum of 250, annealed, skin ground on all four sides and furnished within a variation from a straight line of not more than one-fourth inch in any 5 feet but not to exceed one-half inch times the number of feet of length divided by five with bar ends painted with two colors, one color superimposed, dot on both ends of each bar and heat number or symbol stamped on one end of each bar with a cross-sectional size of eight inches round corner square in quantities of 40,000 pounds or over with a permissible shipment variation of 5 percent and under (or minimum of one full piece) each piece in multiple lengths of 12 feet with a minimum length at least 6 feet; cut with a cold saw with extras and base price subject to change without notice and invoices to reflect prices in effect at the time of shipment FOB the producing plant, Chicago, Illinois, payable net cash in 30 days or with a half of 1 percent cash discount if paid within 10 days of invoice date.

Value to a distributor or retailer in a consumer goods business can include advertising allowance offered, dating (extended payment terms), preticketing (manufacturer places price tickets on merchandise), in-store shelf management, training and literature provided, returns and stock balancing support, warranty coverage, drop-ship direct to the retailer or consumer, promotion allowance, and so on. And value to a consumer can include a complete psychological background of media advertising, peer

[1] Steuart Henderson Britt and Norman F. Guess, eds., *The Dartnell Marketing Manager's Handbook*, 2nd ed., Chicago: Dartnell Press, 1983, p. 82. © 1983 The Dartnell Corporation.

influence, status consciousness, need fulfillment, as well as specific product and service benefits.

Chapter 13 is devoted to balancing the trade-offs (including price) in the marketing mix to arrive at an optimum business plan for a new product introduction. This chapter will provide a background by reviewing creative pricing concepts for new products, traditional techniques of pricing, guidelines for strategic pricing, and ways of reducing risk in new product pricing decisions.

Pricing is often included early in the product development process as a specification or design objective and then ignored until test-marketing or final introduction. Even then, pricing is viewed as more of a financial decision than a marketing tool (price-volume-profit analysis). This is unfortunate because pricing can be a powerful and creative source of innovation in new products. Different market segments can have different value needs, providing an opportunity for combining price and product features in different ways. The airline industry has evolved from basic transportation to different classes of service for different customer segments. The automotive industry has become expert at developing a range of price-value offerings for different consumers. If these opportunities are considered when conceptualizing a product and during its design, price can become a marketing variable as well as a financial tool.

Creative pricing concepts can sometimes build entire industries. King Gillette, the face on the wrapper of Gillette razor blades for many years, didn't invent the safety razor. Dozens of them were patented near the end of the 19th century. But the market economics weren't right: the cheapest safety razor cost $5, and a trip to the barber, although inconvenient, only cost 10 cents. Gillette conceived the idea of designing a razor that could use his patented blades. He sold the razor for 20 percent of what it cost to make, but priced his blades at 5 cents with a manufacturing cost of a penny. And because the blades could be used six or seven times, they were more than competitive with the barber.[2] The key to this marketing creativity was pricing what the customer was buying—the shave.

The copying machine industry is another example where creative pricing strategy created an industry. Xerox Corporation added

---

[2] Peter F. Drucker, *Innovation and Entrepreneurship* (New York: Harper & Row, 1985), p. 246 © 1985 Peter F. Drucker.

the concept of pricing by the copy versus selling the machine and became the dominant leader even though it didn't invent the technology. Cyrus McCormick did something similar in the 1840s when he used installment payment pricing to create a market for the harvesting machine when farmers didn't have the purchasing power to buy it outright.

Following is a checklist of various opportunities for creative pricing during the product conception and development process:

1. *Add optional accessories:* Keep the base product price attractive to interest the largest market, promote extra benefits of accessories, enhance the margin on total sale (durable goods).
2. *Offer service contracts:* Balance lower base pricing with extended warranty or service contracts (durable goods).
3. *Provide installation:* Balance lower base pricing with installation charge (durable goods).
4. *Cash and carry:* Eliminate extra services and support attractive price (the entire home center industry was created on this concept).
5. *Two for one, three for two, six for $1:* Versions of combination packs to reduce unit packaging cost offer consumer a better value and sell higher volume (packaged consumer goods).
6. *Bulk pack:* Extend above concept to 10-pound boxes, 50-gallon drums, truckload or freightcar quantities (consumer and industrial commodities).
7. *Add/delete features, services:* The combinations are endless if considered during development (much more difficult after tooling or a manufacturing system is in place) and can range from complete kits to a "bare bones" product.
8. *Let the customer finish manufacturing:* Offer unassembled, component, partial service, such as knocked-down furniture, unfinished furniture, pasta makers, "kit" automobiles, and electronics, the entire home "do-it-yourself" industry and many consumer durables such as bicycles and toys.
9. *Combinations and tie-ins—*Add another product or service to enhance the value—software packaged with personal computer hardware, supplies packaged with equipment—

or group related services—hotel and car rental with airline reservation, disability insurance with life insurance.

10. *Rent the equipment, sell the supplies:* Examples are copiers, carpet shampoo machines, and industrial cleaners.
11. *Develop a rental business:* Video movies were slow to develop at a $50 to $75 purchase price, but at $2 to $5 overnight rental, a major new growth industry was created.

Thinking of variations like these and others in terms of *cost to the customer* for a specific use expands pricing boundaries dramatically. The design objective for a new product may specify a manufacturing cost to support a price of $200, plus or minus 10 percent. Before casting that parameter in concrete, consider what alternatives might support a price of $20 (per customer usage), or what additional value enhancements might support a price of $1,000. Get creative first, then narrow in on a pricing strategy.

Once a "value concept" for the product is developed, there are a variety of traditional financial-oriented pricing strategies to consider. The Big Eight accounting firm Price Waterhouse believes nine different strategies are worth considering. *Cost-plus pricing* adds a set percentage to the cost of the product in order to earn what is considered an appropriate profit. *Skimming* maximizes short-run profits by targeting customers who place a high value on the new product and are willing to pay a high price to get it. *Low-ball pricing* buys business by offering to sell the product below full cost in the hope of getting profitable followup orders in the future. *Penetration pricing* uses a low price to seize a large untapped share of a market in the expectation that the resulting volume will drive down unit costs and drive up profits. *Opportunistic pricing* raises prices sharply during periods of severe shortage, at the risk of losing customers who badly need the product and will pay a higher price for it, but may get even by deserting when things return to normal. *Loss-leader pricing* cuts the price of selected new products in order to attract customers to take a look at the entire line. *Defensive pricing* is useful in protecting old products or market share by holding prices low to discourage competition or keeping them high when pricing a new product so it won't steal sales from similar, already established products in the line. *Milking*, a short-run profit strategy, is useful if the company plans to leave a market and is willing to sacrifice market share by maintaining uncom-

**FIGURE 12–1** _____
Pricing Strategy

| Uniqueness of product (actual and as <u>perceived</u> by the <u>customer</u>) | High | Premium price: support R&D, communication, and distribution expense. | Premium price: look for added-value through services, combinations. |
|---|---|---|---|
| | Low | Competitive price: look for added-value through additional product features, options | Competitive price: look for added-value through deletions less service. |
| | | Embryonic or growing | Mature or declining |

Growth stage of
the industry

_____

petitive prices with high margins. *Foul-weather pricing* introduces a product at a low price to stay at a level that will cover out-of-pocket costs and make some contribution to overhead, in order to get through a recession or other difficult economic period.[3]

The degree of competition, growth stage of the industry, and the uniqueness of the new product are other considerations affecting an introduction price decision. Figure 12–1 is a matrix approach to analyzing these factors.

Two common considerations for all new products are: a) the product has something unique and different from existing offerings and justifies a higher price (if it has no differences go back to step one in the product development process); b) because the product is new, no one knows about it and the price needs to support an investment in communication. A general guideline is to price any new product at the high end of a reasonable range. This guideline works because some segments of a market will always be willing to pay the price; the company can cover development costs earlier in the life cycle; a safety margin exists to cover design and startup manufacturing cost overruns; and enough margin exists to support sales and marketing expenses. Also, price *decreases* are always easier to implement than price increases.

_____

[3] Carter Henderson, *Winners, The Successful Strategies Entrepreneurs Use To Build New Business* (New York: Holt Rinehart & Winston, 1985), pp. 121–22. © 1985 Carter Henderson.

Pricing too low initially can create a vicious profit trap: demand is far greater than projected; too much investment is made in introduction marketing programs, further aggravating the situation; manufacturing can't keep up with demand, resulting in expediting, overtime, scrap, poor quality, higher vendor prices, and inefficiency; dealers get upset because they can't satisfy customers and refuse to accept any price increases; and the result is a great new product with no profits. The days of double-digit inflation gave companies a cushion to recover from situations like this, but in an era of price deflation, a company can no longer expect to make it up with price increases. The experience of living through this trap on more than one occasion has convinced us that the underpricing risk is far greater and more unrecoverable than the overpricing risk. The difference *can't* be made up on volume.

Following are some additional guidelines for the new product pricing decision:

**Gross margins are like laws of nature—don't fight them.**   Know the industry and live within its margins. If it's a marketing-intensive business (cosmetics, beverages, computer software), the new product better support 50 percent, 60 percent, even 80 percent gross margins or it won't survive no matter how much advanced technology or innovation is incorporated in the product. If the product concept requires high fixed capital investment (new bicycle, paper mill product, railroad car), gross margin is a meaningless number until the company creates enough volume to cover the fixed costs. A low margin of 10 percent, 15 percent, or 20 percent may be more than adequate if it's based on a large allocation of those fixed costs (see numerous books and articles on direct cost accounting methods as a recommended way of better analyzing new products). Check Dun & Bradstreet and similar data sources for financial ratio averages by industry. And if deciding to change "nature's gross margin game," be aware of the risks.

**Lower prices do not necessarily mean higher volume—despite economic theory.**   Ever since Economics 101 you thought a price elasticity curve sloped downward (lower price, higher demand). Not always. Buyer psychology does strange things to those curves. Jewelry, European autos, country club memberships, running shoes, and blue jeans sometimes have upward sloping elasticity

**FIGURE 12–2**

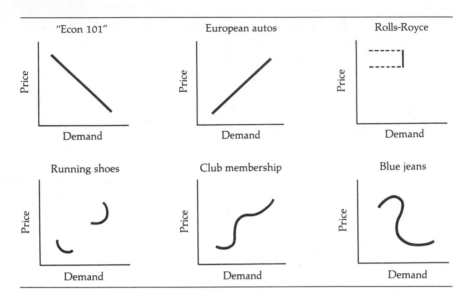

curves. Some curves aren't even curves—Rolls-Royce's elasticity may be a flat line (with discontinuity at each end). Other products may show a dip, then a rise, or a double hump or a "swayback" or any number of variations (see Figure 12–2 for several examples of economic theory gone haywire).

**Don't get too greedy.**   The "high-side risk" on new product pricing is the risk that no one will spend the time necessary to learn why the product is so great. If the price is way out of line with customer expectations of the general category, the product will never get their attention. It might be better to target the product initially at a different class of customer, break the product into optional modules or price variations, or even structure free trials, tests, or other marketing programs to give the product a chance to show its value.

**Start with complete offerings, negotiate downward.**   Pricing to industrial customers and distribution channels always involves negotiation because of the variation in needs and different ways of supporting the product. The buyer's objective is to negotiate for the lowest price and then add on services and extras. Anticipate this by basing initial quotes on a complete package: fully-featured product, minimum order and shipping quantities, max-imum factory support, longest payment terms, most complete warranty, backup inventory with fast reorder filling, store service, engineering support. Then deduct support during negotiations until reaching the right price/support mix to meet customer needs and company profit requirements.

**Always include an introduction "deal."**   A new product requires some customer to be first. Being first means taking a chance, an action to which most customers have a natural reluctance. Yet, the first buyer, the "reference point," the "beta test site," the early adopter, the risk taker is needed to get the momentum started. So dangle a carrot—a special introductory price, on-site factory service for 90 days, extra advertising support, custom installation, dating terms or an opening order, or other incentives. Position that carrot in a way that reduces the customer's risk concern— "support to ensure success, put you at the leading edge of your industry," "an introductory price point to get more traffic into your department, make the whole department look good," "get it now, before every homeowner wants one and the price goes up." Remember, no matter how strong the company image, how unusual the product, or how advanced the technology, "a poor man needs a deal, a rich man loves a deal."

The new product pricing decision obviously requires a knowl-edge of the industry, the buyer psychology, the economics of the technology, and the strategy and objectives of the firm. Some general considerations may push the pricing range lower or higher, however.

A new product can be priced lower if the market is mature, if intensive market coverage is existent if the product is widely distributed, when the company has a very large market share and wants to keep it, if the product requires little or no promotion or it receives a lot of promotional help from wholesalers and retailers, if it's capital intensive versus labor intensive, if it's a single-use product, if product life is short, if it has slow technological changes and short distribution channels, if it has fast inventory turnover, and if the company has a long-term profit objective.

The new product should be priced higher if it's in a new or declining market, if it has selective market coverage or a small market share, if it has heavy promotion expense or little adver-tising help, if it's a labor intensive or custom product, if it's a multiple-use product or has a long useful product life, if it has rapid technological advances or expensive channels of distribution, if it has slow inventory turnover, or if the company has a short-term profit objective.

Another key guideline is to preserve an opportunity to test and adjust the pricing. Pricing new products is much more difficult than a decision to adjust existing product pricing: there is no demand history, no customer base to test reactions, no manufacturing experience to analyze scale economies. If a complete test market with a range of prices cannot be conducted, watch closely for signals during introduction and be prepared to react quickly.

There are basically two aspects to a new product price: the amount and the form of payment. Companies tend to spend too much time thinking about the amount and not nearly enough time on the form. There are several forms of payments.

Direct sale involves payment in cash or credit card or by a third party, such as an insurance company.

Installment sale means credit must be arranged with a lender before sale. Ownership reverts to purchaser at time of sale with the product serving as collateral for the lender.

Through lease or rental, the customer pays for the privilege of using the product without owning it. In a metered or usage charge the customer pays an installation fee to obtain the product on its premises and then pays a monthly fee based on frequency of use.

Subscription means payment is made in advance for the right to receive a future product or service.

In a facilities management contract, the customer transfers the assets of a specified operation or facility—such as a data processing department—to the service provider, who agrees to deliver the specified service for the amount of the annual budget.[4]

Forms of payment and added services are some of the most creative ways to maximize opportunities in new products. IBM is the expert at it. When IBM introduces a new product, its salespeople fan out in several directions to call on a number of potential customers to test the possible price. Upon demonstrating the solutions offered by the new product to the potential customer's

---

[4] A. David Silver, *Venture Capital, The Complete Guide For Investors* (New York: John Wiley & Sons, Inc., 1985), p. 143. © 1985 John Wiley & Sons, Inc.

problem, the IBM salesperson leads the discussion gradually to the subject of price.

> "How much is this product?" asks the customer. "Thirty thousand dollars," responds IBM. Then, if the customer does not bat an eye, IBM continues: "Per Month." If still no eye is batted, nor leg crossed to indicate stiffening resistance, IBM continues: "Plus a service contract of $1,000 per month or $8,000 for the first 12 months." If still no resistance, the salesperson adds: "Plus two days training for $1,500 for each employee trained; plus a parts warranty for $13,600; plus some interesting peripherals and up-grades." Facing no material resistance, IBM continues: "Now let's talk about the software."[5]

A final step in pricing new products is to check the new product objectives and devise a pricing program that supports the achievement of other business goals. For example, following is a program designed to introduce a line of consumer durables to a national market:

1. Simple price structure oriented toward volume distribution and efficiencies of scale.
2. Self-regulating price structure based on order quantities, shipping requirements, and billing procedures (versus attempts to define and classify a variety of distribution channels by function).
3. Price to support mass-market advertising investments, volume-oriented trade discounts (versus personal selling and distribution investments through long discounts).
4. Establish price structure to force small dealer orders and mass merchant fill-ins through distributors versus factory direct.
5. Offer incentives to encourage volume stocking orders before advertising campaign.

New product pricing will always be a challenge with inherent risks, but to ensure survival in the marketplace, keep in mind the following basics: determine if price is a "critical success factor" in the overall product and business strategy; if so, invest in testing and refining the price before market introduction; if not, *always* start at the high end of a range and adjust downward if necessary through deals, added services, or price reductions. Pay back the startup investment first, then push the volume.

---

[5] Ibid, p. 144.

# 13

## The Marketing Attack—Putting It All Together

A new product has one or maybe two chances to succeed in the marketplace. Initial marketing expenses often exceed all of the previous development expenses by three or four times. And the company's reputation and reliability become exposed and at risk based on customer reaction to the product, the product's quality and performance, and the company's ability to deliver on time and create market demand. For these reasons and many others, it is essential that all of the previous market and product research, customer need information, product marketing goals, and pricing and distribution strategy be integrated and documented in a marketing plan. The plan becomes a budgeting and approval tool, a creative marketing synergy exercise, a road map for introduction timing and responsibility, and an insurance policy.

Marketing planning in general, and for new products in particular, has evolved from a numbers exercise in the 1960s, through an emphasis on strategic planning techniques in the '70s (portfolio analysis, cash flow, learning curve theory, life cycle theory), and finally to a philosophy of *strategic management* in the 1980s. Strategic management focuses on action, execution, flexibility, accountability for results, commitment, and creativity. This is especially beneficial in new product marketing because more uncertainties prevail, and new marketing ideas may be essential for a successful launch.

A new product marketing plan can be comprehensive, covering a major national introduction of an entire product line, or be simply a summary of a six-month special promotion on a new product. In either case, it should be easy to understand by everyone who works with it, precise and detailed to avoid confusion, realistic in goals and means of attaining them. The marketing plan also should be adaptable to change, cover all key marketing mix factors, and identify responsibilities.

Characteristics of a good plan were probably best documented by the Department of the Army some time ago in the "Staff Officers Field Manual: Staff Organization and Procedure."

## CHARACTERISTICS OF A PLAN

The essential element of a plan is that it offers a definite course of action and a method for execution. A good plan:

a. *Provides for accomplishing the mission.* Does it accomplish the objective of the planning?

b. *Is based on facts and valid assumptions.* Have all pertinent data been considered? Are the data accurate? Have assumptions been reduced to a minimum?

c. *Provides for the use of existing resources.* Is the plan workable? Are there any resources organic to the organization that are not being fully utilized? Are there any resources available from higher headquarters that should be used?

d. *Provides the necessary organization.* Does the plan clearly establish relationships and fix responsibilities?

e. *Provides continuity.* Does the plan provide the organization, personnel, material, and arrangements for the full period of the contemplated operation?

f. *Provides decentralization.* Does the plan delegate authority to the maximum extent consistent with the necessary control?

g. *Provides direct contact.* Does the plan permit coordination during execution by direct contact between coequals and counterparts on all levels?

h. *Is simple.* Have all elements been eliminated that are not essential to successful action? Have all elements been reduced to their simplest forms? Have all possibilities for misunderstanding been eliminated?

    i. *Is flexible.* Does the plan leave room for adjustment to change in operating conditions? Where necessary, are alternate courses of action stipulated?

    j. *Provides control.* Do adequate means exist, or have they been provided, to ensure that the plan is carried out in accordance with the commander's intent?

    k. *Is coordinated.* Is the plan fully coordinated? When appropriate, has the commander been informed of nonconcurrence or noncoordination?

Typical problems in marketing planning arise frequently because of a lack of quantified objectives, too much time spent on collecting and analyzing historical data in the situation analysis step, and lack of a written plan. No forced trade-off of resource allocation in the strategy plan, no followup to compare results with plans, no commitment by top management to planning, and no involvement by "doers" who will have to carry out the plans also create problems in marketing planning. Keep these factors in mind when developing the new product plan, especially the involvement and commitment of all of the people necessary to executing the plans (more on the "people side" in Chapter 15).

The ultimate purpose of the plan is to allocate resources— people and capital—to most effectively introduce the new product. This allocation of resources is often called "the marketing mix," as shown in Figure 13–1. The mix includes all of the elements relating to the final product configuration, how it gets to the customer, how its benefits are communicated, and how it can be purchased. The mix must be considered relative to the world it operates in and the specific customer targeted. Some questions to consider as a review of previous development efforts before finalizing an introduction plan strategy are:

1. Who are the target market customers?
2. What benefits are there for buyers if they do buy the product? If they buy from a competitor? What product features *really* are important to prospective buyers?
3. What are the competitive advantages and disadvantages in selling the product to specific buyers?
4. What environmental factors pose special opportunities or threats for the product introduction?
5. What are the incremental revenues and costs of reaching various groups of prospective buyers?

**FIGURE 13-1** _____
Outside Environment (Culture, technological, competitive, political, legal, regulatory)

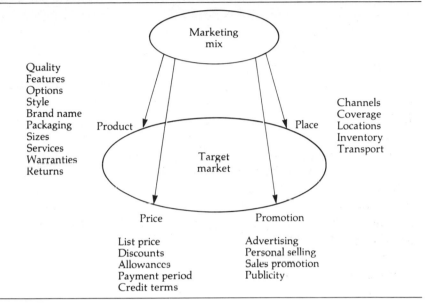

Quality
Features
Options
Style
Brand name
Packaging
Sizes
Services
Warranties
Returns

Product

Marketing mix

Place

Channels
Coverage
Locations
Inventory
Transport

Target market

Price

List price
Discounts
Allowances
Payment period
Credit terms

Promotion

Advertising
Personal selling
Sales promotion
Publicity

6. What marketing factors can be most effective in reaching specific buyers?

The marketing mix must be analyzed and selected based on an explicit definition of the target market. A thorough market segmentation effort dividing all prospective customers into subgroups with similar needs, located in the same area, and re-sponding in the same way to various marketing factors will make a plan more cost efficient as well as more effective. Markets for consumer goods can be segmented by geographic location, be-havioral characteristics of buyers (usage rate, end use, brand loy-alty), personality characteristics, psychographics, benefits sought, and responsiveness to marketing factors (product features, price, advertising, retail outlet). Markets for industrial goods can be divided by geographic location, industry, size of firm, benefits sought, applications/use, and responsiveness to marketing factors (product features, price, quality, delivery, service).

It is especially important to try to identify who the "early adopters" and "influencers" are within the targets. Industrial product success often depends on reference selling using a few leading companies as case histories and demonstration sites. Consumer goods introductions can also be influenced greatly by getting distribution through a few leading retailers, creating pressure on other retailers to take the product in order to stay competitive.

Analysis of market segmentation illustrates how the planning process incorporates two major types of thinking: inductive and deductive. *Inductive* thinking flows from the specific to the general, from detailed facts, analysis, and assumptions to conclusions. *Deductive* thinking flows from the general back to the specific, from strategy, critical issues, and an outline to a detailed operations plan. Analyzing the market segments and moving toward mix decisions is an example of the first part of the planning process—inductive thinking.

The marketing mix offers a choice of many different marketing tools. The *product mix* is concerned with all the elements and ingredients that make up the actual product offered for sale. These ingredients should be integrated to support one another. They include product planning, product development, number of product lines carried, size, color, packaging, warranties and guarantees, branding, labeling, and servicing of each individual product.

The *distribution mix* is comprised of two basic components: channels of distribution and physical distribution. Channels of distribution consist of the institutions and activities involved in marketing products as reviewed in Chapter 11. Physical distribution is concerned with the physical flow of goods to market. The physical distribution mix deals with such factors as inventories, materials handling systems, storage facilities, modes of transportation, distribution centers, and related areas involved in the firm's distribution strategy.

The *promotion mix* pertains to the strategic combination of advertising, personal selling, sales promotion, public relations, publicity, merchandising, and other tools to communicate with the marketplace. And the *pricing mix* is the presentation and establishment of "value" to the customer as discussed in Chapter 12.

The ability to select the right tools, in the right amounts, and integrate them into a coordinated and creative attack is the essence of a new product plan. A simple consumer product could be offered to the market in a seemingly endless combination of alternatives. The concept of "modular marketing" is using the marketing mix and design flexibility to meet the needs of different

**FIGURE 13–2** _____

| Product | Package | Display | Pricing |
|---|---|---|---|
| Basic function | Hanging | Counter | Terms |
| B1 | H1 | C1 | T1 |
| Color variations | Standing | Pegboard | T2 |
| C1 | S1 | P1 | T3 |
| C2 | H1 & S1 (combined) | P1 & C1 (comb.) | T4 |
| C3 | Boxed | Display center | Freight |
| C4 | B1 | DC1 | F1 |
| Trim variations | B2 | DC1 | F2 |
| T1 | B3 | Dump display | F3 |
| T2 | Bulk | D1 | Function |
| T3 | BK1 |  | FN1 |
| Style variations |  |  | FN2 |
| S1 |  |  | FN3 |
| S2 |  |  |  |
| S3 |  |  |  |
| S4 |  |  |  |
| Basic function is the item in raw form. There usually is one basic function.<br><br>Color variations are endless. We designed four possibilities, simply for convenience.<br><br>Trim variations are not as numerous as color.<br><br>Style variations—we indicated four. There could be any number. | Hanging packaging—generally one type.<br><br>Standing package—either a separate package or a combination of hanging and standing.<br><br>Boxed—we indicate several types.<br><br>Bulk pack—only one type. | Counter display—we indicated one. There could be more.<br><br>Pegboard could be separate or a combination of counter & peg.<br><br>Display center could be one, two or more types.<br><br>Dump display—we only indicated one. Could be any number. | Terms—We indicate four:<br>T1-T2/10 EOM<br>T2-Net/30<br>T3-3/10 EOM<br>T4-2/10/N/30<br><br>Freight could be prepaid or F.O.B. factory or full freight allow.<br><br>Function—would be whether goods are brought into a warehouse, drop-shipped, etc. |

market segments (consumers and retailers).[1] Figure 13–2 shows how only four elements—product variations, package, store display, and distribution pricing—could be combined in different ways for different retail customers.

The varieties and variations of promotion programs are also limitless. Some examples are: sampling; couponing; price packs;

_____
[1]A concept created by one of the authors, Edwin E. Bobrow, and described in various publications.

bonus packs; on-pack, in-pack, or near-pack premiums; refund packs; free mail-in premium; bonus packs; "two-for" packs; price packs; prepriced packs; multiple-proof premiums or refunds; contests and sweepstakes; self-liquidating items; and on-pack couponing good on next purchases. Advertising can include: network television, cable TV, spot market TV, network radio, spot radio, general interest magazines, vertical market magazines, newspapers, newspaper inserts, billboards and other outdoor media.

A variety of imaginative forms of communication can be used, such as TV monitors displaying commercials in supermarkets, video commercials in movie theaters, commercials incorporated in videotape movies and shows, ads on buses, display ads on accessory giveaways, and sports sponsor use of branded products. An imaginative farmer with land on a busy highway was reportedly even selling sign space on the sides of his cows!

The subject of marketing communications is beyond the scope of this book, and a good advertising agency or specialist should be used to help put together a media plan. Following, however, are the general advantages and limitations of each major communication form.

Television gives near universal coverage of homes; appeals to both ear and eye for dynamic selling; provides power of demonstration with sight, sound, motion, and color; develops strong levels of reach; reaches both selective and mass markets; and is highly merchandisable to distribution customers. Television's *limitations* include perishability of messages, high total costs, limited availability of good programs and time slots, and firm commitments are required.

Radio is the only medium that appeals to ear alone. It reaches special kinds of target audiences—ethnic, farm, teenagers, religious—efficiently. Radio offers timing flexibility and is mobile, permitting listeners to do other things. Radio provides good local coverage, and if necessary copy can be changed overnight. In addition to these advantages, radio has certain limitations. Audience size is limited because there are many stations in any one market. The message is perishable and has no eye appeal. Good time periods are limited, and the necessary frequency is expensive to develop, with much wasted circulation.

Newspapers provide immediacy, local appeal, dealer tie-ins, and flexibility, reaching a metropolitan area or town. Newspapers also penetrate all income groups and are a high-interest medium for influentials. Shorter closing dates allow for crash campaigns and last-minute changes. Daily newspapers provide high frequency opportunity and section selectivity. Large page size offers certain amount of creative scope. But newspapers have a short life span and color varies from paper to paper. Also, the pass-along audience is small.

Outdoor advertising has several advantages, including large coverage (reach) of local markets, flexibility in market-by-market coverage. The huge size and brilliant color permits successful product identification. Around-the-clock frequency of exposure, and brief, simple copy, making it easy to read. The message has a long life, extending into a year, and low cost per exposure. Outdoor advertising has limitations too. The message is limited to a few words (usually six or less). There is no selectivity of readership. The ban on posters is a problem in some areas. Also, the prestige value of outdoor is not high. The cost per thousand people reached is low but total costs are relatively high.

Unlike mass media communications, direct mail can be personal, "Dear Mr. Smith," and private. It is selective, with the advertiser exercising precise control over the delivery of his message. There is little competition with other advertising messages, and direct mail offers considerable production flexibility in size, color, message, and talent. The medium also can offer unique promotion opportunities (free demonstration, dollars off-coupons, contests), and it is easy and economical to test and evaluate. But direct mail can be very expensive, accuracy of mailing lists limits some delivery, and personalization of the envelope and letter is slow and costly.

Personal selling is a key element of the new product marketing mix. Whether company employees or independent agents are used, introducing the product with excitement, thorough product training, and all supporting materials available is critical to effective use of the selling tool. The best way to leverage the personal selling effort in a new product introduction is to utilize trade shows effectively. They can be the best way to demonstrate a new product, get a customer's attention in a dramatic way, and close an order on the spot. This technique will be covered in greater detail in Chapter 14.

A final key element is publicity. This will also be covered in Chapter 14 relative to maximizing the impact of an introduction. If executed properly, public relations can be one of the most effective tools in a new product plan. News releases can be written on a variety of aspects concerning the new product and presented (either by mail or personal visits) to both end user and distribution channel publications.

In addition to selecting the right mix of marketing elements, a new product plan must specify a budget (or allocation of resources). This is the beginning of the deductive planning process—moving from strategy back to detailed operations plans. There are several ways budgets can be determined. The budget can be established based on a percentage of expected sales—related to total marketing experience for the company. This method is popular because it is easy to defend, but it really looks at the question backwards (sales are the result of marketing, not the cause). The budget also can be set in relationship to competitor budgets in the same product category. It is important to consider competition, but that ignores the product's competitive strengths. A fixed sum per unit bases the marketing budget on using a value per unit times the volume of sales expected. It can overlook territory or market segment differences. Profit objective bases the budget on the difference between expected sales revenues and profit contributions and a target profit amount.

All of these methods, although important to consider, fail to answer the basic question: what must be spent to successfully reach a specific customer with the new product? Budgets should be "objective driven" to ensure survival of new products in the marketplace. Some examples of market introduction objectives are:

- Get at least two models stocked by the three longest retailers in automotive and hardware channels by April.
- Install test systems in one large manufacturer in each of the following trade classes by June—automotive, large appliance, small appliance, precision instruments.
- Reach 50 percent of adults, age 25 to 44, living in the top 50 metropolitan markets, with an average of three exposures to the product.
- Complete sales presentations to 25 percent of the customer base by August.
- Reach 50 percent of all distributors and dealers at least twice during the first six months of introduction.
- Get trial product use by 10 percent of the target market in the first three months of the campaign.

Clear development of objectives in each element of the mix is the difficult part of a marketing plan and requires experience in the industry, judgment, and creativity. The easier task is determining the cost and budget to achieve the objectives.

An example of a sales manpower budget plan would have as an objective to close 20 accounts in three months, based on assumptions of closing 20 percent of contacts, taking three calls to close/reject, with two hours per call and 25 sales hours available per week. This means to close 20 accounts, the salesperson would need to call on 100 accounts, making three calls to each account for a total of 300 calls, at two hours per call, for a total of 600 hours. At 25 hours per week, it would take 24 sales weeks. (The number of salespersons depends on geography, other time requirements, strategy relative to timing, and so on.)

A media advertising plan could be structured as follows: The objective is to generate 5,000 sales leads for new product XYZ over six months. The assumptions are a .05 percent response from general trade magazines; .15 percent response from professional magazines; and .15 percent response from vertical industry magazines. A media mix analysis indicates the following combination generates lead objective at optimum cost, frequency of exposure, and reach of the target market.

| Media | Insertions | Circulation | Sales Leads | Cost per Thousand | Cost per Lead |
|---|---|---|---|---|---|
| General | 3 | 1,500,000 | 1,500 | $25 | $75 |
| Professional | 6 | 200,000 | 1,800 | 50 | 33 |
| Vertical industry | 6 | 200,000 | 1,800 | 60 | 40 |
| | | Total leads | 5,100 | | |

(Company brand awareness, competitive advertising, relative quality of the leads, and other judgmental factors would also influence the specific magazine selection.)

A consumer product media mix decision might be based on an analysis including target audience demographics/psychographics, reach versus frequency (depending on product and communication challenge), continuity (seasonality factors), regionality (product usage), media cost, media quality, media effectiveness, and media availability.

The creative side of a new product marketing plan involves selecting a balance between mix elements so they reinforce each other, build and intensify a campaign, and achieve objectives at an optimum cost. Most consumer product introductions utilize a balance of consumer media advertising and price promotions sampling (if nondurable goods), public relations, sales literature, distributor and dealer incentives, and occasionally store displays and demonstrations. An example is the introduction of a new line of light bulbs by North American Philips Corporation, which acquired the Westinghouse lamp division in 1983. The mix included:[2]

1. Redesigned packaging to make a transition from the Westinghouse to the Philips brand and introduce a new T-bulb shape.
2. A regional TV campaign to achieve 50 percent reach.
3. A second-year national TV campaign extending reach to 98 percent.
4. A public relations campaign including TV talk shows and news programming.
5. Store changeover of entire line by sales personnel.
6. Retailer promotion support (newspaper inserts, point-of-purchase material, and allowances).
7. Computer-generated planograms (visual drawings of suggested shelf layout) designed to help retailers optimize shelf productivity.

Industrial product plans tend to use many of the same elements, but the balance may be much more heavily skewed toward personal presentations of the product benefits through trade shows, sales calls, demonstrations, test installations, or engineering evaluations. An industrial equipment manufacturer introduced a new line of portable electrical products with the following mix:

- A volume-oriented pricing structure to distributors.
- An early-order and extended payment terms program to get distributor stocking before the season.
- Magazine advertising designed to reach 75 percent of the target users.
- A sales and service training program for distributors.
- A repair parts stocking program for distributors.
- A free accessory offer to the end user during the initial three months of the introduction.

---

[2] *Marketing News*, November 22, 1985, p. 26.

- A direct mail campaign aimed at the largest businesses in the target market.

A critical issue in most new product marketing plans is the risk of overspending or underspending. Ongoing business can be adjusted quickly and easily to plan spending errors, but new products are fragile and can explode and die a quick death from errors in either direction. For example:

### Overspending

Demand exceeds supply.

↓

Customers can't find product; brand credibility suffers.

↓

Dealers can't meet customer demand; their credibility suffers.

↓

Dealers look elsewhere for product.

↓

New competitors enter market to meet unfilled demand.

↓

Manufacturing chaos.

↓

Quality suffers.

↓

Cost overruns due to expediting, scrap, returns.

↓

Dealers increase orders to hedge availability.

↓

Manufacturer finally catches up.

↓

Dealers cancel hedge orders.

↓

Manufacturer has excess capacity and overhead cost, quality problems, low margin, dealer dissatisfaction, customer dissatisfaction, new competitors, and reduced market share.

↓

Management kills the product and fires everyone involved.

### Underspending

Customers aren't aware of the product, so don't ask for it.

↓

Dealers can't move their inventory, so start cutting prices.

↓

Manufacturer has excess capacity and inventory, so starts cutting prices, adding more dealers.

Sales force loses interest in product.

Dealer price war ensues; manufacturer credibility suffers.

Customers see inventory stacking up, gathering dust, so begin to perceive that product has a problem.

Everyone begins to believe that the product may be a dog.

Management tries to sell the tooling and product rights to some unsuspecting third party, usually without success.

Management kills the product and fires everyone involved.

(Notice that the eventual outcome is *identical* in either case.)

The spending decision is always difficult and requires a participative planning effort to get the maximum judgment applied to the issue—there is no easy solution. Every industry has characteristics that require major commitments before introducing a new product: tooling, manufacturing capacity, advertising, sales force, service organization, store facilities, and so on. The key to the spending decision is to do a thorough product development job, make sure the product is right and a market need exists, and have the judgment, fortitude, and capability to react *fast* when market or product conditions don't follow plan.

A well-structured new product plan will help get the market attack started in the right direction. Figure 13–3 shows the frequency various categories are covered in marketing plans for consumer, industrial, and service firms based on surveys by The Conference Board.[3] Although this information applies to general marketing plans, new product plans include most of the same elements but might emphasize to a greater extent field sales plan, pricing, advertising, and distributor or dealer.

Following is a sample outline for a new consumer product plan:

---

[3] *The Marketing Plan,* (New York: The Conference Board, 1981), pp. 37–40. Copyright 1981 The Conference Board.

## FIGURE 13–3 _____

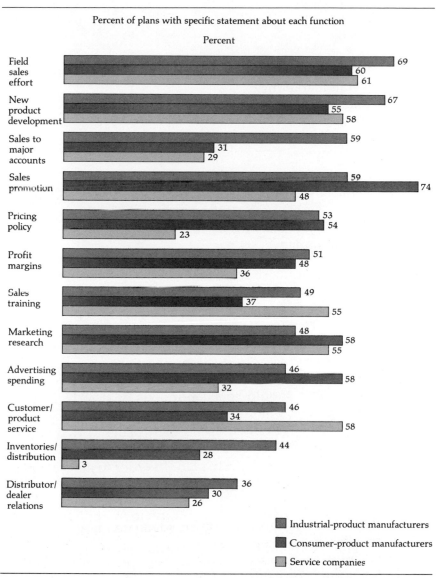

Percent of plans with specific statement about each function

Percent

Field sales effort — Industrial 69, Consumer 60, Service 61

New product development — Industrial 67, Consumer 55, Service 58

Sales to major accounts — Industrial 59, Consumer 31, Service 29

Sales promotion — Industrial 59, Consumer 74, Service 48

Pricing policy — Industrial 53, Consumer 54, Service 23

Profit margins — Industrial 51, Consumer 48, Service 36

Sales training — Industrial 49, Consumer 37, Service 55

Marketing research — Industrial 48, Consumer 58, Service 55

Advertising spending — Industrial 46, Consumer 58, Service 32

Customer/product service — Industrial 46, Consumer 34, Service 58

Inventories/distribution — Industrial 44, Consumer 28, Service 3

Distributor/dealer relations — Industrial 36, Consumer 30, Service 26

◼ Industrial-product manufacturers
◼ Consumer-product manufacturers
◻ Service companies

SOURCE: The Conference Board, *The Marketing Plan.* © Sales & Marketing Management.

A. Final product development
   Specifications
   Name
   Package
   Price
B. Market objectives and strategies
   Overall marketing
   Creative blueprint
   Media
   Promotion
   Packaging
   Pricing
C. Establishment of budget (advertising/sales promotion; payout plan)
D. Advertising pretesting
E. Promotion plan
   Calendar
   Plan/materials
F. Distribution plan
G. Research plan

Figure 13–4 illustrates a more comprehensive outline example for a major new product introduction.

The final step in the marketing attack is to sell the plan to those involved. This should be a continuous process throughout product development, but ultimately a budget must be approved.

Marketing executives often "sell" their plans to two key audiences: management (for resource commitments) and all employees critical to carrying out the plan. In order to accept a plan, senior management must be convinced:

1. Something must be done.
   • Benefits outweigh costs by an adequate margin.
   • Inaction is unacceptable.
   • Objectives are consistent with higher management's goals.
   • Risks are acceptable.
2. The best alternative has been selected.
   • We've objectively assessed others.
   • Decision criteria are reasonable.
   • Outline risk profile.

**FIGURE 13–4** _____
New Product Marketing Plan

_____

    I. Plan overview
   II. Situation summary
      A. Industry
      B. Market
      C. Company
      D. Competition
      E. Environmental
      F. Key performance indicators
  III. Issue review/key assumptions
      A. Problems
      B. Opportunities
      C. Critical issues
      D. Key assumptions
  IV. Objectives summary
   V. Advertising/public relations
      A. Overview
      B. Objectives
      C. Tactics
      D. Public relations
      E. Summary media
      F. Planning implications
  VI. Pricing/channel programs
      A. Overview
      B. Channel pricing
      C. Price Lists
 VII. Promotion/merchandising
      A. Promotion background/Programs
      B. Key buyer program
      C. Point-of-Sale display
      D. In-store demonstration program
      E. Store Plan-O-Gram service
VIII. Distribution/sales objectives
      A. Distribution objectives
      B. Sales/account goals
      C. Top 50 accounts
  IX. Market Information/Research
      A. Objectives
      B. Strategies
      C. Budgets
   X. Final product development
      A. Specifications
      B. Name, packaging
      C. Line strategies (options, accessories, supplies)
      D. Product schedules
  XI. Service
      A. Situation summary
      B. Critical issues
      C. Key assumptions

**FIGURE 13–4** _____
(*concluded*)

---

    D. Goals
    E. Major programs
  XII. Foreign market plan
    A. Overview
    B. Products
    C. Key accounts
    D. Advertising
    E. Pricing/channel programs
    F. Financial
      1. Price margin analysis
      2. P & L
      3. Marketing budget
 XIII. Manufacturing
    A. Resources planning
    B. Inventory summary
    C. Capital expenditure plan
 XIV. Sales forecasts/financial
    A. Price margin analysis
    B. Monthly sales forecasts
    C. Income statement
    D. Marketing budget

---

  3. It *can* work.
    • It's logical.
    • We've done our homework.
    • We've considered all the significant factors.
    • It's realistic.
  4. The product is right.
    • It does what we say it will do.
    • The cost is right.
    • The quality is right.
  5. It *will* work.
    • We believe in it and want it.
    • We'll accept the responsibility and accountability.
    • We're committed. We'll "bet our jobs."

    Visual aids can be extremely useful in selling the plan (a picture is worth a thousand words, a model, ten thousand). Early in development, concept sketches used in research and bread board prototypes can be used in presentations. Later, full-scale models and samples of marketing materials can be helpful. The objective is not to hype the product, but to ensure that the concept is perceived identically by everyone and to avoid misunderstandings. It also helps present the product in the same way the customer will ultimately see it and aids management judgment.

Selling the plan to everyone involved in executing it depends on one key element: participation. Get people involved early and frequently, even at the risk of confidentiality. No one likes surprises or change in their work environment for which they are not prepared. Sales representatives and even customers will be much more receptive to a new product if they have had the opportunity to contribute to the process. This involves some risk but if handled effectively, early customer involvement will go a long way toward making a marketing attack successful.

# 14

## Wagons Ho! Market Introduction Techniques for a Fast Start

The new product has survived every attempt to kill it along the pioneering road. The right goal has been selected, the right spirit and organization structure has supported the generation of a great idea, and thorough analysis has confirmed that it should be a winner in the marketplace. The product should be on the homestretch, but that is the very point it is most vulnerable to a final attack and market failure. Several barriers to success can trip a new product in the final stages of introduction.

Timing may be off. Introducing before the product or market is ready or after competition has intensified, prices have eroded, or the opportunity has passed by can mean failure.

When it's introduced, a new product gets maximum attention from the press, the investment community, the employees, the distribution channel, and especially, the customer. Early poor performance can quickly kill any future interest in the product.

A major investment is made in executing the introduction plan—advertising, training programs, literature, sales meetings, and so forth. Failure to have all materials and steps happen in concert can waste precious resources and eliminate a second chance.

Prototypes and even pilot operations are easy; the real test is whether the product or service can be produced *in volume, on time.*

Creating great excitement in the marketplace will only backfire if the company cannot deliver a quality product on schedule.

The market doesn't share the developer's excitement—a new product means change to the production organization, the sales force, and the distribution system. That change can be viewed as either a positive or a negative. The way the product is introduced can help make sure it is perceived as a positive.

The target can move. The product is planned with careful study of an existing market opportunity. Unfortunately, the market is constantly changing—new competition, new pricing, distribution changes, even changes in customer buying habits and tastes—and the product may miss the mark.

The map may be wrong. Analysis, research, and product planning was based on some facts, some judgment. Because few companies or managers are infallible, some signals may have been misjudged and the product ended up on the wrong road.

This chapter deals with understanding these introduction dangers, recognizing them, and taking steps to manage them.

Bad timing has been a major killer of great ideas throughout history, starting with the wheel. Wheels have been found on children's toys in Mexico in the pre-Columbian period, but no evidence of practical use exists until after the Spaniards introduced horses to pull carts. Charles Babbage conceived the idea of an analytical engine (the first "computer") in 1823, but without the electronic technology to support it, his idea of using mechanical rods, levers, and cogs to perform binary calculations was unworkable. Modern examples include the introduction of exercise equipment in the '60s before exercise and health were popular or the introduction of new programmable calculators shortly after personal computers became popular and low-priced.

One technique for analyzing and judging the timing issue earlier in the development process is to look at the trade-offs between opportunity cost and development risk. Opportunity costs are high when there is:

1. Significant risk of not being the market leader.
2. Significant risk of volume or share loss.
3. Risk of losing key customers to competition.
4. Risk of losing control over distribution channels.
5. Risk of losing sustainable advantage because the products are no longer the standard of the industry.

If these risks and opportunity costs are high, the company should concentrate resources on short development and fast, national introduction. When IBM began to see personal computers growing rapidly in the mid-1970s and being installed at customers IBM considered its own, IBM decided the opportunity costs were high enough to justify uncharacteristic action. It put together a crash program and a separate division, sourced most of the hardware and software from external sources, and introduced a PC line in 15 months instead of the customary four-year cycle. In addition, IBM introduced the product line nationally using network television advertising—another first for the company.

Another technique to accelerate development and buy time with customers is to announce an entry to a market or product category *at the beginning* of the development process. This can get customers to stick with the company and can light a fire under internal personnel, but it certainly carries some risk if the product doesn't develop.

Development risks are high when:

1. The future market demand or value to the customer is very uncertain.
2. The right product design is highly uncertain.
3. The technology is new and unproven or significantly advances the state of the art.
4. The breadth of the product line or breadth of product features to be offered are highly uncertain.

When development risks are high, the strategy should be long development, test-marketing, local and regional introductions, and placing a premium on longer term competitiveness through getting the right product to the right market at the right cost.

This relates to another critical introduction risk—the product doesn't work. The introduction represents a great opportunity to put a new product in the spotlight, and good performance is essential. Following are some guidelines to assure good performance:

**1.** *Personally check prototypes and pilot production samples before exposing to customers.* Odd and embarrassing things can happen with early production—motors can get left out, parts can be assembled wrong, wrong models can be shipped to customers, tolerances can stack up and prevent proper performance, parts can fall off. Don't assume anything!

**2.** *Take duplicates and triplicates of everything to trade shows, press conferences, and major customer previews.* Despite best efforts to check everything out ahead of time, something will go wrong when the switch is turned on or the product picked up and put in a customer's hand. Have extra products, parts, and even a few engineers behind the curtain if it can be arranged.

**3.** *Prepare extra customer support.* Set up a "strike force" to leap on early customer problems and get them resolved quickly. Don't give the product a chance to develop a bad reputation.

**4.** *Train the sales force on demonstration techniques.* If the sales force can't show the ability to use the product or maximize its performance, the customer can't expect anything different.

**5.** *Never send early samples to customers without hands-on control.* Don't take any chances that the head buyer of a major customer will get a poor sample or be unable to properly use the product, especially if the buyer is personally not part of the target market. Stay in control of the situation and try to arrange a personal demonstration.

**6.** *If manufacturing can't get it right, stop production.* A delayed introduction may hurt credibility and cause a great amount of anguish and reaction within a sales force and distribution system, but it won't kill a new product. Shipping hundreds or thousands of defective products will.

Scheduling and managing a new product launch can make the planning of the Normandy invasion in World War II seem like child's play in comparison: Eisenhower only had to worry about one market—France! A good product introduction is often the result not of creative flair so much as it is an outcome of good planning and coordination. The best public relations people often get that way through attention to detail and organization skills, not creative genius.

A key activity in managing an introduction is to address the question: who is the audience? It could include employees, top management, board of directors, sales force, service or organization, distributors and dealers, investment community, media, and the ultimate customer.

Each audience segment has a particular requirement for information about the new product and can be reached through different communication techniques. Internal employees can be exposed to the product at a demonstration event, an auditorium presentation, or even given samples. All of these techniques help build excitement in the product and pride in the company and help ensure a successful introduction.

The sales organization should be "sold" just as thoroughly as the customer. That means a complete marketing presentation, including the business plan, samples of the product, advertising and promotion materials, audio visual sales aids, and a motivational kickoff meeting with special sales incentives for a fast start on the new product. Distributors and the investment community also require similar materials and information.

These intermediary and supporting groups must be convinced that the time spent on the new product will directly benefit them. Remember, with these audiences, the product isn't the tangible new item, it's the *increased business* that will result. This requires a balanced communication effort. The audience must be convinced that the product is innovative, works well, and provides a useful benefit. Then, quickly move on to who needs the product, why, how big is the market, how fast is it growing, and what the company is going to do to support the marketing of the product.

An example of failure to communicate business benefits is a presentation we made to a national organization covering an exciting new line of products, complete with hard-selling packaging, improved performance, and a major advertising campaign. The first reaction from the buyer was, "I'm going to have to add 32 SKUs (stock keeping units) to the computer . . . that'll take forever! Why should I?" The second response was, "What are *you* going to do with my existing inventory?" Obviously we were more excited in the product and the market opportunity than the customer, and we failed to anticipate what the change meant to him, and why it would benefit him directly. (Benefits could include increasing traffic and business in the entire department, improving margin performance in the department, demonstrating the buyer's ability to source and promote exciting new categories, and other results making the buyer a star.)

Don't become enamored with the technical features of the product: this audience needs to know how it will create growth and profitability, and what's in it for them.

The trade show presents an opportunity for answering these questions in a dramatic fashion for most industries. It can also provide a reason for getting things done on a critical path and with a sense of urgency. Without an annual sales meeting or trade show creating the need, it's questionable whether some companies would ever get a new product launched. The trade show also presents one of the few marketing mediums in which the prospect is actually coming to the new product developer, with an open mind, and actively seeking information. Following are some ways to manage the medium to support the new product introduction:[1]

1. Define the objective—communicate to key customers, generate leads for later followup, demonstrate to large volumes, research interest.
2. Design the exhibit based on the objectives.
3. Analyze the attendance at the show and maximize the communication effort.
4. Promote the product's presence through advance mailings, sales force communication, incentives, and so on.
5. Select and train the booth personnel. Working the booth is not the same as field sales; it takes special skills to move quickly through introductions, qualifications, presentations, and close.
6. Establish a followup system. Trade show leads, when properly qualified, are hot. Don't let them get cold.
7. Evaluate whether the objective was achieved. If not, why not? What can be done quickly to get the introduction on track?

A trade show booth doesn't have to cost $100,000 to successfully introduce a new product. Careful planning, advanced mailings, a good product idea, and enthusiastic booth personnel can get a great deal of attention and interest. A large, expensive booth with no one in it or, even worse, bored and tired personnel will not get nearly as much attention.

The investment community can be an important audience for any public company and even private companies can benefit by reviewing new products with their investors. If the new product is a major innovation, a formal introduction to security analysts and other investors should be arranged. Analysts are interested in:

---

[1] *1980 Portfolio—Sales & Marketing Plans* (New York: Bill Communications, 1979), p. 33. Copyright 1979 Sales and Marketing Management.

1. Marketing strategy: What market niche is the product targeted at? What kind of impact on the customer base? How does it fit in the product line? Market size? Distribution channels?
2. Technical specifications: performance, test data, durability, and what distinguishes it from competitors?
3. Financial strategy: pricing, terms, and likely impact on sales and earnings.
4. Demonstration: Analysts consider a demonstration crucial to really understanding the product.

Analysts tend to err on the side of high expectations, so a straightforward, factual presentation with a degree of conservatism may be the best approach. The investment community will also be interested in how the product actually does in the marketplace, so periodic followup communications are essential.

The news media can be one of the most productive and valuable audiences for a new product introduction if used properly. Depending on the magnitude of the innovation, various publications can be targeted. These include industry journals, general business publications, consumer special interest and general publications, local newspapers, national newspaper releases, and local and national TV releases.

These targets can be reached in a variety of ways depending on the importance of the product and its newsworthiness:

- Product news release (8-by-10 black and white photographs of product with a one- to three-page description).
- Marketing news release (details of marketing program for industry and marketing publications).
- Syndicated newspaper release (services that manage releases to city and suburban newspapers across the country).
- Snydicated radio release (similar to newspaper services).
- Video news release (increasing in popularity, especially if product demonstration is helpful).
- Editor meetings (personal review).
- Media tours (traveling presentation to media in local markets).
- Press conference.

In order to get editor attention, product releases should be truly newsworthy. No matter how much advertising the company may buy from a publication, the editor won't give the product coverage unless it truly represents a new concept that would be interesting to the publication's readers. The release also should be designed to make the editor's job easier. Copy should be written with the most important points summarized in the first paragraph; photo prints should be provided in black and white, and company contact and phone number should be provided for answering any questions. The product release should arrive at least three to four months ahead of market introduction or desired editorial coverage. Magazines have long lead times (90 days or more) and editors don't appreciate rush jobs.

A formal press conference can be scheduled if the product is a major innovation with a variety of potential markets and interest groups. Managing the conference requires complete attention to detail and thorough followup activity. A personal computer in the marketing department can be a very handy support element. Tom Dombrowski, marketing manager at S. S. White Industrial Products, described in *Business Marketing* magazine how, in running a press conference to introduce a new abrasive machine, he used a microcomputer for:

1. Preparing the major release (six pages) with a word processing program written for our own use and stored for our editing and subsequent printout.

2. Preparing "shortie" releases (two pages) in similar fashion for editors who don't have much space to devote to the new product and don't want to exert the effort it takes to chop down the big release.

3. Generating "punch lists" (a term borrowed from the construction industry) to show: who is responsible for which facet of press conference preparation; target dates for task completion; panic dates at which tasks *must* be completed; notation of steps accomplished.

4. Preparing the total mailing list of all editors to be notified of the new product, whether by personal attendance at the press conference or receipt of a press kit mailed to those who do not come. The list included editors' names, publication names, and addresses.

5. Preparing the invitee list. Out of 85 editors on the total list, we invited only 37. We did not really expect to see more than 12 to 15 of them, generally those near New York City.

**6.** Writing invitation letters—three of them starting with the first one three months before the event, followed by two more at regular intervals. Each letter was personalized by name matched by a personalized envelope.

**7.** Preparing additional items for the press kit, all stored in computer programs for easy changing, editing and updating: lists of new product applications by industry; specification sheet; comparison chart to show advantages of new product over existing products; captions for 19 photos; list of S. S. White personnel attending the press conference.

**8.** Writing rules, regulations, and entry blanks needed for a contest to be run during the press conference.

**9.** Following up with thank you notes, sent the day after the press conference to every editor who attended. Again, each note was personalized, with first name drop-ins throughout each note.

**10.** Keeping track of the actual attendance list of editors and publications for our records.[2]

A final and most important audience is the ultimate customer.

Advertising and other marketing techniques as discussed in the previous chapter are all part of the communication effort to make the end user aware of the product and its benefits. The initial introduction of a new product can offer some interesting creative opportunities, however. Apple invested about $1 million to produce and run a unique, 60-second TV commercial during the Super Bowl coverage introducing a new personal computer. The company utilized a series of *Wall Street Journal* ads for several weeks before the game as teasers, building suspense and interest in the announcement.

A small computer software company, Brown Bag Software of Campbell, Calif., tried an unusual approach of binding its new word processing product into an issue of *PC* magazine, set up with coding so it would run a limited number of times. If the consumer decides he wants to buy the software, it's $89 to unlock it and get the manual and spelling checker.

Thousands of unusual and theatrical stunts have been created to introduce new products. Some work; a lot don't. Following are some guidelines:

---

[2] "Computerizing The Press Conference," *Business Marketing,* June 1984, p. 70.

**1.** Match the technique to the image of the product and company. If the company is introducing a new 200-ton automated punch press, go-go girls may not be in order! (However, Selma Weiser introduced her first Charivari high fashion boutique in Manhattan with a go-go dancer in the window and is now grossing more than $10 million in six stores.)

**2.** Look for the "big idea." Focus on a unique activity that dynamically communicates the major benefit of the product (Krazy Glue holding up a car, an elephant stepping on a Timex watch, a lawn mower cutting a grass strip from Houston to Dallas).

**3.** Provide a public service if possible. These get media attention and contribute to the community.

**4.** Plan in detail. The best publicity event looks simple because someone paid attention to the details.

**5.** Set objectives and measure them. Generally these include awareness and coverage (recall of the event, association with company and product, media time and space coverage).

**6.** Use a good communications adviser. Public relations firms and consultants are experienced at producing publicity that achieves business objectives and doesn't backfire.

Scheduling publicity events, press releases, advertising materials, production startup, sales meeting introduction, product samples, and a myriad of other details, all to be completed at the right time, in the right place, and the right quantity, is like conducting an orchestra—the result can be either Mozart or mush. Some companies are fortunate in having a few key people skillful at juggling 20 balls in the air and never dropping any. Most companies have to adopt some scheduling techniques, however, to cope with a new product introduction. The key is to provide adequate lead time—usually three to six months before market introduction. Figure 14–1 shows a "Gantt" chart covering typical marketing activities six to eight months before media and trade show exposure of a new industrial product. (Consumer products generally require a much longer lead time on ad development if a substantial new advertising campaign is planned.)

Thomas Publishing Company has developed a comprehensive critical path planning system consisting of 19 primary new product introduction tasks, each consisting of numerous activities essential to their completion. An example of the system are the tasks included in the introduction phase:

**FIGURE 14–1**

| Publication | Month 1 | Month 2 | Month 3 | Month 4 | Month 5 | Month 6 | Month 7 | Month 8 | Month 9 | Month 10 | Month 11 | Month 12 |
|---|---|---|---|---|---|---|---|---|---|---|---|---|
| **Fact findings** | | | | | | | | | | | | |
| Engineering inputs | X | X | | | | | | | | | | |
| Outside research | X | X | | | | | | | | | | |
| Roll-out plans | X | | | | | | | | | | | |
| Model design | | X | | | | | | | | | | |
| **Public relations** | | | | | | | | | | | | |
| Backgrounders | | X | | | | | | | | | | |
| Photography | | | X | | | | | | | | | |
| Feature(s) | Place | | | | | Appear | | | | | | |
| Technical article(s) | Place | | | | | Appear | | | | | | |
| Featurette(s) | | | | Place | | | Appear | | | | | |
| News release(s) | | | | | Place | | | | Appear | | | |
| User article(s) | | | | | | | Place | | | | Appear | |

198

Marketing communications schedule (Gantt chart):

| Activity | 1 | 2 | 3 | 4 | 5 | 6 | 7 | 8 | 9 | 10 | 11 | 12 |
|---|---|---|---|---|---|---|---|---|---|---|---|---|
| Mgmt./co. article(s) | | | | | | | | | | | Appear | |
| Trade show PR | | | | | | | | | | Show | | |
| **Marketing support** | | | | | | | | | | | | |
| Sales presentation | | Prepare | | | | | | | | | | |
| A-V presentation | | | Prepare | | | | | | | | | |
| Preliminary data sheet | | | Prepare | | | | | | | | | |
| Brochure(s) | | | | | Prepare | | | | | Place | | |
| Direct mail | | | | | | Prepare | Mail | | | | | |
| Sales meeting | | | | | | | | Hold | | | | |
| Trade show | | | | | | | | | Show | | | |
| **Media advertising** | | | | | | | | | | | | |
| Ad development | | | | | | Prepare | | | | | | |
| Media research | | | | | | Prepare | | | | | | |
| New product ad placements | | | | | | | | | | | Appear | |

SOURCE: *Business Marketing*, November 1983.

1. Develop publicity.
2. Develop advertising program.
3. Develop direct mail program.
4. Prepare other communications.
5. Prepare literature.
6. Prepare sales aids and training.
7. Start sales, distribution, and service.
8. Start manufacturing.
9. Develop and implement inquiry handling system.

The system is described fully in a booklet, "A Guide To Marketing New Industrial Products," available from Thomas headquarters, 250 W. 34th Street, New York, N.Y. 10119.

These techniques combined with communicating the right information to the right people can reduce most of the introduction pitfalls mentioned at the beginning of the chapter, but they won't do anything to prevent aiming for a moving target or using the wrong road map. The only way to manage these introduction problems is to track early results closely and be prepared to change, refine, and try again.

Talon zipper looked like a winner when it was introduced at the turn of the century, but customers refused to buy for various reasons: "Can't see increase in cost of garments," "too much trouble to take up with pants makers," "shop people want more money for applying it." Talon should have been discouraged, but instead began pushing zippers for use in products other than clothing. This broke the market open.[3]

Fred Smith started Federal Express Corporation with an inauguration ceremony in Memphis, Tenn. The initial fleet of Falcon jets flew in from an 11-city pickup network and unloaded six packages, one of which was a birthday present from Smith to a company employee. The introduction was a bust, so some Federal Express managers locked themselves in a room and rebuilt the network from an 11- to a 25-city system and launched the company again one month later. This time the Falcons flew into Memphis with 186 packages aboard. Since that quick reaction, Federal Express has grown to handle more than 450,000 pickups and deliv-

---

[3] Carter Henderson, *Winners* (New York: Holt, Rinehart & Winston, 1985), p. 29. Copyright 1985 Carter Henderson.

eries per day.[4] Sometimes a little twisting and refining soon after introductions can make mush into Mozart!

Without a good product concept, no amount of introduction, planning, managing, and publicity will provide market survival. With a good concept, a stage, a spotlight, and a full house audience, a fast start is guaranteed.

---

[4] Ibid., pp. 132–33.

# 15

# The Human Element

A frustrated new product manager was once heard exclaiming after a heated committee meeting, "This project would be so easy if it weren't for the people involved!" This statement could easily be applied to all business, but businesses as well as new products depend on the interrelationships of good people to be successful. New product development is unique, however, as a business activity that cuts across every function of a business and requires skillful communication management to avoid breakdowns and product errors.

The process can also provide a great opportunity for management to develop teamwork in an organization, broaden understanding of the total business, and cross-train people in other functional areas. A new product committee or task force can develop either friction and disagreement or enormous team spirit and motivation depending on the leadership and communication management provided. This chapter addresses the interpersonal relationships that occur in new product development, the potential areas of conflict, and the management skills and techniques that can turn conflict into teamwork.

The product development process by its very nature requires a series of trade-offs and compromises to achieve an optimum business solution. These trade-offs must occur among various functional areas in the company and people who tend to have different objectives based on the focus of their departments. Advanced R&D departments have a natural desire to achieve a major scientific breakthrough and prefer creative freedom and minimal restrictions on goals. Engineering departments generally prefer long development phases in order to perfect the design and achieve a product recognized as a triumph of performance and reliability.

Purchasing and manufacturing organizations would prefer to minimize the number of models and component parts; utilize standard, inexpensive components and materials; and run lot sizes of at least 2 million each. Finance departments would like to see a product priced at 80 percent gross margins, minimal tooling and equipment investment, and tight project budgets. And marketing and sales people would like the product yesterday, before the competition runs away with the market.

With these often conflicting objectives and motivations, it's a wonder that a new product survives within the company let alone the marketplace. Figure 15–1 shows the range of interests and differences that can exist between typical marketing organizations and other functions.

Design of a small plastic product illustrates the detailed trade-offs that occur in a development project. Good appearance is an essential requirement for successful sales. To the mold maker, good appearance means perfectly matched parting lines, flawless cavity polish, and no gates or ejectors on outside surfaces. To the plastic processor, good appearance means the absence of flash, sink marks, and plastic warpage, but balanced against the struggle to achieve fast mold cycle times and high production rates. To the design engineer, appearance means more complicated contours to calculate and draw, the hiding of assembly devices, squeezing parts into smaller spaces, using nonstandard fasteners, and sometimes being asked to defeat the laws of physics.

The industrial designer would like to see an appearance that represents good form, color, balance, and proportion and sets a new standard for the category. Management and finance would like an appearance that generates a lot of sales and profits—the only goal that perhaps everyone could agree to as desirable.

Any product that depends on appearance to sell in the marketplace (and that would include most consumer durables, the packaging of nondurables, and even some industrial products) will require an endless series of trade-offs. The members of the project must have a shared incentive to produce the best product through a cooperative effort. If each member honestly tries to give the other member as much as he can, the result can be a fair

**FIGURE 15–1** _____
Summary of Organizational Conflicts between Marketing
and Other Departments

| Department | Their Emphasis | Marketing's Emphasis |
|---|---|---|
| R & D | Basic research | Applied research |
| | Intrinsic quality | Perceived quality |
| | Functional features | Sales features |
| Engineering | Long design lead time | Short design lead time |
| | Few models | Many models |
| | Standard components | Custom components |
| Purchasing | Narrow product line | Broad product line |
| | Standard parts | Nonstandard parts |
| | Price of material | Quality of material |
| | Economical lot sizes | Large lot sizes to avoid stockouts |
| | Purchasing at infrequent intervals | Immediate purchasing for customer needs |
| Manufacturing | Long production lead time | Short production lead time |
| | Long runs with few models | Short runs with many models |
| | No model changes | Frequent model changes |
| | Standard orders | Custom orders |
| | Ease of fabrication | Aesthetic appearance |
| | Average quality control | Tight quality control |
| Inventory | Fast-moving items, narrow product line | Broad product line |
| | Economical level of stock | High level of stock |
| Finance | Strict rationales for spending | Intuitive arguments for spending |
| | Hard and fast budgets | Flexible budgets to meet changing needs |
| | Pricing to cover costs | Pricing to further market development |
| Accounting | Standard transactions | Special terms and discounts |
| | Few reports | Many reports |
| Credit | Full financial disclosures by customers | Minimum credit examination of customers |
| | Low credit risks | Medium credit risks |
| | Tough credit terms | Easy credit terms |
| | Tough collection procedures | Easy collection procedures |

compromise and an optimum product. Engineers and manufacturing and finance people need to understand and develop an appreciation for appearance and its impact on the marketplace, and designers and marketers need to be bottom-line and quality and reliability oriented as a balance.

The ability to empathize and project into the other person's environment and professional objective is key to managing a new product through its development. In the beginning stages of a project, R&D departments are usually involved. If they are good, they are staffed with creative personalities who share the characteristics of all creative people—inquisitive, need variety, sometimes sensitive, occasionally disorganized. The key management technique with this group is to give plenty of support to their ideas, don't pass judgment prematurely, and stimulate their imaginations by bringing a lot of ideas from the marketplace and the general business world. If efforts seem to be going in the wrong direction, a gentle nudge back on course can be given by suggesting a new idea to work on, but without killing current ideas—just shelve them temporarily. They may just be ahead of their time.

Market research staffs are another group involved early in new product development. This profession tends to attract analytical personalities and can bury a good idea with too many numbers. Working closely with market researchers and helping to ask the right questions is critical to a new product success. Probing the researchers for interpretations of study results is also a useful technique. They can shed light on critical development questions if given a little appreciation and a chance for input on project decisions. Another key management technique is to balance the need for research with its cost. Many researchers will want to take the time and spend enough money to produce the most reliable research result they can, and this occasionally needs to be balanced with timing and budget trade-offs.

Once a product idea is generated by R&D or market research, it moves into the engineering design phase (or operations development if a service, or formula and process development if a nondurable good). Engineers or their equivalent in other industries are a special breed of people. They are right in the middle of the new product process, but often seem to have the greatest desire to *not* release a new product to the market. This is probably because of a basic contradiction in their profession. Engineering is a science and generates a desire for precision and exactness, but it requires dealing with uncertainty in new products—working with new materials and new processes, combining components in new ways, and creating new physical properties. The natural inclination of an engineer is to try to eliminate as many of these uncertainties as possible through analysis, testing, and retesting, stretching out a development schedule and budget.

Another difficulty with the engineering profession is a natural focus on function and technology. This focus can overshadow other key criteria such as cost, function trade-offs with customer wants and needs at a price they can afford, appearance, serviceability, and human factors. A product that will last for 25 years, provide performance 150 percent above average usage, and call for precision machining of parts in order to provide a technically elegant assembly might represent an engineering triumph, but the one unit eventually manufactured will sit in the company museum.

Engineers can be the single greatest factor in the success of a new product, however, if managed and integrated properly. They bridge the gap between the raw idea and a product that can be manufactured economically, maintain a quality image, and provide a real benefit for thousands of users. The best way to manage the engineering effort is skillful and frequent integration with project management decision making and exposure to the market. If engineers participate in the key trade-off decisions, they are exposed to all factors in a design issue, develop an understanding of other criteria, and are better able to make good engineering decisions. Another extremely useful technique is to involve engineering personnel in market research and field customer test activity. It's amazing what an awakening can occur after a few hours behind a one-way mirror in a market research focus group listening to customers point out what they don't like about the engineering triumph or what they wish "whoever's engineering those darn things" would put into the design. Another great awakening is to send a junior project engineer out to live with a customer for a few days as he tries to utilize a prototype in a live environment. He comes back as an instant "senior engineer."

Getting a new product accepted by a manufacturing group is another of life's great joys in pioneering. Manufacturing folks love standardization and simplicity (Henry Ford led the trend by offering the Model T in any color you wanted—as long as it was black). A complicated assembly might be rejected even if it's what the customer prefers, or a feature that distinguishes the product in the market might be viewed as "adding unnecessary cost" or "too complicated—takes too long to design the tool." And then there's the standard lead time that seems to exist for every tool ever built—the "16-week tool."

These reactions occur because of an inherent resistance to change built into the manufacturing profession. A manufacturing function thrives on repeatability and standardization—allowing products to eventually reach a group of customers at a price they can afford. A good manufacturing organization is very good at delivering this critical skill. We believe the best way to manage manufacturing planning in a new product environment is through organization techniques. Separate the new product responsibility into an "advanced manufacturing planning" group with industrial engineers, quality people, and tool designers assigned and given the sole responsibility of supporting new product development. Trying to use the day-to-day operations people on new product work may prevent the product from ever reaching the market or, worse yet, may destroy efficiencies in the ongoing business.

Finance departments are usually quite accommodating through most of the product development process, but only because not much money gets spent until the later stages. When it's time to ask for tooling investments or market introduction and advertising budgets, that's when the new product gets their attention. Unfortunately, that is also when they start asking the tough questions that need to be asked early in the process: Why is the unit cost so high? Why didn't you design it to use more of the existing tooling or excess line capacity? What about the component inventory of the product it's going to replace? How can you be sure you'll really sell that many? Why is the gross so low? Why do you need 90-day terms to get it into the market?

Finance departments have a professional interest and responsibility in preserving the assets of a company versus spending them to generate more assets somewhere in the future. This is an essential role in any company that wants to survive in the marketplace. The questions posed by this group can be very helpful in introducing a new product that also survives—from a profitability standpoint. The right way to use a finance group in new product development is to get them involved early in the project—not just when it's time to ask for the money. They can be extremely helpful in guiding a product toward financial success, especially in estimating and monitoring projected unit cost.

Marketing and sales departments are certainly not without fault in a new product effort. The most common danger this group brings to a project is the direct result of a characteristic inherent in their profession—optimism. A good marketing organization thoroughly and completely believes *it cannot fail*. This attitude is necessary or many new products would never see the light of day. But the attitude can also result in overly optimistic sales projections for the new product, pricing lower than it has to be, and a desire to rush the product to the market before it or the organization is really ready.

This group can be managed by slowing it down a little or asking for a second or third analysis from a different angle, a contingency plan, a test market, or a customer field test. But ask for these in a way that doesn't lose the excitement and enthusiasm in the idea. The excitement is contagious and needs to spread frequently and thoroughly throughout the new product team and the rest of the company. If the marketing group needs to slow even further, assign it another two or three new ideas to work on.

A variety of general management techniques are helpful in new product pioneering. Some of the most essential are behavior analysis, communication barriers/bridges, organization structure, and team building/leadership.

Behavior analysis is a technique based on human psychology and has been adapted to business communication and management theory by a number of different training organizations. It is usually presented in a grid format where people are clustered in one of four grids in a matrix based on their most common behavior style. The grid is based on two axes: the degree of control individuals like to exercise and the degree of emotion they express in communication. The theory is that everyone has a different behavior style that falls into one of the grid sections, and the better the managers are able to understand the predominant style and how it may differ from their own, the better they can manage the interpersonal relationship.

For example, individuals who are high in controlling but low in emoting tend to like detailed analysis and proof and may be reluctant to make a decision. The management technique in this case would be to carefully document the facts and assumptions and give the individual several choices for ease of decision making.

Someone high in controlling and emoting likes to make decisions without wasting time, so give them the facts quickly. A high emoting but low controlling type likes to make decisions based on trust in the people relationship, so take the time in this case to build a relationship. Finally, a low emoter and controller wants to move very slowly and carefully, develop a relationship and a comfort in the numbers, and may need a little push to move to the next phase of the project. Figures 15–2a, 15–2b, and 15–2c illustrate the behavior style grid, the techniques for relating to people with each of the styles, and ways to support them in decision making. A good understanding of behavior styles and an attempt to manage within them, not from a manipulative sense, but from an honest desire to understand and relate to differences in decision-making nature can be useful in new product management.

Building bridges to overcome barriers in interpersonal relationships is a variation of the matrix approach to managing communications. In this technique, the two key variables are ex-

**FIGURE 15–2a**
Anticipating Actions Toward Others

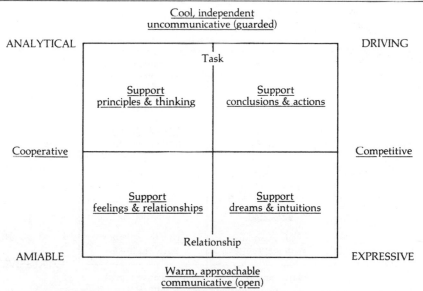

SOURCE: Wilson Learning Corp., Minneapolis, Minn. © 1975.

**FIGURE 15–2b** _____
Anticipating Actions Related to Use of Time

Cool, independent, uncommunicative (guarded)
Disciplined about time

| ANALYTICAL | | DRIVING |
|---|---|---|
| | Support principles & thinking<br><br>Time to be accurate | Support conclusions & actions<br><br>Time to be efficient |
| Cooperative slow actions | | Competitive fast-actions |
| | Support feelings & relationships<br><br>Time to be agreeable | Support dreams & intuitions<br><br>Time to be stimulating |
| AMIABLE | | EXPRESSIVE |

Warm, approachable—communicative (open)
Undisciplined about time

SOURCE: Wilson Learning Corp., Minneapolis, Minn. © 1975.

**FIGURE 15–2c** _____
Anticipating Actions in Relation to Decision Making

Cool, independent, uncommunicative (guarded)
Disciplined about time
Uses facts

| ANALYTICAL | | DRIVING |
|---|---|---|
| | Support principles & thinking<br><br>Time to be accurate<br><br>Provide evidence with service | Support conclusions & actions<br><br>Time to be efficient<br><br>Provide options with probabilities |
| Cooperative slow actions avoids risks | | Competitive fast actions takes risks |
| | Support feelings & relationships<br><br>Time to be agreeable<br><br>Provide guarantees with assurance | Support dreams & intuitions<br><br>Time to be stimulating<br><br>Provide testimony with incentives |
| AMIABLE | | EXPRESSIVE |

Warm, approachable, communicative (open)
Undisciplined about time
Uses opinions

SOURCE: Wilson Learning Corp., Minneapolis, Minn. © 1975.

**FIGURE 15–3** _____
Bonds and Barriers

Organization distance

|  | Close | Far |
|---|---|---|
| **Close** | Bond<br>Bond | Bond<br>Barrier |
| **Far** | Bond<br>Barrier | Barrier<br>Barrier |

Geographic distance

pressed in distance; first in terms of physical distance between project team members, and second in terms of organizational distance between them. Figure 15–3 shows this matrix and illustrates that a team can have a distance bond, barrier, or combination, depending on the two variables.

If the team members are close in terms of both geography and organization, they will probably communicate and work well together on the project. Any distance in either of the variables will require some overt management attention through task force meetings, review sessions, or personal control of the effort. Distance in both variables is probably a high-risk situation that may not be controlled through normal management processes and may need to be changed. Consider reorganizing to create a venture team, physically move some of the players, or do both. Sometimes even shifting offices to get engineering and marketing groups next to each other can make a great difference in their teamwork. Having people scattered all over the town or the country is a sure road to project disaster.

In some cases, the timing or the magnitude of the project is so critical that an organization structure is created to provide maximum bonding between team members and optimum communication and consistency of goals. Venture teams, task forces, and other variations were discussed in Chapter Four. The basic concept is to force total shared goals by integrating both the people and their communication into one organizational unit.

Another organization structure that can be used to facilitate fast action is to include the chief executive in the task force. Kellogg Co. used that technique to develop a decaffeinated tea and was able to hit the market with a full-blown consumer campaign in six months. It formed a crash task force of five people—an R&D man, a marketing manager, a sales manager, a production manager, and the division president.[1] Xerox has been able to react to intense competition in the copier business by integrating new product development teams at low levels in the organization. At one time Xerox enjoyed a 70 percent share in the copier market. In recent years that share fell to 36 percent and is now back to 39 percent and growing because of a rapid pace of new product development. The low-level integration helped Xerox cut its development cycle by more than 50 percent.

Some guidelines to managing the human factor through organization theory are:

1. Pick good people—intelligent, inquisitive, creative, persistent, and able to coordinate their work with others.

2. Give the group authority—within strategic guidelines.

3. Give the members in the group a sense of participation and thus responsibility.

4. Establish an informal working relationship in the group. Avoid the feeling of formal reporting channels.

5. Pick people who can be trusted—new product decisions require a great amount of subjectivity. Management must believe in the people as much as in the research.

6. Recognize and reward the efforts of those involved.

Finally, top management can have an ultimate impact on the interpersonal relations of a new product team. This is not a business function that runs well in a top leadership vacuum. The CEO must continuously communicate throughout the organization what is expected in the new product effort—timing, technology, quality, and performance. Uncertainty is prevalent enough in new product development without trying to guess at top management goals for the organization.

---

[1] *Marketing News*, 19 (November 22, 1985), p. 26.

There is no substitution for "eyeball" control and communication. Tours through the lab, visits to customer trial sites, participation in market research evaluation sessions, and personal use of first and second prototypes is *not* excessive control; it's good management and essential to understanding the activities that represent the future of the company.

An example of very clear management communication of goals and getting motivation and teamwork out of it is Sony's long and eventually successful effort in the compact audio disk market. Norio Ohga, Sony's president and a former opera baritone, insisted the disk size be increased over early prototype concepts to enable it to hold Austrian conductor Herbert von Karajan's slow, 72-minute version of Beethoven's *Ninth Symphony*. And Kozo Ohsone, an audio engineer in charge of the project, decided his team could pack that recording in an even smaller player. He went to his lab and made a block of wood about five-inches square and about an inch and a half tall. That, he surmised, was the minimum necessary size for a disk player.

"To persuade the engineers," he says, "I just made the model and placed it in front of them. I told them we would not accept the question, 'Why this size?' That was our size, and that was it." To be sure that no crafty engineer stole the wood and replaced it with a bigger model, Mr. Ohsone signed his name on the back and left it out for all to see. The researchers grumbled, but they got to work and designed the most compact disk player on the market and, in addition, worked with manufacturing to enable it to be totally assembled with robots.[2]

Some ways to recognize when the new product team is running smoothly and when the human factor needs some work are the following indicators. Effective interpersonal relationships are evidenced when professional needs and management objectives are integrated; diversity of ideas is encouraged; goals are clearly defined, understood, and accepted; members of management are interdependent; initiative is often shared by several team members; team members are accepted for what they are and what they can contribute; resources among team members are identified and used effectively; and team members genuinely respect one another. Ineffective relationships are marked by mistrust and fear; a "play it safe" attitude; conflict being suppressed, smoothed over,

---

[2] *The Wall Street Journal*, 95 (February 27, 1986.), p. 1.

denied, or avoided; ideas faltering because of lack of support, examination and/or understanding; many hidden feelings; members wanting others to assume responsibility; counter-dependence; occasional fights over leadership of the project; some team members wanting to be told exactly what to do; and too much emphasis on who is a "winner" and who is a "loser."

If these danger signs exist, step in and get the pioneering back on track. If the project seems to be going well, stay out of the effort (but not the evaluation and observation). The larger a business becomes, the more difficult it is to leave people alone to do their jobs. Layer and layer of management review gets created and eventually smothers the spark of creative thought as well as any sense of responsibility. Product development needs management goals, priorities, and strategy, and then it needs the freedom to create and execute as a responsible and committed team.

# 16

## On Being First

*"It must be considered that there is nothing more difficult to carry out, nor more doubtful of success, nor dangerous to handle, than to initiate a new order of things. For the reformer has enemies in all those who profit by the old order, and only lukewarm defenders in all those who would profit by the new order, this lukewarmness arising partly from fear of their adversaries, who have the laws in their favor; and partly from the incredulity of mankind, who do not truely believe in anything new until they have had actual experiences of it. Thus it arises that on every opportunity for attacking the reformer, his opponents do so with the zeal of partisans, the others only defend him half-heartedly, so that between them he runs great danger."*

1513 A.D. MACHIAVELLI

Machiavelli could have related very well to the dangers of pioneering new products in today's business world. These dangers, fears, adversaries, and attackers take the form of a variety of people and special interest groups, both within and outside the corporation. Unfortunately, the reaction of professional managers in too many cases has been to take refuge behind excessive numbers, analysis, and short-term earnings performance rather than staking a claim for the future.

The result, as Tom Peters, author of *In Search of Excellence*, says, is "they have become ensnared in a thicket of portfolios— cows and dogs and stars, mergers, expected value thinking, concern for profit growth—this quarter, obsessive and equal attention to every stockholder (instead of, it sometimes seems, to the customer). Gimmicks and techniques have replaced love of the product and the people who make it. And lost as well is the intensity and commitment.

When management begins to view profit as the "means" rather than the "end," it gets into serious long-term trouble. Financial performance is the scorecard and the "winnings in the game," the return to the investors, "cold cash," but the way it happens is by *creating customers and innovating products.* Peter Drucker has gone as far as saying the *purpose* of business is to create a customer. A pioneer would probably say that getting to the gold is the first priority, but creating markets is the essential business activity.

The mid-1980s has ushered in a period of huge corporate mergers and acquisitions. Big companies are buying smaller companies, large companies are swallowing big companies, and giant corporations are marrying other giants. This phenomenon is occurring in every industry—consumer goods, industrial goods, banking, airlines, retailing, even emerging growth industries such as health care. Investment bankers are making fortunes, stockholders are doing OK, and the general business community seems to nod in agreement to rationale such as "increasing stockholder value," "eliminating excess industry capacity," and "eliminating the expense of entering a new market by buying into it." David Ogilvy would not quite agree with this reasoning based on his statement regarding such activity:

> You can judge the vitality of a company by the number of new products it brings to market. I have known chief executive officers who made enough profit from the products they inherited from their predecessors to obscure their failure to introduce new ones of their own. It is not uncommon for such men to grudge a measly million dollars for developing a new product, but to shell out $100 million to acquire somebody else's product, without turning a hair. Their borrowing power is greater than their brainpower.

Why does the merger and acquisition game seem to take precedence over new product pioneering? There are a number of half-legitimate reasons:

- The financial markets have created an artificial situation making "buy versus make" a good financial decision.

- Deregulation has intensified competition in a number of industries, forcing out weak players and eliminating artificial supports.
- Excess capacity has plagued mature industries suffering from decreasing markets and international competition.
- The cost of advertising and other marketing efforts needed to establish a brand or distribution system has escalated to the point where it seems to be more attractive to buy an existing brand or distribution system versus building one.
- All of the other risks outlined in this book.

These are financial justifications, however, and gain credence and support quickly because buying is *easier* than building and occasionally more fun than fighting the Machiavellian enemies of "a new order of things" inside the company. There are situations where mergers make perfect sense. An only caution would be to ensure that opportunities for building markets from within have been exhausted or at least funded in balance before departing the business at hand as the company hits the acquisition trail.

Another major factor affecting new product pioneering is the perennial American focus on short-term results and the lack of patience for long development cycles. Manufacturing technology is visible and can have short-term and well-defined paybacks. Cost reduction is easy to justify. Liquidating assets generates quick cash. Buying businesses generates instant products and markets. Pioneering new products, especially breakthroughs, can take a long time and have no guarantees of success (but reading this book will help).

The Sony Corporation spent 15 years working on a laser recording and compact disk player after N.V. Philips, the large Dutch electronics company, figured out the technology in 1970. N.V. Philips and several U.S. companies, including RCA and Zenith, gave up on the project after investing hundreds of millions of dollars in disk research. Sony persevered and eventually brought out the first successful minisized, laser-operated disk player that is sweeping the consumer market and starting to find a host of applications in computer storage and the military.

Sony had numerous failures along the way. Its first four years of effort ended in a nonworkable system, and the project was put on the back burner. It was brought to life again in 1977 when a new disk material was developed. By 1979, Sony's chairman, Akio Morita, was visiting New York securities analysts with a dummy disk and proclaiming it the medium of the future. But the first machines introduced in 1982 were still too big and expensive to generate a large market. Sony combined its creative engineering with its manufacturing skills, redesigned the product around high-volume, low-cost production and compact components, and hit the market in 1984 with its ultimate success. Today, Sony dominates a rapidly growing business.

It isn't so much that Sony succeeded, but the others failed. RCA still produces a few special systems for the Defense Department, and MCA Inc., which made video disk players in the 1970s, sold its factories to Pioneer Electronic Corp. of Japan. Zenith dropped out without producing anything. Although U.S. companies produced some of the basic research, Sony officials say they no longer consider the U.S. a competitor. Novio Ohga, Sony's president, says, "We were really impressed with innovative U.S. technology after the war. In the past, a U.S. company would really stick with an idea if it thought it was a good one. They don't do that now."[1]

This discouraging statement on the perception of American business by an outsider has a ring of truth. The same capital markets that do such a wonderful job of providing money for starting new companies and developing great ideas have just the opposite impact on the efforts of major corporations. Instead of supporting these institutions in using their great human and technology resources in the pioneering of new ground, the capital markets force the executives to produce financial results on a three-month deadline. It might be productive for the business and investment community to start promoting a whole series of new indicators in addition to the traditional earnings, margins, dividends, and debt ratios. How about a series of growth and development indicators such as:

- Customer base and growth rate.
- New product ratio—revenue from products introduced in the previous five years as a percent of total revenue.
- Innovation quotient—number of patents awarded annually.

---

[1] "Japanese Triumph," *The Wall Street Journal*, February 27, 1986, p. 1.

- Market development—new S.I.C. codes and/or geographic markets developed (revenue and profits generated from new markets annually).
- R&D investment compared to industry and foreign averages.

If the investment community demanded performance in these indicators equal to short-term financial performance, an innovative edge might be restored to American business. For this to happen, the pension funds and institutional investors that control the capital markets must start holding for long-term appreciation versus reacting to the securities industry desire to drive up trading volume on Wall Street.

What can you do about being first while waiting for the corporation to adopt the same behavior? You can be an initiator of change from within. The term "intrapreneuring" was coined to describe the activity of creating change and growth inside a corporation. It's a way to have a role in pioneering new ground in any company and industry, regardless of outside pressures for short-term financial performance or industry cutbacks. It depends on individual perseverance more than anything else, but there are some guidelines on successful intrapreneuring:

**1.** Develop the habit of looking at problems as opportunities. Formulate solutions and step in and offer to implement them.

**2.** Study the corporate culture and determine how to work the organization. Figure out how to create change "with the flow" rather than using adversarial tactics.

**3.** Build value credits. Go the extra mile when asked to do something—it develops sponsors for later innovations.

**4.** Develop and hone your people skills. Use the techniques in Chapter 15 to find out other's needs and develop win-win strategies.

**5.** Generalize. Explore other related functions, activities, technologies; broaden your horizons. If you are in engineering, take some time to learn something about sales and marketing; if you are in R&D, get out in the field and learn something about customer operations.

Some guidance from the leaders of business (Thomas Watson, IBM; David Ogilvy, Ogilvy & Mather; others) may be less pragmatic but can add some inspiration to your intrapreneuring efforts:

**1.** Strengthen your "risk muscle." Everyone has one, but you have to exercise it or else it will atrophy. Make it a point to take at least one risk every 24 hours.

**2.** Develop the hunter's attitude, the outlook that wherever you go, there are ideas waiting to be discovered.

**3.** You are doing things nobody has ever done before. Therefore, you are going to be making mistakes. Make your mistakes, but make them in a hurry.

**4.** The way to succeed is to double your failure rate.

**5.** If you want to double your growth rate, you must more than double your efforts.

**6.** Rules are for the obedience of fools and the guidance of wise men.

These rules and guidelines may help you pioneer within your company and develop new products that survive in the marketplace, but they may not eliminate personal risks and ensure your own survival. That goes with the territory. There are ways to reduce personal risk, however, and still be an innovator and a change agent. For any idea to be successful, it must not only have committed people working on it, but also the commitment of the top people in the organization. Someone at the top has to buy into it and share in the ownership. Almost every major pioneering effort has problems in the beginning. If no one at the top has bought into it and has a personal stake in it, you are on your own. And as soon as you run into trouble, either you'll start getting out or that decision will be made for you.

Some other indicators of your business can give you a clue as to what degree of risk to assume:

**1.** Is your business developing or mature? A larger proportion of risk takers is needed by a developing company.

**2.** Is your business capital or people intensive? The greater the capital intensity, generally the more control must be exercised. Too many risk takers can cause chaos.

**3.** Are your company's business goals ambitious or conservative? Align your risk taking with the environment you operate within.

**4.** Is the business high or low technology? High-technology businesses frequently operate on the borders of the unknown and require a disproportionate number of risk takers. Low-technology industries may be unable to absorb a fast rate of change, no matter how supportive your company may be.

**5.** What are the dominant motivation patterns of your management group? Speed of decision-making and degree of change in history can indicate the boundaries of comfort.

These are indicators of how much personal risk you may be assuming on a project. They are *not* rules on how much risk you *should* assume. Only you can answer that question. Every business needs a balance of risk takers and risk reducers. Top management's primary responsibility is to create, maintain, and protect that balance on both sides. If you are in the product pioneering game, however, you should be a risk taker or your new products may not survive in the marketplace.

A fair question at this point may be, "What's in it for me. Why risk my personal survival on being first in the market?" There are some very practical reasons as well as personal rewards. People who can create change, innovate, and build new ideas get noticed and rewarded, if not by their companies, then within their industries or the business community. Grey and Gordon of Hay Associates even documented this in a study of the promotion history of 700 individuals in a large multinational company.[2] Figure 16–1 clearly indicates that risk takers tend to rise more rapidly (their study correlated the number of promotions received with a score on a risk-taking scale). Also, they further documented, as shown in Figure 16–2, that risk takers can be more effective managers. This may support the theory that successful executives are those who are motivated more by the need to make their own decisions than by their desire for assured employment or steady income.

Aside from career and monetary rewards, there can be an enormous personal reward in being a new product pioneer. It is the best way to learn and develop in a business because it covers the entire spectrum—both inside and outside. New products can be a personal expression of creativity, a tangible result of an imaginative mind. They take on a life of their own as they enter the marketplace and begin to provide pleasure, ease, better living, or

---

[2] Dr. Ronald J. Grey and Dr. George G. Gordon, *Management Review*, (November 1978), pp. 9–13. Copyright © 1978, AMACOM, a division of American Management Association.

**FIGURE 16–1**
Risk Taking and Career Mobility

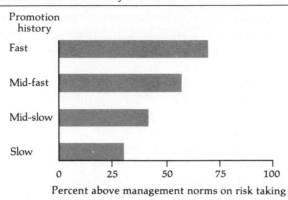

Percent above management norms on risk taking

improved productivity for customers across the country or the world. If they survive in the market, it's because they are improving that market in some way, making it a better environment for living or working, creating economic growth that translates into employment and productivity.

Tom Peters talked about this feeling of personal attachment to a product in describing some of the great pioneers of business. Ray Kroc, McDonald's founder, said, "You've gotta be able to see the beauty in a hamburger bun." Forrest Mars reportedly once

**FIGURE 16–2**
Risk Taking and Management Effectiveness

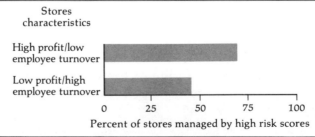

Percent of stores managed by high risk scores

got on his hands and knees at an officers' meeting and offered a prayer to M&Ms. Freddy Heineken is "personally offended" by a single sour bottle of beer. J. Willard Marriott Sr. read all customer complaint cards until he was well into his 80s. Sam Walton of WalMart visits each of his stores every year. David Ogilvy reportedly has every piece of creative work copied to him in France and reviews every campaign (with a few caustic notes to offices around the world now and then). A senior officer remembers Bill Hewlett of Hewlett-Packard Company sticking the first hand-held calculator prototype into his shirt pocket and, finding it didn't fit, sending it back for more work. Digital Equipment Corp.'s Ken Olsen similarly spent hour after hour worrying over the screen tint of Digital's new personal computer. These pioneers had one thing in common—they cared or care deeply about their products.

Contemporary business seems to have lost this love for the product in too many cases. Emphasis gets placed on formality, measurement schemes, and a belief in the benefits of large scale versus "skunk works." Larger businesses tend to breed these tendencies as a natural consequence of size, but it doesn't have to happen. Minnesota Mining & Manufacturing Co. is a prime example. Insiders occasionally joke about their efforts at producing "yesterday's products, tomorrow, maybe!" But they know 3M is a leader of industry in pioneering and technical innovation. The company does it by operating as a cluster of small, entrepreneurial companies, each with a marketing group operating side-by-side with a product laboratory (a real skunkworks) as defined by Tom Peters. Hewlett-Packard, Emerson Electric, Digital Equipment, and even IBM have managed to keep a spirit of thinking small and maintaining an environment where people can still take risks as individuals and develop a close association with their products.

Jack Welsh of General Electric describes the feeling and sense of purpose and satisfaction that can come from being a new product pioneer:

> Only the market vision, the *outside* cause, can rally people *inside* . . . can mobilize and animate a company. Only the market vision—with its focus on life, not things; on people, not numbers—can give meaning to what we do. . . . The issue will be, do we have the people

---

[3] Grace Hawthorne and John F. Wilson, *The Electric Sunshine Man.* Copyright © 1978, Somerset Press, Carol Stream, Ill. 60187.

in our organizations who will see constant change and have the courage to demand constant innovation?

One author attended his son's fifth grade play recently, which was a musical about the life of one of Welsh's predecesors at General Electric—Thomas A. Edison. The title of the musical is "The Electric Sunshine Man" (music by John F. Wilson, words by Grace Hawthorne, copyright 1978 by Somerset Press, Carol Stream, Ill.). Some of the lyrics should be an inspiration to every would-be new product pioneer:[3]

> Once upon a time the world was not too bright,
> Sunshine ruled the day, but darkness ruled the night! . . .
> You would not believe the things we could not do.
> We couldn't see a movie, or play the radio, or listen to a record, or watch a TV show;
> Pick up the phone, turn on the light, borrow the car,
> go on a flight!
> Man! What a life!
> Yesterday we couldn't, but today we can!
> Thanks to the Electric Sunshine Man! . . .
> There was nothing he couldn't do.
> He had a dream, and it all came true.
> The Electric Sunshine Man!

And on Edison's formation of the first skunk works at Menlo Park:

> If it's never been done we can do it! We can do it!
> Yes, in—deed!
> If it's never been thought, We'll think through it,
> Yes, in—deed!
> If there's a design that you have in mind, then this is the place, this is the place to pursue it, yes, in—deed!
> This is the invention factory. Where we make things that never was.
> If it's impossible, bring it to us!
> That's what this factory does! . . .
> There's nothing we can't do if we're determined to.
> Our talent and skill, talent and skill pay the rent here! Yes in—deed!
> If it's impossible, bring it to us!
> That's what this factory does!

And a final message for future generations of inventors and pioneers:

Eighteen seventy-seven, they said, "That's impossible!
No one had ever heard of a phonograph before," but he did it! Yes,
he did it! . . .
Eighteen seventy-nine, they said, "That's impossible!
No one had ever owned electric lights before," but he did it! Yes,
he did it! . . .
Eighteen hundred ninety, they said, "That's impossible!
No one had ever seen a picture show before," but he did it! Yes, he
did it! . . .
And now it's not impossible any more, Oh no! Oh no!
What do they tell you is impossible now?
Maybe it's just that no one knows how!
But someone will make the impossible true!
And it's possible that "someone" may be you! . . . .
Nothing is impossible—If you try.
You'll be sure to work it out—by and by,
Just never say "quit," Never say "die."
So, why don't you give it a try?

# INDEX